LONG RIDE TO THE END OF THE WORLD

A Lonely Long Rider's 7,500 km Journey to the Land of Fire

FILIPE MASETTI LEITE

Copyright © 2020 by Filipe Masetti Leite

Ebook ISBN 978-1-927607-73-2

Paperback ISBN 978-1-927607-72-5

Published by Ex Parte Press

First Edition June 30, 2020

Second Edition August 18, 2020

Cover design: Cristiano José de Campos Leme – Design Grafico Rodeio

Cover photograph: Sebastián "Toti" Cichero

Project Manager: Peter Hawkins

Developmental Editing: Robert Chazz Chute

Editorial services: Gari Strawn of strawnediting.com

For media inquiries and to arrange author appearances: DM instagram.com/filipemasetti.

LONG RIDE TO THE END OF THE WORLD

A Lonely Long Rider's 7,500 km Journey to the Land of Fire

Filipe Masetti Leite

DEDICATION

For Life, Doll, Cautiva, Andariega, Picasso, and Sapito: my children.
For Mark Maw, Mario T. Luna, Ramon Bastias and Sebastián "Toti" Cichero:
my brothers in arms.
For Peter Hawkins, my mentor and friend who has been by my side since
day one.
And for Clara Victoria Davel, my flor del pago who taught me how to love
again.

PROLOGUE

Day 420 - Tierra Del Fuego, Argentina.

Only one hundred kilometers from the end, the dream becomes a nightmare.

"All the horses and all the horsemen in the universe, please help me save my son... please, please, please," I desperately chant the mantra into the night's dark sky as I run my hand down the soft dark blond hairs of Sapito's forehead. Sitting in the icy snow, frozen in time yet shaking in panic, I focus on the thick vapor shooting out of my Criollo's nostrils in a frantic rhythm. My fingers burn with pain as I try to put another IV bag of saline into his veins. Deep red blood drops stained the crisp white snow. Bubbles of drool dribble from his lips.

It was the alfalfa cubes from last night! A little treat and now my pony is writhing in terrible pain. He is going to die. The thought enters my mind like a knife, and I fight to rid myself of it.

I am in Tierra Del Fuego, Argentina, only 1,000 kilometers from Antarctica, the end of the earth. One of the coldest places in the world, right now, it feels like a frozen hell. It is four a.m. and -16°C. Already, fourteen hours have passed since we began fighting for Sapito's life, but he is deteriorating. I feel sick to my stomach. I can taste my puke. My lips and limbs are numb from the extremely low temperatures. Panic pumps through my veins. My heart, tight and tense, is ready to burst into a million little pieces of ice.

Suddenly, as if given a shot of adrenaline, Sapito fights to stand. I help by pulling on his gray, frozen lead rope with all the strength I have left in my fatigued body. He almost rises but his back end slides on the ice, and he drops hard on his right side. The heavy thump shakes the ground and the sound makes me cringe.

He scrambles to stand again and this time, letting out a deep grunt, he manages to get up. Shaking, using all of his vigor to keep himself off the ground, he begins to defecate. He has terrible diarrhea. With my arm under his head, his neck leaning on my right shoulder, I help hold him up.

"We are going to get through this, buddy," I whisper. "I love you so much."

I begin to cry once again. Heavy tears freeze against my burning cheeks. We maintain this position as long as both man and beast can hold. Eventually, both give out and return to the frigid, white carpet beneath.

"All the horses and all the horsemen in the universe, please help me save my son..." I moan my mantra over and over again, as wild-eyed as a mad man. The silence of the night is heavy, pushing against my skin, driving me crazier.

At seven a.m., after several hours trying to stand with no luck, with all his might, he shoots his stocky, golden body up and stands shaking once again. Then, while I hold his head, he begins to walk forward, as if his heart is moving his legs. With every beat, he inches forward a centimeter.

My body fills with hope for the first time since the sunset. Helping my horse walk one small, stiff step at a time, I think, *Maybe the Universe heard my prayers... maybe Sapito will be ok after all.*

PTSD

I awoke to the sound of muffled voices in the next room. My eyes fought their way open as I began lifting my head from the pillow. The once pristine white pillowcase, glued to my face by the dried blood oozing from my mouth, lifted with me. I peeled it from my swollen lips and examined the round, dark red stain for a second. Confused as to why I was bleeding, I felt my front teeth with the tip of my tongue. I could feel the broken, sharp edges on several of my pearly whites. My lips were cut and puffy.

Attempting to stand, my pain only allowed me to sit on the bed. My entire body was sore, and my mind was in a complete haze. My head pounded. Struggling to remember what happened the night before, images began to race through my mind. Drinking. Music. Rain.

I remembered getting into my truck and driving down the winding, narrow, muddy road. Shards of glass exploded all around me, and I heard the sharp sound of bending metal. Cold rain hit my face as I lay nearly lifeless with my head propped on the passenger seat.

"I crashed the truck."

The realization hit me harder than my face had struck the steering wheel several hours earlier. I felt so embarrassed. Stupid. Irresponsible. When I mustered enough courage, I walked out of the room where I had slept and made my way into the old farmhouse's kitchen. My friend, Potato, whose parents owned the farm, welcomed me with, "Look who's alive."

Everyone in the small kitchen stared at my broken face. The sunlight drowned me, making me feel my hangover for the first time. I felt sick to my stomach.

"I crashed the truck last night, didn't I?" I half-asked, half-stated, trying to hide my broken teeth behind my swollen lips.

"Crashed the truck? You totaled it, my friend," he responded with a mischievous smile on his potato-shaped face. "Here, drink some coffee. It will help." He passed me a cup of strong, black coffee.

Sitting around the breakfast table, my friends gave me a play-by-play of the previous night. I had drunk way too much vodka and hit on every girl at the party. Then, for no apparent reason, I had decided to drive my drunk ass home. Just one hundred meters before getting on the main road, I lost control of the truck and crashed.

Realizing the shame I felt, Potato said kindly, "Count yourself lucky to be alive."

Alive was the last thing I felt at that moment.

The moment I stepped down from the saddle, my life began to fall apart. Trying to reintegrate myself back into society after spending 803 days on the road, traveling at four kilometers an hour, thirty kilometers a day with only my horses was anything but simple.

The first few months after my journey, I experienced symptoms of post-traumatic stress disorder (PTSD). During my long ride home, I had to fight to keep myself and my horses alive in some of the most grueling places on earth.

I'd seen two people shot dead. I'd witnessed a husband trying to kill his wife, and looked into the cold eyes of a drug lord. I'd come face to face with an immense grizzly bear. I'd seen my pony, Frenchie, get hit by a roaring Ford F-250 on a desolate road in southern Mexico. I watched as Dude, my blond mustang, fell into a cattle guard cutting his left front leg down to the bone. I'd fought for nearly two hours to dig my Quarter Horse, Bruiser, out of a deep ditch in New Mexico.

Several times I feared for my own life and the lives of my horses. We'd felt the painful wrath of thirst and hunger more than once. I spoke to God truthfully for the first time in my life at those moments. And I learned the most important lessons I would ever learn during those low points.

After that journey, life became hell. The experience left a deep scar on my inner being: anxiety, nightmares, and early signs of depression. Like many people who return from real wars, I turned to alcohol. It was too easy. I drank as much as possible as a way to drown out the ugly feelings that threatened to boil over. My desire to numb myself to those feelings caused me to nearly kill myself in that truck.

A few days after my accident, in between Christmas and New Year's, after five years of dating, living some of the happiest moments of my life with Emma, she broke up with me. In large part, it was my fault. Once I started the Brazilian portion of my Long Ride Home, I quickly noticed my parents' dislike for her. It was subtle at first: a roll of the eyes here, a sigh there.

"Your parents hate me," Emma muttered to me when they met us along the way.

I tried to deny it. "No, they don't, babe." I wiped tears from her porcelain skin. "It's all in your head."

But as we got to Barretos, the truth was evident. Every time someone focused on Emma, I saw anger in my mom and dad's eyes. I knew why. She was the girl who was going to take their golden son away again. They didn't see the unwavering support, the determination to see me through my journey, the sacrifices. They only saw someone who bewitched me.

One day, when my mother told everyone I would ride to my hometown after the rodeo finished, Emma spoke up to voice my concerns. "Filipe doesn't want to keep riding because he has a bad feeling about the trucks. The roads in Brazil are dangerous, and this is the end of his journey."

Emma's tone with my mother sounded more aggressive than she'd intended. Thankfully, I wasn't there for this scene. Later, I was told my mother burst into tears at the table and then began praying with my aunt as if Emma was the devil. To them, she was just that.

After my ride ended at my parents' ranch, it only got worse. Emma and I spent some time living with them. Every night, my girlfriend would cry. "It's so uncomfortable the way they look at me. I can feel their hate," she told me over and over.

It became so unbearable, we moved into a friend's beach house for a month. There, I began writing my first book. After two months in Brazil, Emma flew back to Toronto where we planned to reunite after Christmas.

"I'll see you soon, babe. Love you!" I said, giving her one final kiss.

On a rainy afternoon, sitting in my bedroom, I opened up to my father. I told him I was thinking about marrying her. "I love her so much. She has supported me since day one."

"Are you crazy?" he asked, red in the face. "Marriage? You don't even have money to buy a car. How will you afford a family? You're too young."

Staring at my hands, my mind was 16,000 kilometers away from that stuffy room. If I had the money to buy a car, I thought, I probably would have already asked Emma to marry me. I love her with all of my heart!

My father was twenty-one when he married my eighteen-year-old mother. His comments were so hypocritical, so stupid. I was furious, I wanted to punch him in the face.

Then, one day while driving home from an event at my little sister's school, the tension between me and my parents came to a head. A full-out fight broke out when I told them I planned to fly to Canada after the holidays.

"You're just going because of that girl! She is the devil who came into our lives to try to ruin our family!" my father yelled.

Next to him, my mother wept. Fuming, I yelled back, asking him what the hell he was talking about. When we got home, my father ran into his room. He and my mother returned with a stack of papers.

"We love you, Filipe," my mother said. "We thought about not showing you these to protect your feelings, but you need to see them."

My father passed me the pieces of paper. I began examining them, unsure of what I was looking at. I was so confused. They were screen-shots from my iPad. As I looked closer, I found they were conversations Emma had had with her mother over iMessage.

They hate me.

Going through the pages, the comments only got worse and worse. In these private conversations with her mother, Emma complained about how my parents were treating her and that she hated them for it.

My mother sat at the edge of my bed, looking distraught, as if someone had stolen her child from her arms. "You see the things she said about us."

Flabbergasted, I didn't know what to do or say. I asked my parents how they got these, and my father explained he ran into them acciden-tally. "I was using your iPad one day and opened iMessage by accident, and the messages were right in front of me." He'd taken the screen-shots, sent them to my mother and got them printed. Together, they showed the entire family.

Confused, I immediately called Emma on Skype. I was angry. I couldn't believe my parents snooped through my iPad. I couldn't understand how Emma could have been so stupid as to say those things. Leaving iMessage open for anyone to read was even worse.

We fought.

She yelled.

I cried.

Our relationship ended.

∼

The next few days, I cried myself to sleep and woke with swollen eyes. I spent several hours a day thinking about my disaster of a life. My mind always raced to Emma. Her golden blonde hair smelling of wild-flowers blowing in my face on a Kenyan beach. Looking out to sea with our entire lives ahead of us, we'd been surrounded by peace, love, and positive energy. I fell in love with her quickly and deeply. I remembered searching the dirt floor under a wooden restaurant table in the sacred valley of Peru. One of her earrings had fallen from her left ear. I'd wanted to impress her so badly, over and over I prayed, "Please let me find it, please let me find it, please let me find it."

This stream of memories clouded my thoughts, always returning to Calgary, Alberta. My ride out of the Calgary Stampede played out in my mind over and over. The final thing I said to her on that tense July 8 was, "I'm so sorry, babe." I looked back after fifteen minutes of riding, seeing her in the distance. She gripped her blonde ponytail over her chest in both fists, her face soaked in tears. I felt like I was leaving the love of my life behind that day. And somehow, I just kept riding... And for what?

Sitting in my cluttered room with photos and articles from my journey plastering the walls, I blamed myself for ever going on the ride. It was my fault our relationship ended. If I had just gotten a normal job in Toronto, this never would have happened. I would still be with the love of my life, the woman I imagined walking down the aisle toward me. My muse, with her gorgeous smile and powerful soul, was gone. Distraught, I had never in my entire life felt so low and empty.

And yet, things needed to get worse before they got better. On the final day of 2014, we were at the ranch when my father announced he was going for a ride. He asked me if I wanted to join him and I refused. It was about six p.m., and I was getting ready to go to town to celebrate the New Year. After about half an hour, I heard my little sister Izabella yelling hysterically. When I ran to the front door, I saw Frenchie saddled and running loose. My father lay on the ground.

Frenchie bucked him off, I thought. Panic began to creep in.

I ran toward my father. I knew it was bad immediately. He screamed in pain, white as a ghost, sweat dripping from his brow. He lay, holding his upper half off the tall grass at a 45-degree angle, elbows dug into the red dirt. His head dipped back in pain. Several flies lit on the thick layer of sweat pouring down his face. His left leg pointed south, but at the ankle it made a 90-degree turn due west. I almost puked when I saw his Wrangler jeans going one way and his ostrich-skin boot the opposite.

"My leg broke! My leg broke!" He yelled over and over again, his eyes squeezed tight in pain. "I heard it, it snapped like a branch!"

I froze for an instant, then I ran to Frenchie and untacked him in what seemed like two seconds. Then I ran up the hill to my house and arrived out of breath.

While my mother cried uncontrollably, I got the keys to my parents' truck and drove down to get my dad. I parked the truck right next to him. When I moved to lift him, both hands under his armpits, he yelled as if his foot was hanging off of his leg by a single muscle.

"Stop, stop, stop! My foot is going to fall off!" he screamed.

I tried once more, but it was impossible. I couldn't actually see how bad the break was. He was wearing a cowboy boot with a tall barrow, and his jeans were over them. Judging by his reaction when his leg began to lift from the ground one centimeter, it was really bad.

I stayed by his side while my mother called the fire department to send an ambulance. It took about thirty minutes for the ambulance to leave my hometown, drive the fourteen kilometers of winding road, and climb a small mountain. It felt like three days.

We spent New Year's Eve in the institutional green emergency room with a family who yelled and threw themselves on the floor after finding out their son had been stabbed to death. The mother's piercing cry of agony was the rawest manifestation of pain I have ever witnessed. It was as if her powerful scream could lift her son from the dead. It was like someone had reached into her chest and squeezed her heart in a tight fist until it exploded.

I could feel her pain as if it had a shape and weight, an object, pushing against my chest, making it hard to breathe. At that moment, that woman's pain became my pain. With the smell of rubbing alcohol clogging my nostrils and leaving a bitter taste in the back of my throat, I prayed for this mother. I prayed for my father. I prayed for happiness to find its way back into my life.

I whispered to the Universe, "Happy New Year."

HOME

During the beginning of 2015, I found myself in Espírito Santo do Pinhal, Brazil, the town in which I was born. It was supposed to be home, yet it felt like anything but.

The town of 40,000 people, located in the state of São Paulo, only a few kilometers from Minas Gerais, was absolutely breathtaking. Rolling hills covered in vegetation that danced through various shades of green surround the small town. Coffee farms, eucalyptus plantations, and small cattle ranches began where the main road ended.

A large church was located in the city center. Built in 1849 on land donated to the city by my great-great-great-grandfather, Romualdo de Souza Brito, the church still stood proud.

Igreja Matriz do Divino Espírito Santo e Nossa Senhora das Dores was so beautiful and intricate in detail, it looked like it should have been built in Rome. The cathedral, painted pale yellow with white details, had a freestanding campanile with four large angels playing flutes guarding the colossal bell at the top and a large dome. It was surrounded by a traditional town square, with manicured lawns, cement benches, and tall *Araucaria* trees.

My parents' ranch, only fourteen kilometers from town, was heaven on earth. Built on top of a mountain, it had a rain forest that formed a half-circle, covering the back and sides of the home. The front faced a gorgeous green valley with the *Río Manso* snaking its way through the middle with strong brown rapids.

Even though I was born in this peaceful and beautiful corner of the globe, I couldn't help but feel like a fish out of water. No conversation I had seemed worthwhile or interesting. The women did not attract me. Colors seemed less vibrant. Nothing tasted good. Anxiety, lack of motivation, sadness, confusion on what to do next...These were just some of the feelings boiling deep within my core.

When I went out with friends, they would boast to every girl at the bar how I was the *"Cavaleiro das Américas,"* the cowboy who crossed the Americas on horseback. I hated them for it. I just wanted to be Filipe again. I did not feel comfortable in my own skin. While dealing with all of these emotions, I was trying to finish my book, *Long Ride Home*.

At the same time, I was forced to become my father's nurse. After spending New Year's Eve in the emergency room, my father underwent surgery to put two large titanium plates in his leg along with thirteen screws. He was bedridden for three months.

"Filipe, can you help me? I'm going to shower now," my father would yell from his bedroom.

I would stop writing, walk down the long, dark hallway to his room, and help him off his bed. His room smelled like medication and baby powder. I helped him hobble to the bathroom. While I waited, I would lay on his bed and stare at the ceiling. When he announced he had finished doing his business, I helped him tie a plastic garbage bag over his leg and assisted him into the shower. Then I would wait outside again. When he finished showering, I helped him back to his bed.

It was nothing more than my duty as a son. This man had changed my diapers how many times? My father had worked outside in Canada's -30°C February days to offer me the best life possible. It was totally my obligation to help out my old man.

However, due to everything that had happened with Emma just a month before, this was not an easy period. I was very angry with him, and his actions saddened me. At that moment, I felt like he and my mother had been selfish. Even though they firmly believed that they had acted in my best interest, I resented them. After all of the suffering I had endured, this was how they welcomed their son home? By chasing his one great love away?

Feeling shitty about myself and everything that had happened, it was hard to have to help him several times a day every day. Yet I had to put my feelings aside. I catered to him for ninety-seven days. Eventually, he got better. I finished the first draft of my book and, using my last $1,000 CDN — made from a Burger King commercial — I bought a plane ticket to Canada.

When the Air Canada Boeing 787 touched down at Toronto Pearson International Airport, I let out a sigh of relief. It was like I had finally arrived home. In Canada, my life began to change. Being around my friends, the guys I grew up with, started to make me feel something I had not felt in months: happiness.

They came to pick me up at the airport. I stayed at my friend Terry's apartment, and every weekend we got together to chat, drink beer, laugh, and chase skirts. I was slowly becoming Filipe again.

It wasn't all flowers. The money I'd had disappeared quickly. Some days, being my stubborn self and full of pride, I went to bed having eaten one bagel — and *only* one bagel — that day. My friends were already helping me so much, I didn't want to bother them for money. I needed a job ASAP.

Since I was in Canada on a tourist visa, I didn't have a work permit. It was tempting to look for odd jobs, but my mother forbade against doing any work under the table. "Filipe, you are a journalist. You have written a book. There is a statue of you! There are *two* statues of you, for God's sake! Find something to do that honors who you are!"

Only two weeks later, true to my mother, I got a tremendous opportunity to speak at the Pan American Games in Toronto. I gave a motivational speech on my Long Ride Home to 200 people. Still, money problems plagued me.

What about Emma, you're wondering?

I would be lying if I said I didn't see her. We met secretly on several occasions. I didn't tell my friends. She didn't tell hers. It was surreal. At times, it felt like what had happened in Brazil was nothing but a nightmare we had now awoken from. But, at the same time, it was different. She was different. I had changed as well.

On our final date in Toronto, I noticed her glance at me shiftily as a text came in. I grabbed her phone. It read: *I love you, too, babe.*

My heart was broken yet again. I stormed out of the pub, calling her every bad name I could muster at that moment. It was not a pretty scene. After everything we had been through, I was so angry she hadn't been honest with me and sad for the guy she was sending loving messages to while having me on the side.

Love? Love? Love? How could she fall in love so quickly? We never saw each other after that.

It took me a long time to judge my own behavior as harshly as I had judged hers.

A NEW DREAM IS BORN

When I arrived at the Barretos Rodeo in 2014, I asked to visit Barretos Children's Cancer Hospital. I'd heard some extraordinary things about this state-of-the-art institute that offered free care for patients from all over Brazil and wanted to see it for myself. When I walked into the cancer hospital, I felt like I was in another country — a First World country to be more specific.

The walls were white with colorful drawings, paintings, and flowers. In the middle of the reception area, there were big bright red and baby blue comfy couches. Purple, blue, red, and yellow swirling art hung from the ceiling. In front of the waiting area, there was a McDonald's-style restaurant and a playroom filled with books, toys, televisions, and games.

Dr. Luiz Fernando Lopes, the doctor in charge of the children's hospital, took me for a tour of the building. I met many children and their families and learned more about this extraordinary hospital. While touring the facility, Dr. Luiz told me two numbers that constantly played out in my mind for the months to come. The first was that the hospital needed to fundraise around $13 million Reais ($4.5 million US dollars) monthly to keep its doors open.

The second statistic was that at St. Jude Children's Hospital in the

United States, out of one hundred kids who were diagnosed with cancer, they tended to save around ninety-five. Out of one hundred kids who were diagnosed in Barretos, we lost about thirty to forty. I was shocked. How could this be happening at this extraordinary hospital?

"The children we treat here in Barretos are arriving too late," the white-haired doctor said in his slow and low voice. He wore round-framed reading glasses that needed to be adjusted often after sliding down his nose. According to Dr. Luiz, we were losing a tremendous number of children in Brazil because when they finally began the treatment they needed, the cancer was already too advanced. Even with this state-of-the-art hospital, there was little he and his colleagues could do.

"We have started an initiative called *Passos que Salvam* (Footsteps that Save Lives) to try to change this reality," he explained.

This walk, which happened in cities and towns all over Brazil every year on November 24, not only helped raise money for the hospital. It also educated people on the importance of an early diagnosis. They passed out brochures listing the early signs of childhood cancer and some easy tests parents could do at home.

At the same time, the hospital brought one doctor from every city that participated in the event to their facility in Barretos. In 2019, the fifth annual walk, more than 900 cities and towns around Brazil participated. The goal was to educate these professionals on how to properly diagnose childhood cancer.

It wasn't the fancy machines or colorful walls that had the biggest impact on me. It was meeting the children under Dr. Luiz's care. I colored photos of princesses and dogs with these extraordinary kids all day. Some had lost all of their hair. Others lost limbs. None of them had lost their ability to smile.

Seeing these kids face such a difficult future with such positivity left me much lighter than when I walked in. I needed to do something to help.

When I learned that the hospital had sprung from a dream of a rancher and that of his son, Henrique Prata, I was in awe. Henrique was a cowboy who roped calves and rode saddle broncs in his youth (now a pickup rider at rodeos). As director, he was taking this institution to another level.

"Our goal here is to offer a humanized treatment to every patient who walks through the front doors, no matter the color of their skin or balance of their bank account," Henrique later told me during a meeting in his spacious office.

The walls held photos of him, a wide smile on his thin face, next to celebrities who had made large donations to the hospital over the years. Black and white images of Xuxa, Fernando e Sorocaba, Ivete Sangalo, and even Garth Brooks among other Brazilian celebrities and politicians were plastered on the wall.

Henrique had skinny arms, a receding hairline, and a long, thin nose that curved down like a hawk's beak. To me, this cowboy was a superhero! He told me about his dreams to take the hospital to other cities in Brazil. Three hospitals are already up and running, with one near the Amazon rainforest. Dismayed at the corruption which plagued our country, he offered free housing for the families who came to treat their children from afar. He even secured jobs for the fathers.

"Childhood cancer doesn't just affect the child. It rips the family apart. They need our support," the director said while checking his emails on his phone and signing papers his secretary had placed in front of him. He did not stop while I was in his office. It's not easy offering 100 percent free treatment to 6,000 patients daily!

The moment I walked out of Henrique's office, I vowed to do everything in my power to help this courageous cowboy save lives. A light bulb went off in my head.

I could go on a Long Ride to raise awareness and funds for the hospital. Just like the walk they organize!

One day while checking my emails in Toronto, there was a message from OutwildTv, the production company that sponsored my first journey. They asked if I would be interested in going on another Long Ride, this time to Tierra del Fuego, Argentina. As soon as I finished reading the email, the Barretos Children's Cancer Hospital jumped into my mind. It was perfect. It was what I needed to do next. However, I still remembered very well how hard the first journey was. Almost a year had passed since I crossed the finish line and only after all that time was I getting back to my old self. As inspired as I was, it was still a hard decision.

"Should I stay or should I go now?" I asked that question of many friends and people whom I respect. The majority answered yes.

PBR World Champion Guilherme Marchi and my good friend four-time world tie-down champion Tuf Cooper encouraged me. "Heck, yeah, brother, get to the bottom of it!" Tuf said in his thick Texan accent with his Ken doll smile.

In the end, I went with my instincts. As much as a part of me feared jumping back into the saddle again, a larger part just wanted to keep riding forever.

"Cowboy is another word for freedom," an old Mexican *vaquero* once told me over a bottle of *maguey*. I loved being free. That why I ride.

PLANNING

Planning an expedition of this magnitude was difficult. It took months of phone calls, emails, reading maps, working on shedding weight, gaining muscle, and convincing people to help. With the first ride under my belt, this time around I didn't get called crazy or told I would die as I had in the planning stage for my Long Ride Home. But it was far from easy!

The first thing I did was secure my mounts. Doll O'lena was lent to me by Lincoln Arruda, a Quarter Horse breeder who became a close friend. Lincoln was another incredible human being put in my path! He had purchased the saddle I used on the first journey at an auction for the Barretos Cancer Hospital.

During a delicious lunch at his house in Jaboticabal, Lincoln, a man the size of a bear, told me, "It will be a great honor to be a part of your ride."

In his midfifties, the cattle rancher raised Quarter Horses, grew soybeans, and was a philanthropist. He was also a black belt in judo who had studied agricultural sciences in my hometown. "I know Espirito Santo do Pinhal very well — at least the bars," he said, making me laugh hard.

My second mare, Topaz Life, came from the Brazilian Quarter Horse Association president, Fabio Pinto da Costa.

Next, I contacted the Long Riders' Guild (LRG) and told them about my new plan to ride to the end of the world. CuChullaine O'Reilly, the founder of the Guild, put me in touch with Benjamin Reynal, an Argentinian Long Rider, who lived in Bariloche and had ridden across his country several years before.

"Filipe, it will be a pleasure to help you plan your route through my country," the bubbly Argentinian businessman told me over Skype.

With my tentative route underway and my new mounts secured, I moved on to equipment. The packsaddle lent to me by the LRG for my first journey was in great shape, but I needed a new riding saddle. I contacted one of Brazil's oldest and best saddle makers, Ronaldo Paião, or *Baixinho* (Shorty) as he was known. He agreed to make a saddle especially for my journey.

Because Brian Anderson from Copper Spring Ranch had given me a Wade saddle in Montana during my first ride, I decided to use one for this journey. It was super comfortable to sit in, and it never caused saddle sores on my horses' backs.

The Wade saddle sits lower than others with a prominent lip in the front and a larger horn. Sitting lower over the withers, it causes less stress on the horse's back. The bars are wider for more surface area against the horse so it stays in place better, and it doesn't need to be cinched as tight. In my experience using it, I found that it distributed the weight of the saddle and the rider much better across the animal's back.

Baixinho ran his rough hands over the chestnut-leather saddle the day I picked it up. His fingers were stubby like sausages, with many cuts and calluses. "I made this saddle as light as possible for your mares' comfort. The deep seat and placement of the Wade's stirrup will help ease the pain in your knees and back on those long days."

The final thing I needed for my departure was a support vehicle and a support driver. During my first Long Ride, I spent countless nights rolling around in my tent, unable to sleep with the fear my horses would colic and die because there was no water to give them. Some days, I tied them to a lonesome tree in the middle of the desert with nothing to graze on. On a few stretches, I spent days without seeing or speaking to another human being. These moments of solitude, fear, and anxiety — above all else — left the deepest scars on my psyche. From the moment I decided to undertake this second immense challenge, I promised myself I would only do it with a support vehicle and a driver.

The vehicle was lent to me by my sponsors, Os Independentes, the group that put on the Barretos Rodeo. It was a white, 2000 Renault Master cube van covered with photos of me riding from my first Long Ride, along with my name. The sixteen-year-old vehicle looked like it should be delivering flowers. It had a three-person seat in the front, and a thin piece of plywood served as a partition to the back. With a six-foot ceiling, the back of the van was spacious and offered a lot of room to carry hay, feed, medication, and equipment needed for the horses. It wasn't the newest or prettiest vehicle in the world, but for what I needed it was perfect.

The driver was not so simple to find. During the early stages of the planning, a journalist and her husband came to me full of excitement and vigor and offered to drive the vehicle for me. They knew someone who would sponsor their portion of the journey and assured me repeatedly that I didn't need to worry. A month prior to departure, they called me and said they weren't going to be able to go. Their sponsorship had fallen through.

When I said I was going to ride a horse from Canada to Brazil at the age of twenty-three, no one wanted anything to do with me. They laughed in my face. They called me crazy. They said it was impossible. However, I believed in myself, and I knew that quitting was never an option. I kept on working and working and working until one day I had everything I needed. That was the secret to life. Work. Dedication. Commitment. Focus. Determination. Discipline. I was sad they couldn't find a way.

As always, my budget was only enough for the essentials. With one month to find someone to drive the van and willing to work for no pay, my best friend Mark Maw came in to save the day. While I contemplated what the hell I would do, Mark offered himself. "Bro, I can drive the van for you."

After the Pan American Games, Mark had flown to Brazil with me and lived at my parents' place for several months. My first Canadian friend, he and I had been through a lot together. We were more like brothers than anything else. A natural comedian with a big beer belly who cared more about his friends than himself, he was completely addicted to hockey, especially the Toronto Maple Leafs.

I asked Mark several times if he was sure about this commitment. Being brothers, I knew that Mark and the word commitment didn't sit well in the same sentence. He had a track record of disappearing sometimes. He would screen calls for days and not answer texts, or blow off birthday parties, volunteer gigs, and dinner plans due to a big night out. I created the title "Went Hard the Night Before," for his memoir which I planned to write one day.

Beaming a confident smile on his round face, hacking a dart, he replied, "Yeah, bro, I mean, how hard can it be? Plus, it will help me work on my Portuguese, and I will get to see Brazil."

I looked hard into my Sancho Panza's green eyes as he coughed up a lung and announced, "Let's go, Marky."

The Long Ride was on!

I met my mounts ten days prior to leaving. Lincoln dropped off both mares at 3G, a stunning ranch outside of Barretos. The family who owned it raised Senepol Cattle and Quarter Horses and were close friends of his. When I arrived, the worker told me where my mares were, and I ran to them.

"Hey, girls," I called, staring at them from the gate.

Both mares turned their muzzles up and smelled the humid air, ears pointing my way as straight as an arrow, grass hanging from the side of their mouths. When I made my way into the pasture, they both took off like rockets, bucking and whinnying around the field. It was as if they were trying to tell me that winning over their trust and hearts would be a challenge. They were the saucy high school girls out of my league.

I wasn't worried. I had worked with several mares during my tie-down roping days and knew what "playing hard to get" was all about. After about five minutes, I managed to catch my feisty mares and gave them the first of many pats on the neck.

I first caught Doll O'lena and immediately blew in her right nostril. An old-timer once told me this was the most polite way to say hello to a horse and it ensured the animal would never forget you. I did it with Frenchie, Bruiser, and Dude, the three horses I rode from Canada to Brazil on my Long Ride Home, when I first met them.

I must say it worked! When I returned from Canada, after working on the Pan Am Games, all three horses smelled my skin, all over my hands, arms, and neck, giving me goosebumps, as if remembering where they knew me from.

"Hey, beautiful girl, nice to meet you," I said, scratching Doll's star. Her eyes opened wide to take me in. Doll was as flashy as they came. She was a five-year-old, red-roan Quarter Horse. Standing at 14.2 hands, she was all ginger, a darker red on her head and legs, with a half pastern on her back left leg. She was slim, gorgeous, and full of spirit. Doll was the feisty redhead.

After tying her up, I blew into Life's left nostril to introduce myself. I scratched the side of her head and gave her buckskin fur a kiss. Life was a six-year-old Quarter Horse standing at 14.3 hands. She was stocky like a bulldog, with a star on her forehead and half pastern on her back right leg and a sock on her back left. Her dark golden body was stunning. In the middle of her back, like a zebra, a dark brown line ran from where her mane ended to where her tail began. Her mane was a mixture of dirty-blond and red. At the tip of her ears, her fur went from golden brown to a darker brown color, as if someone had painted them using a thin paintbrush.

After introductions were made, it was time to get started. I put the saddle on Doll first, rode her around the pasture, and then did the same with Life. Both mares were excited at first, but after a few minutes they calmed right down. I then took them out and ponied one around while riding the other. They did great! Some horses did not like to follow another animal so close and some hated being followed. This could become dangerous to both rider and animal when one tried to bite or kick the other on the side of a busy road or on a narrow trail some 11,000 feet high.

The following morning, I introduced the packsaddle to Life. When I untied her, I held my breath waiting for her to start bucking and explode with the orange panniers on her back just as Frenchie had. He had nearly killed me in Calgary several years before when I started my first Long Ride.

Nothing. Life put her head down and started grazing. I was astonished at how calm she was while she carried the pack behind Doll and me.

I started adding kilometers that afternoon to get these equine athletes used to the rhythm we would carry out during the journey. On average, I rode thirty kilometers a day. You couldn't expect a horse that hadn't been doing anything to cover that amount of ground right off the bat. I started with five kilometers the first day, then seven kilometers the second, ten the third, and so on until they built their conditions naturally to adapt to thirty kilometers a day.

Another important aspect of getting horses ready for a Long Ride was adapting them to car traffic. Because I rode thousands of kilometers on my journeys, it was impossible to avoid busy roads. Before leaving, I needed to get my mares bombproof. One freak attack by the mares could send me and them into oncoming traffic.

On our fourth day of training, I took them out into the scary world outside of the ranch. As they began to hear the rattle from the colossal trucks blowing by in the distance, they started to tense up. I did, too. It was hard to explain the feeling of being atop a skittish animal next to such large vehicles moving so fast, but it was something like meeting a mighty grizzly bear — scary as hell!

When we finally reached the road, I took a deep breath and kicked them up to the grassy patch next to the highway. We were pretty far from traffic, but every vehicle that went by made Life run up. As the clunky pack hit Doll in the ass, she, too, would want to take off running. I had to hold her up and give a couple of jerks to Life's lead rope to stop both mares. This lasted about half an hour. Eventually, they both calmed down and learned that nothing would harm them.

For the next couple of days, I continued working with the mares from sunup to sundown. Slowly, patiently, I added more kilometers to our test runs as the sun tried to kill us with its murderous rays. As the temperature neared the forties, I rode drenched in sweat all day, my skin burned, and my mouth parched.

What had I gotten myself into — again!

ON THE ROAD AGAIN

I t was an overcast morning. A powerful wind blew, making a mess of my horse's mane and forcing me to tilt my head forward to prevent my cowboy hat from flying off. In front of us sat a long, gnarly bridge. I applied pressure using my left leg and moved my horse as close to the guardrail as possible.

Taking an extra-tight grip on the worn-out leather reins and moving my boots back so that just the tips sat in the stirrups, we began crossing the structure, some fifty meters above a shallow river. As we neared the halfway point of the bridge, my biggest fear appeared on the horizon: a screaming transport truck.

Every muscle in my body tightened as my horse's head shot up. The noise of the truck and my tense muscles already warned the animal of the danger ahead. When the truck got about twenty meters from us moving at about 120 kilometers per hour, my horse stopped in his tracks and began to dance nervously from left to right, bending his right front leg at the knee, then his left, then his right again.

Everything happened too quickly to react, but inside me, the world transitioned into warp mode. When the truck went to pass us going the opposite direction, my horse turned his head to the right and, on instinct, reared up, tucked his two front legs under him, and using all of his force, catapulted over the guardrail. In a millisecond, we were free falling toward the rocky river beneath, man and beast, tangled in a desperate dance in midair. Just as I was about to hit the river, I opened my eyes, startled by my own scream.

After my first Long Ride ended, waking up to a nightmare involving my horses became a normal thing. Some nights, I searched and searched and searched for water with no luck. Other nights, we were being chased by armed men in a dark forest. None of those tense dreams replayed themselves like that nightmare. It plagued my dreams during the months prior to jumping into the saddle. Each time, that vision of me free falling with the dark horse left me more convinced I would die on the journey.

Opening up for the first time about the deadly premonition I held deep in my core, one night I confessed to one of my friends, "I feel like I won't survive this one."

"You can't go, Filipe. If you feel this way, you can't go on this trip," a close friend protested, holding my right hand so tight my fingers turned white.

I struggled with this thought for weeks on end. It was tearing me apart. Was she right? Was I being an absolute moron to jump into the saddle harboring such a deep feeling it would kill me? Was I not listening to the Universe?

I wasn't sure what I should do until I visited the Barretos Children's Cancer Hospital one last time. Making my usual rounds to paint with the kids, tell them horse stories, or just to try to get them to crack a smile, I met a little boy named Arthur. Standing just over three feet tall, he was small for a seven-year-old, pale, bald, and extremely frail. Thin purple veins appeared on his forehead. A strong wind could knock him down. However, his aura, his smile, and his energy made him a giant.

"I don't cry at the needles anymore because my mom told me they turn me into a superhero." Despite the dark rings around his eyes. Arthur's smile was contagious.

On one knee, looking him straight in the eyes, I told him he was already a superhero to me. Gazing at my black felt cowboy hat, he smiled wider. He then grabbed my hand and pulled me to his toy station.

Arthur was battling Acute Myeloid Leukemia. The chances of him winning this fight were slim, but he and his family were not giving up. This extraordinary hospital was giving them a real shot.

It was at that moment I realized that this ride was much more than just a project or an adventure. It was my destiny. My journey was meant to help these children. If I died doing it, so be it. My life was no more important than Arthur's or the hundreds of children being treated or the thousands who might receive their diagnosis too late.

Before leaving the hospital, that little superhero threw his arms around me so tight I could feel his heart beating against my chest. His thin arms locked like a pretzel around my neck. I took a deep breath, closed my eyes tight, and promised I would see him after my journey ended. Now, it was my turn to try to become a superhero.

Had I known I would never see Arthur in this life again, I would have held that hug just a little longer.

On April 10, 2016, after several months of planning, I began tacking my mares.

"Bro, I feel like I could fry an egg on top of my head right now," Mark said. Thick lines of sweat flowed down the sides of his face from his sideburns.

It was a hot and humid Sunday, like most days in Barretos. People from all over the state and the country had come to send me off on yet another adventure. My parents, friends, the president of the Barretos Rodeo, the mayor of Barretos, my sponsors, the media, and the president of the Quarter Horse Association all wished me well. It was a chaotic scene.

My mares pranced around nervously as I tried to calm them with my words. The large sound truck directly in front of us played a song written for me loud enough for the entire town to hear. That did not help.

He comes in riding.
With faith and courage.
Along trails of passion.
Behind the wind.
Under the sun.
With reins full of emotion.
Arriving where the land kisses the ocean.
Under heavy rains or bathing in the moonlight.
He is the Horseman of the Americas.

Hundreds of riders were around me. People wanted to take selfies, ask for autographs, and wish me a good journey. Since my first Long Ride ended, I had been interviewed by all of the big television and radio shows in the country. Burger King had centered one of their new television campaigns around me. Two statues were raised to celebrate the journey — one in Barretos and another in the state of Paraná.

Public appearances like this one were a complicated ordeal. Amidst the craziness, an elderly man brought forward a gilt replica of Our Lady of Aparecida — the patron saint of Brazilian cowboys — as an offering.

I dismounted Doll and kneeled on the hot asphalt, removed my straw hat, raised my right hand to the saint's image, my pale fingers touching her black feet, and dropped my head.

I whispered, "Please look after my mares and me on this journey. Please guide me to green pastures and fresh water. May we all return healthy and alive."

It was a big task. I would spend a year traveling with my horses to Tierra del Fuego, the end of the world. Crossing Patagonia in its entirety, from north to south, I dared to ride through one of the wildest and inhospitable places on earth. Long stretches of nothing, harrowing mountain passes, ferocious pumas, and screaming winds at over one hundred kilometers per hour awaited us. If I broke my leg falling off one of my steeds as my father had months back, the closest hospital might be days away. In Patagonia, simple things could become big problems. But first I had to leave Barretos.

I remounted, sliding onto my brand-new Wade saddle. With a kiss from my spurs, Doll walked forward, and Life followed closely behind. We were off. I was taking the first stride on a journey of 7,500 kilometers.

A peace that I had not encountered in a long time descended upon me. The thought I would die on this ride was still there, lodged deep in the back of my mind, yet it no longer bothered me. I felt at home atop that mare. I felt complete once again. Purpose had returned to my life. When I was not in the saddle, I felt like half a man.

What should have been a day of celebration turned into our first problem. Only two hours after the kickoff to our journey, we encountered our first worry on the road. Life was lame.

I jumped off Doll's back and made my way toward the golden mare who carried the pack. When I lifted her front right leg, the reason for her pain stared back at me. A sharp piece of metal wire stuck out of the bottom of her right front hoof. It had pierced her sole, on the right side, where her soft frog met the hard sole of her hoof.

Frustrated, I yanked the metal out. Looking up at the clear blue sky, my eyes burning from sweat, I protested, "With hundreds of horses here, this thing had to go into my mare's hoof? Damn!"

I arranged to have Life transported in a truck to our rest stop, the Barretos Rodeo grounds, and continued the ride with Doll. I kept smiling for the cameras, but I was worried. After a delicious lunch complete with live music, dancing, and cold beer, I rode the final five kilometers to the rodeo grounds where Life was resting.

After untacking Doll and taking more photos, I soaked Life's leg in ice water for forty-five minutes and gave her an anti-inflammatory injection. Now we needed to wait. I slept fitfully, exhausted from the day's hectic ride and blazing sun.

I rose at 6:30 am to the cheerful chirping of a *tico-tico*. The sun was just starting to rise, yet the heat was already making it hard to live. Before brushing my teeth, I went to my girls to feed them and check on Life. Thankfully, the treatment had worked. Life was fine, for now.

We rode south.

~

My first week on the road took me down the same land I had traversed at the end of my first Long Ride. And as fate would have it, I was accompanied by the *comitiva* which used to be a group of cowboys who traditionally worked the large ranches in Brazil, but today had become a club of sorts. It was for men and women who love to go on day rides or longer journeys on horseback. They were called *Água do Peão,* the same folks who had entered the arena with me in 2014.

Milton Liso, the leader of the *comitiva,* had light eyes, a thin white and gray mustache, and the square body of SpongeBob. He was a calm, soft-spoken man you didn't want to see angry. His importance in the group could be observed by the way everyone, young and old, respected him. He had a deep love for mules and burros and the cowboy way of life, but his heart beat to the sound of his grandson's high-pitched voice. Guilherminho was his biggest pride, and the two went everywhere together. His grandson rode right next to him atop Granfina, a bombproof, buckskin mule.

"This is where all of the cattle used to travel through on foot as cowboys pushed them to the Barretos slaughterhouse, one of the first in the country," Milton told me as he sat atop a large, sweaty, dark mule.

Fact was, this kind and loving *vaquero* told me the same thing last time, but it didn't matter. Having his bright, familiar face riding next to me felt comforting.

Just as with the final days of the last journey, filled with too much meat and beer for one man to handle, the new ride had begun. Every day ended with a huge barbecue, tons of people, and copious amounts of alcohol being passed around. Music was always blaring from an old speaker or a torn-up guitar.

After riding for eight to ten hours in 40°C plus weather and covered with red dust, the cold beer felt exquisite as it made its way down my dry throat. However, the next morning, having slept only four hours and hungover, I regretted ever picking up the first can. My head banged to samba drums.

The only difference was that this time, my best friend Mark Maw was there driving the support vehicle. "I had no idea people would take us into their homes like this," he said one night while we shared a dusty room in an old farmhouse.

Mark had never traveled like this before. Like most Canadians I knew, his idea of a vacation was going to an all-inclusive in Mexico, Jamaica, or the Dominican Republic where the most amount of culture offered was the tacky "traditional" dance on display at the hotel bar while you got to know a family from Texas.

"I really like seeing how these people live... what they eat... It's so different from my life back home," he said, sipping on a cold *Brahma*. Mark loved beer so much, he carried "emergency beers" under the driver's seat.

Mark's favorite part of that first week on the road was watching the *comitiva's* cook work. Partly because he was always hungry, and partly because it was truly a spectacle.

Joao Rozetta was like a character even Shakespeare would have had a hard time bringing to life. One of the happiest and hardest working individuals I have ever met in my life, the fifty-three-year-old cowboy lost his left leg in a work accident several years before.

"I was putting sugarcane through a grinder to make feed for the cattle," he told me while boiling a big pot of beans. "Some of the stalks got jammed, and when I went to push it through the machine using my foot, they became loose and my leg went through the grinder."

A champion bull rider, the accident changed his life. He had to have his leg amputated up to the calf, ending his rodeo career. Looking down at the knot in his filthy jeans' left leg, he said, "It was hard at first, but I realized that I was lucky to be alive and needed to continue on with my life." That was exactly what he did.

Every night I watched as the tanned cook, who always looked

darker from the dirt glued to his skin, hopped from the sink to the oven, back to the cutting board, and back to the sink while he cooked delicious meals for us. All the while, Joao sported a huge smile on his wide face. He drove a standard car, rode horses, made knives, and did intricate leatherwork. He was more capable than most people who have both legs! A true inspiration.

In his house, built from the ground up with his own hands in the small town of Guapiaçu, Joao hosted Mark and me for a night. After a delicious barbecue dinner, he came into the cluttered room where we would rest wearing tighty-whities and holding a thick photo album.

"I want to show you guys some photos," Joao said as he used his crutches to hobble to a nearby couch.

He was so comfortable with his body it made me uncomfortable. He stood with his sly smile stamped across his dark face. His beer belly protruded over his tighty-whities. With both crutches snugged deep in his armpits, his right foot sat on the cold cement floor while his left stump hung there for all to see. The skin folded over at the end where his knee once sat, creating a cone, like a bald man's head.

Joao raised his voice with excitement as I looked over the photo. "Look at this bull! I scored eighty-nine points on him and finished second in Barreto's that year."

He never won Brazil's largest rodeo, but he definitely won in life. Seeing the love he had for his wife and children, and the way they looked to him with eyes full of admiration and love, it was clear how much he had won. They lived a simple life, one without many comforts or possessions. However, like in many of the simple homes I entered in the Americas, there was something much more powerful than money could ever buy. A purity. An essence of life. Light hearts and big smiles. True happiness.

On another hot afternoon, while Mark waited for me in the middle of nowhere surrounded by sugarcane, he saw a man walking up to the van through the mirror on the driver's door. As he studied the tall, shirt-less, dark figure, he noticed a large metal object hanging in his right hand. When Mark inched closer to the mirror, he realized the object was a large knife.

Holy shit! This guy is coming to rob me, the Canadian thought to himself. Mark quickly locked both doors and rolled up the windows. With sweat dripping from his brow, he awaited the man's arrival. He hoped he would continue walking by and not bother him. No chance. When the man arrived at Mark's window, he said hello. He was the size of a fridge! Speaking little Portuguese and afraid for his life, Mark tried to make the man understand I would be arriving soon.

"*Cavaleiro das Americas*," Mark said over and over again, pointing back with his right hand.

The man wanted him to step out of the van.

"He was gesturing for me to get out of the van and follow him," my friend told me with a wide smile. Coming from Mark, the story sounded more like a stand-up routine.

Eventually, Mark came to the conclusion that if the man wanted to, he could break the window and drag him out with ease. Mark opened the door and followed the strong fellow into a collection of trees a few meters back.

"When we entered the small forest, I thought I was going to die. I was sure of it." After following the man for five minutes, he gestured for Mark to stop, reached into a large, white bag, and pulled out two oranges. He used his large knife to peel both, cut them in half, and, with orange juice dripping from his dirty hands, handed Mark one of the oranges.

"I couldn't believe it. I was so scared of him, and he just wanted to give me an orange!"

Together, this Brazilian man who worked the fields and a Canadian Early Childhood Education grad sucked on delicious oranges, side by side, under the shade of a big mango tree. Somehow, they conversed without speaking the same language.

"He told me these were the best oranges in the world and asked if I liked them."

They each had three oranges before Mark said goodbye and returned to the van.

~

Doll and Life took on the first 120 kilometers of our journey like pros. They easily navigated both rickety wooden bridges and highways of roaring traffic. I could feel them maturing beneath me. That was until Life's sharp teeth snapped that thought in half. On a scorching after-noon on a dusty country road, I walked in front of the mares to give them a break. I was exhausted. Staring at the horizon in front of me and thinking about nothing but a cold shower, I felt a sharp pain on the top left side of my back.

"What the?" was all I managed to blurt out before jumping forward and snapping my head back.

Life had tried to take a chunk out of my back. An actual scrap of my flesh. I had a cannibal pony on my hands.

"Why the hell did you bite me?" I demanded. She didn't give me any answers, but she did leave a nasty purple bruise on my back to remind me never to turn my back to the feisty mare again.

During this stretch, crossing large sugarcane fields that stretched for hundreds of kilometers in all directions, the flies nearly drove me mad. The farms used a liquid extracted from the cane to spray the fields. Smelling sweet like honey and full of nutrients, the concoction acted as a natural fertilizer. What it also did was create a perfect breeding environment for flies.

Hundreds. Thousands. Millions of the small black flies landed on my face trying to enter my mouth and eyes all day. It was extremely annoying. I rode or walked flailing my arms around like someone who was just burned by acid. I knew it looked funny, but it was brutal. After five hot days on the road, dusty and tired, we arrived in Rio Preto. Our first resting point was Milton Liso's beautiful ranch.

My body ached from my hair to my toes, and my skin was badly burned, but I was happy. I had missed life on the road more than I realized. I loved meeting new people every day, listening to their wild and intriguing stories, and sharing my own.

I enjoyed being immersed in nature, spending the entire day outside. Hearing the birds chirping nearby elevated my spirits. Feeling the soft wind kiss my face calmed me. I meditated to the sharp hollow sound of my mares' hooves hitting the road. Smelling like horse sweat, being one with my ponies, flies and all, it was so real. My life was magical.

ROAD TO PRESIDENTE PRUDENTE

In Rio Preto, I got a chance to rest at Milton's ranch and speak to the media about my mission to help the Barretos Children's Cancer Hospital. I even attended a rodeo. Mark and I also used our time off to organize the support van. It was already a mess.

"It looks like a bomb went off in here," he said, using his hands to imitate an explosion that started at his belly button and rose up until his arms were spread far apart above his head. Having my best friend by my side felt comforting. Just to have someone to talk to at the end of a long day made all of the difference in the world. Since Mark was the funniest person on this planet, even on the shitty days, he managed to make me laugh with his dad jokes.

"What does a bee do when it is hot out like this?" he asked me one afternoon as we sweated like construction workers in a tropical heatwave during our first week on the road.

"I have no idea, Mark."

"He takes off his yellow jacket."

Let's all groan together!

With the van organized and the mares feeling fresh, Mark and I also rested before we continued our ride south.

Milton Liso, alongside his *comitiva,* bid me farewell with a strong hug. "You take care of yourself, Filipe. Thank you for representing our culture so well! We are going to miss you!"

I would miss those boys, as well. However, just like when I said goodbye to them at the end of my last journey, I knew this would not be the last time we saw each other. The horse made brothers out of people who came from different lands and realities. That brotherhood could not be broken by time nor space. It may take another year or two for us to meet on some dusty trail, but when that day came, it would be like before, as if we had never left each other's side.

On our third week on the road, with our escort long gone, the weather changed dramatically. Heavy rains and single-digit temperatures punished us. On a cool morning, heavy, angry clouds hung low over my cowboy hat. They moved quickly, with a strong wind blowing from east to west.

Before jumping into the saddle, I thought about putting on my blue rain poncho, the same one I wore when I entered Honduras on my first Long Ride. However, the thought of the flapping plastic scaring Doll didn't seem enticing. That morning, she was feeling too good for her own good. In heat, the mare called out repeatedly and thrust her head from side to side in search of a non-existent stallion. Her tail lifted up, and she pranced around the pasture in a rhythmic trot as if she had Arabian blood.

"Relax, Doll! There are no studs here," I said, trying to calm the excited mare down as she walked sideways in search of her Prince Charming. After only half an hour in the saddle, thick raindrops began to fall from the dark sky, building in intensity.

Luckily, I spotted the support van pulled over on the right side of the road 200 meters ahead. I kicked Doll up and, with Life next to us, we trotted toward Mark. He sat in the back of the cube van with the doors open looking like he was scheming a joke.

Quoting the movie *Old School*, Mark passed me the blue poncho rolled up into a neat cylinder. "Don't beat yourself up over this, Mitch.

It's not your fault. Dammit, Blue was old. That's what old people do. They die."

"You're my Boy Blue!" I shot back. Laughing, I placed the poncho on my lap, but as I went to open it, Doll shot off to the right like a cat. Her quick movement ripped Life's lead rope out of my right hand, and the spooked mare ran onto the road.

Panicked, I worried she would get hit by a vehicle. I tried to throw the poncho off the saddle, but Doll bucked and it slipped under my left leg.

This is not good, I thought to myself, already looking at the ground beneath me, preparing for the worst.

I tried to step off quickly, but Doll swooped the other way and threw me down hard. I landed on my back, holding onto the rein with a tight grip. My attempt to hold her was futile. Doll ripped the leather rein out of my soggy left hand and took off after Life.

I jumped up from the wet grass and scrambled after them. Luckily, they both stopped in the middle of the asphalt as if nothing had happened, and thankfully, no car was in sight. Letting the heavy rain-drops hit my face, I looked up at the gray sky and thanked the Universe. My back throbbed in pain, but my girls were okay, and that was all that mattered.

For the rest of the morning, I got soaked. The feeling of being thankful the mares were okay had long passed, and I was now livid. Doll had gotten her way. The "scary" blue poncho would remain off her soft fur while the idiot on top of her got drenched.

The rain, now heavy, drove a deep chill down my spine and into my legs. My clothes, soggy and dense, clung to my skin and made every movement in the saddle extremely uncomfortable. I rode south shaking in the saddle like an angry diamondback snake's rattle. Luckily, there was a family waiting to share their lunch with us. I found refuge under their roof.

"You need to get out of those clothes, or you're going to get sick," the matriarch of the family said. She sounded as anxious as my own mother.

Sitting around a long wooden table filled with meat, yucca, rice, beans, salad, and *farofa* (a toasted yucca or corn flour mixture), I wore a dry shirt lent to me by one of the three sons. I let the family's love warm my soul. It was exactly what I needed.

After lunch, two of the sons and a few other cowboys from the community decided to ride with me in the afternoon toward the town of Buritama. It was great to have the company but, even better, with their help, I would be able to use my poncho and keep dry.

With Doll's lead rope dallied around his worn-out saddle horn, an old-timer in the group gestured that it was safe for me to get on. The skin on his face looked like the worn leather of his saddle. His droopy brown cowboy hat, covered with red specks of mud, sat low on his head. His small, glossy eyes seemed to carry all of the wisdom in the world. I trusted him.

Holding the bottom of the blue poncho bunched up together with my right hand, I used my left to pull myself up onto the saddle. Doll looked back at me, wide-eyed and unhappy at what I was attempting to do. As soon as I swung my right leg over the Wade saddle and found my seat, she tried to take off as she had a few hours earlier. With her lead rope safely fastened around the old-timer's horn, she wasn't going anywhere.

"Easy, girl, We ain't gonna hurt you," he whispered toward Doll, who pranced on the spot, eyes wide and full of fear, her head nearly on his lap.

I slowly opened the plastic I had bunched up in my right hand, allowing the poncho to cover the saddle and Doll's back end. She protested immediately, trying to take off once again. The old-timer began walking forward, and she followed his big mule, uncomfortable with the blue plastic touching her.

The mule, with his primeval head, shot her an annoyed look once in a while as if saying, "Relax, you prissy city girl."

After about five minutes, the feisty mare realized the poncho was not going to eat her, and I was able to go back to riding solo while ponying Life.

～

With a sore back from the previous day's fall, I rode out of Buritama. The temperature which just two days prior sat in the high 30s was now in the low 10s. The cold did not help the pain. The drastic change in temperature, along with riding in the rain, left me with a sore throat and a runny nose.

In Gabriel Monteiro, a town of 2,000 people, I was welcomed with a spectacle in the sky. Riding down a country road on the outskirts of town, I was blessed with one of the most beautiful sunsets I had ever seen. As the sun dove toward the edge of the earth directly in front of my mare's ears, the sky burned orange, bright yellow, pink, and purple. It was simply breathtaking.

With *fim-fim* birds flying to their refuge for the night, their bellies and the top of their heads a bright yellow and the rest of their bodies a bluish black, I closed my eyes and gave thanks. They whistled a long-lasting, high-pitch chirp as if to say, "Hello!"

I whistled hello back.

"The wide open spaces are my church, the Universe, my religion, Nature, my God," I said aloud, letting the setting sun kiss my face goodnight.

Just before the golden globe disappeared under the horizon, I arrived at the farm where we would spend the night. Mark and our new host José Eduardo Bortoloci came to the gate to welcome us.

"I told all of my friends you were coming, but no one believes me!" Shaking his head in disbelief, the excited teenager chewed tobacco with vigor, spitting out the brown liquid every few seconds. "Heck, I can't even believe that the *Cavaleiro das Americas* is staying at my farm."

José was a tall and wide team roper in his late teens. He had dark eyes and a friendly smile. He moved slowly on the ground, with a bit of a lazy hunch, dragging his cowboy boots. However, atop a horse, José was as quick as lightning.

He helped me fill a large bucket of water for the mares and gave me a bale of hay. "Save your hay for when you are down the road."

After untacking the mares and feeding them, we made our way to a bright orange house in the center of the property. Empty bottles of beer sat on a white table on the porch where Mark and José had spent the past hour trying to communicate. Judging by the number of empty bottles, they drank more than they talked.

"I have no idea what your friend is saying but he's hilarious," José said, his arm around Mark's shoulders as if the two had been buds for years. I didn't know how, but Mark managed to be funny in Portuguese, speaking only four words. In every town, he became the center of attention. Everyone wanted to meet the real Canadian guy, teach him bad words, and ask him questions using hand gestures and Google translate. Mark acted like the cool guy in high school, a cigarette hanging from his lips. With a cunning grin, he usually donned his tinted aviators.

Mark's right arm had a gnarly scar running from the middle of his hand up to his shoulder caused by a terrible car accident that nearly cost his life. It was always part of the conversation. It bothered him.

"I don't understand how they aren't embarrassed to blatantly point at my arm and ask about the scar," Mark opened up to me after a barbecue while resting at a host's home. The truth was the accident had a big impact on Mark's life. I would never forget the day I found out about it. I was in Kenya, shooting a documentary and doing volunteer work when my father told me over a phone call what had happened to Mark.

"It was bad, Filipe. He is in the hospital but he's going to be okay," my dad assured me. The news rocked me. We had known each other since Grade 4. We grew up playing mini-sticks in my basement and egging homes during those warm Bolton summer nights. Finishing elementary and high school together, our friendship only got stronger when we went off to university. We were inseparable. He was my best friend. My best friend was badly injured, and I was on the other side of the world. I wanted to be by his side. I felt like I had let him down, as if I could have prevented the accident somehow had I been there that night.

It was a humid Friday night in the middle of the summer. Mark was at a house party with many of our high school friends playing beer pong when they ran out of alcohol. His partner, a big, curly-haired guy in his early twenties who loved cars, offered to drive to his house to get another two-four. Mark agreed and offered to go with him. They jumped into a 1990s Mercedes Benz and in the first turn, driving drunk and way too fast, the owner of the vehicle lost control and rolled the car several times. Both teens were wearing their seat belts.

When I returned from Africa a month and a half after the accident, Mark recounted what happened. "When the car finally stopped rolling, landing on its side, I panicked. The driver was knocked out and wouldn't respond. I thought he was dead."

Mark was wearing a white plastic brace around his upper body as he retold the story. He had broken his back. In a panic, Mark couldn't open his passenger door so he punched a hole through the window, ripping his right arm apart in the process. He rushed to a nearby house to get help.

Mark lost a lot of blood and had to have skin grafts taken from his legs and placed on his arm. His back was in rough shape, but thankfully both boys survived.

"When the firefighters saw the way the vehicle ended up, they said we were extremely lucky to be alive. Had it not been for the Mercedes' strong chassis, we would have probably died."

It was understandable that he didn't want to tell complete strangers about the menacing scar on his arm. As always, he resorted to comedy to get off the uncomfortable topic. Early on in the trip, Mark made up a new story. Holding out his arm, showing off the wide, darker-skinned scar tissue running up his arm, the chubby Canadian would announce, "It was a shark attack!"

People went wide-eyed in amazement. They nearly drooled at the story in excitement. He told them about the terrible moment when he single-handedly fought a Great White out at sea and survived to tell the tale. People actually believed him.

His hook at the end always made everyone laugh. "You should see the shark!"

～

We arrived in Gabriel Monteiro two days before the annual horse parade.

"Please, Filipe, stay to ride with us. It will make the parade so much better," José's friend Tiago, a skinnier version of José, said to me with big puppy eyes. What I have learned on my adventures was that the most significant parts of a journey were the moments you didn't plan or expect. On my last Long Ride, I was always in such a hurry to get to the finish line, at times my anxiety didn't allow me to truly enjoy the journey.

"Okay, I will ride out tomorrow, leave the mares resting at a farm, and return to ride with you guys," I said. "Can you lend me an animal?"

"Yes, yes, you can ride my mule," Tiago quickly responded before beaming a proud smile. Two days later, there I was in the middle of hundreds of riders, parading through the small town on my tall, dark, and handsome mule.

Elderly men, women, and children rode their horses, mules, and even saddle bulls. Riders wearing matching shirts held banners proudly announcing the names of different ranches. With a sound truck blaring music in front of us and too many cold beers being passed around — causing more than one cowboy to fall off his mount — I sang and laughed with my new friends.

The morning after participating in Gabriel Monteiro's horse parade, we continued on toward the city of Presidente Prudente, São Paulo.

In the 1950s, the King Ranch, one of the largest and oldest ranches in the world, bought land near Presidente Prudente. Based out of Texas, the operation sent workers, machinery, seven mares, and a Quarter Horse stud by the name of Saltillho Jr. to the South American country. There were different European breeds of horses in Brazil at the time, but the Quarter Horse revolutionized work in the field. The animal's athleticism, cow sense, and intelligence made it the perfect fit to work the large pastures of Brazilian ranches.

On March 31, 1968, the King Ranch held the first Quarter Horse sale in the country. It was at that moment that the breed took off in Brazil. Ranchers from Presidente Prudente and the surrounding area began purchasing horses from the King Ranch Remuda and crossing them with their own animals. Within a few years, the number of pure Quarter Horses grew significantly in the country. The Brazilian Quarter Horse Association was born.

The day before arriving in the birthplace of the Brazilian Quarter Horse, I heard a noise I detested: a loose horseshoe clanking. Every time Doll's front right hoof hit the ground, the sound of loose metal made me cringe. *Clank. Clank. Clank.*

I was forced to stop at a gas station, borrow a hammer, and nail the shoe back on. Just after four p.m., with an empty stomach sounding like a ferocious lion, I saw the sign for the Quarter Horse Ranch, our home in Presidente Prudente. The blue sign made my back straighten and spread a smile on my long face. I had made it. Or almost.

Just as I passed the sign, relaxing my tired body, a truck sped by us dragging a short chain on the road. The sound of the rattling metal scraping against the coarse pavement made my mares explode into a gallop that nearly knocked me out of the saddle. I managed to stop them and, with my heart pounding a million beats per second and my hands shaking, I remembered a lesson from my first Long Ride: It ain't over 'til it's over.

The moment you relaxed in the saddle, you put yourself in danger. Letting out a long breath, I asked my girls, "Can we try to arrive alive?"

HOME OF THE QUARTER HORSE

Having trekked 396 kilometers in one month and one week, I felt proud of my mares. I thanked Life and Doll for all of their hard work as we rode into the large ranch where we would rest in Presidente Prudente. I promised them fresh water, tons of feed, and shade. The president of the ranch, Heitor, a big man with an even bigger heart, greeted me warmly.

"Filipe! Welcome to the Quarter Horse Ranch. We are so proud to be hosting you and your mares."

His hand was big and puffy like a bread roll. He wore a red baseball cap that looked just like Donald Trump's "Make America Great Again" but with the ranch logo on it. His shaggy, dark brown hair poured out of the sides. I liked Heitor right away.

When I stepped off Life's back, a sharp lightning bolt shot up from my knee, up my leg, and into my torso toward my heart. My lower back felt like it was on fire. Tight and sore from the long days in the saddle and nailing Doll's shoe back on, my body desperately needed a break. The Quarter Horse Ranch was the perfect place for a cowboy to rest his horses and his soul.

We fed the mares and found refuge in the shade of the main office. Drinking a tall glass of cold water, Heitor told me that he had organized a welcome party for me that night. He explained how several members from the ranch would be present along with influential people from the city.

"You can give your motivational talk about the first journey from Canada to Brazil and meet our members. Then, we will have a big barbecue to celebrate your arrival." My new friend ran off to prepare everything for the night's event.

All I longed for was a bed and a shower. Instead, I was given a microphone and a stage.

Fortunately, the adrenaline from public speaking and cold beer gave me new life, and I ended up having a great time at the event meeting some wonderful Quarter Horse breeders from the region.

The next morning, the current president introduced me to the Ranch's first president, Mr. Ruy Terra. In his late eighties, Ruy told me about the rich history of the ranch, started by the first breeders like himself in 1974.

"We started the ranch so there was a place for the Quarter Horse and the cowboys and cowgirls to evolve and grow." Ruy ran the index finger on his right hand over his chaotic, bushy, snow-white eyebrows as he spoke.

Home to Latin America's largest indoor arena, he told me how everyone was against him when he decided to build it. Ruy was a visionary and pioneer, a man with a dream bigger than the average man could comprehend.

"They didn't have the vision I had back then," he told me as we walked the ranch. The skin sagging over his right eye, the deep lines running across his face, and his slight hunch all disappeared behind the fire blazing in his eyes.

After he gave me a tour, he invited me to his own farm. We got into his white Jeep Cherokee, and his driver took us to a large property about a half-hour away. Wearing a beige baseball cap with the words *Haras Terra* stamped on the front in brown, he showed me every detail of the facility he'd built recently and the horses housed in it.

After showing me one of his best studs, a great big gray horse, I asked him why he had decided to breed Quarter Horses more than four decades ago.

Patting the gray stud on the right side of his thick neck, Ruy told me, "The Quarter Horse is the family's horse. When you go to a competition, you see the kids riding and competing alongside their parents and grandparents. That's what I love about this horse."

Since I was only sixty kilometers from the state of Paraná, I needed to get the mares' health exams in order before continuing on. Every time I crossed a state line in Brazil, I had to get the animals tested for *mormo* (glanders disease) and equine infectious anemia. This caused me to layover in Prudente for an entire week as I waited for the mares' blood work to return from a lab in São Paulo.

On a chilly Thursday night, some new friends invited us to go out to the new bar in town. It was a mixture of a country saloon with a fifties rock and roll feel. Cowboy boots were glued to the ceiling as if invisible people were walking around up there. The tables were made from black metal barrels, and Harley Davidson signs hung in the bathroom. It was a cool place.

We started the night with some Budweisers while we got to know the thin blonde who invited us out with her brother, a medical student, and her girlfriend, a personal trainer. Both the girls had their charms.

The thin blonde wore a brown fur vest over a tube top and a mini skirt. She was skinny but fit with toned arms and legs. Her light blonde hair was long and straight, pulled back with a black barrette.

The personal trainer was a beautiful, but curvier, woman. She wore a skintight black-and-white dress showing a lot of cleavage and her dirty-blonde hair caressed her chest with every turn of her head.

To say Marky and I were excited was an understatement! After weeks hanging out in horse barns with bloated old men discussing which color of mule we preferred, this was a welcome break.

"Bro, I will take the one you don't like," Mark said excitedly while the pair went on a bathroom trek. Truth was, I actually thought we had a shot. However, when the thirsty gals ordered a dangerous bucket of ice filled with cans of Red Bull and a bottle of Smirnoff vodka, we had a bit of a false start. We went too hard, too quick.

Just after midnight, I placed Mark into an Uber. His eyelids hung low and his chatter didn't make any sense. I begged the driver to take him to our hotel. When the Uber arrived, Mark had passed out. We found out days later that the staff had to put Mark on a baggage cart and wheel him up to our room.

I lasted an extra half hour at the bar but lost focus on why I was drinking in the first place and ended up going back to the hotel alone.

While Life and Doll rested, I was taken to several Quarter Horse ranches where I saw some of the best animals in the country. It was such an extraordinary opportunity for a lover of the breed like myself.

The most memorable ranch I visited that week was 4M. Owned by Adilson José de Almeida, he was known in the area as the Scrooge McDuck of the horse world. The stunning property was home to some of the best cutting and barrel racing bloodlines in the country. Over a delicious barbecue, Adilson showed me his grand stallion, Tilly Playboy, a short and thick flashy bay Quarter Horse with a long mane and soft kind eyes. He looked like a mirror image of Adilson!

"I spent over $100,000 Reais (Brazilian currency) on this stud more than ten years ago. Everyone thought I was crazy, but he became the highest-earning cutting stud in Brazil," Adilson told me with pride as the majestic horse ate alfalfa.

After getting on Tilly bareback and taking some photos, Adilson and his friends walked me to the front of his home. Standing there chatting, a worker appeared with a beautiful bay colt. He walked the animal to where we were, and Adilson began telling me about the young horse.

"This right here, Filipe, is a very special colt. He is a son of Tilly Playboy with Sonora Song, the best cutting mare in Brazil. His name is Tilly Song," the short man told me as he patted the horse's neck with his left hand while holding a Brahma bottle with his right.

I could tell something was up by the whispers and laughter all around me. I couldn't put my finger on it, but I knew something big was about to happen. The air was electric. When Adilson finished talking about the colt's bloodlines, he paused for a second, looked over at me with his big brown eyes and said, "Tilly Song is a present to you."

I froze. My heart beating forcefully, my gaze stuck on the colt.

"What? No ... you're crazy," was the only logical thing I could say at that moment before tilting my cowboy hat back.

"No, no, I'm not. What you have done is not easy, son. It shows how much dedication, determination, and heart you have. You are an inspiration to all of us. You deserve this present."

I gave him a tight hug. In my world, Adilson had given me a Ferrari. This colt, only one year and six months old, was valued at $20,000 Reais. Tilly was the son of the best cutting horses ever born in Brazil and he was mine!

I have been given a lot of presents on my Long Rides. A dog, knives, belt buckles, saddles, cowboy hats, booze, a Mustang (the horse) — The list went on and on. This was by far one of the greatest gifts I had ever received on the road. Weeks later, I was given a second colt! But that was to raise funds for the Barretos Children's Cancer Hospital. We named the small, months-old baby Che and sold him for $2,500 Reais. I felt blessed.

PARANÁ

The morning when I went to get the mares for our ride out of Presidente Prudente, they didn't want anything to do with me. After a week off eating and sleeping, my ponies were as rebellious as teenage girls. They ran around me, tails pointed up, heads held high, whinnying loudly, and bucking every third stride. In horse lingo, they were giving me the middle finger!

I missed my boys from my first long ride. Frenchie, Bruiser, and Dude were always the same. Every morning when I went to get them, they were calm and waiting for me. I walked up to them, and they stood still watching me. When I arrived, they smelled me to see if I had treats, and they let me catch them, no problem.

Life and Doll, on the other hand, changed their mood with every phase of the moon. One day they loved me. The next they wanted to kill me. Then they wanted nothing to do with me, only to love me again. Their temperament was completely different from my boys.

Even the mares' urine smelled different. Every time they stopped to piss, an acrid smell would rise and nearly choke me. It was sour, acidic, and rank, a mixture of vinegar and rotten vegetables. I could feel the odor clawing at the back of my throat.

Riding south from Presidente Prudente, we traveled down the

"Quarter Horse Corridor," a thirty-five kilometer stretch of highway with ranches on both sides of the road. Trekking on a wide grassy shoulder, we passed several beautiful gates leading to even prettier ranches. In the late afternoon, we rode by a stunning *Ipe Rosa* (pink trumpet tree). Completely covered in light pink flowers, it looked like a work of art.

With the sun setting behind us, we rode into *Fazenda Dois Irmãos*, our home for the night. Renata Prata and her two daughters took photos of the mares and me as we made our way down the long driveway. I tried not to blush as I gave the three a quick kiss on each cheek. I didn't want them to smell the horse sweat that permeated my burned skin.

They were stunning women in a way only extremely wealthy Latin Americans can be. Perfectly silky hair, the skin of a baby, the smell of tropical fruits and honey, dressed to perfection with the posture and air of a supermodel. I felt embarrassed in my ripped jeans, dirty and sweaty skin, and worn-out cowboy hat.

The ranch, home to some world-class cutting and barrel horses, was owned by Antonio Renato Prata. He was Renata's father and the first president of *Os Independentes*, my sponsors and the group that put on the Barretos rodeo.

When I rode into the pasture where the mares would rest, Mr. Prata was there waiting for me. The tall and thick elderly man wore blue jeans tightly fastened to the middle of his stomach with a thin brown belt. His light denim long-sleeve shirt was folded up at the arms, and he wore a white straw cowboy hat tipped down in the front. The eighty-six-year-old stood with a slight hunch, both hands placed on top of his wooden cane.

Stashed in his left breast pocket was a worn-out pad of paper and a blue Bic pen. When I stepped down from the saddle, we shook hands. It was always easy to sniff out a real horseman by the way he acted around my animals. Before asking me any questions about my journey or destination, he wanted to make sure the mares were tended to with all of the feed and water they needed to rest that night.

Sitting in the rustic yet elegant living room of his ranch's home with antique silver stirrups hung on the brick wall above a flat-screen television playing the news, Mr. Prata told me, "I bought my first Quarter Horse in 1970 from the King Ranch sale."

A legend among Brazil's horse and cattle breeders, we spent an hour chatting about the rodeo he helped create in Barretos and his award-winning animals. It was a real treat for me. I absolutely loved talking to old-timers. These cowboys held wisdom the twenty-first century seemed to have lost. Some of the greatest lessons I had learned came from men wearing raggedy cowboy hats over their snow-white hair.

Before he and his family left us to rest, Mr. Prata advised, "You have seen a world very few people will ever experience, son. Keep on going. Use your horses' energy to keep you going when things get hard."

He was right! The horse had awarded me the opportunity to enter people's homes all over the Americas and learn their stories. I had broken bread with millionaires, farmhands, prostitutes, and drug lords in twelve nations. Thanks to these majestic animals, I had learned not to judge anyone until you had walked a mile in their boots. My time in the saddle had also taught me that my limit was much further than I ever imagined.

The biggest gift I had gained from these experiences as a Long Rider was my connection with the natural world. Only men like Marco Polo, Charles Darwin, Aime Tschiffely, and a few other explorers who were part of the history of the Long Riders' Guild had seen the world as I had.

When riding, you were at the perfect height to see the world around you. Traveling at four kilometers an hour, you didn't miss anything on your route. The animals, insects and reptiles, the fauna and flora, the geology — from the saddle you saw it all! And since the horse didn't have an engine, you were able to hear the birds chirping, the bees buzzing, and the wind blowing. The rain soaked you. The desert choked you. The rain forest was alive, sounding like a symphony and smelling of wet dirt and chlorophyll.

These experiences along with the daily dose of adrenaline of not knowing where you would sleep made it exciting. Would that bear up ahead eat you? Would you make it to the summit of the mountain you were fighting to climb? This way of life was extremely addictive. This was why I felt like half a man when I was not in the saddle. Once you had tasted life as a saddle tramp, life on foot was not as sweet.

After two long days on the road, we arrived at the bridge that crossed the Paranapanema River to enter the state of Paraná. The bridge stretched out at half a kilometer. I didn't have much time to enjoy the gorgeous view of the wide, brown river beneath. With giant trucks blowing by, we kept moving as quickly as possible. My body tense the entire time, I wondered if this was the bridge from my recurring nightmare.

After a long ten minutes, we finally crossed and entered the second state on our journey. I rode up to the MAPA (Ministry of Agriculture) office on the right side of the road and handed them the mares' exams. Luckily, everything was in order, and we were able to enter Paraná. That night, with no farms, ranches, or towns in sight, we were forced to camp at an old gas station. Not my favorite place to set up the tent, that was for sure.

We put up the tent right next to the gas station bathroom. Mark observed, "This place is filthier than a garbage dump!"

I tied up the mares to a fence line and gave them both an abundance of hay. After eating some noodles for dinner, Mark and I hit our own hay.

The next day, with the sun setting, we arrived in the rodeo capital of Paraná state.

Renan Almeida, a local bull rider, met us as we rode onto his ranch. "Welcome to Colorado!"

Located in the northern part of the state, Colorado had hosted forty-two consecutive rodeos since its humble beginning in 1973. Today, the event gave out thousands of Reais in prize money and featured some of Brazil's top country singers and bull riders. The rodeo drew giant crowds.

"The people here love western culture and rodeo. That's why it has been such a success," the tall, muscular cowboy told me as we looked at his photos from the most recent ride.

I was in awe of a sequence of images where a big, white bull with curved horns rammed Renan in his left cheekbone with great force. When the bull's sharp horn moved away from the cowboy's face, a prominent hole could be seen. In the later images, while the bull rider was spurring the bull for ninety-plus points, a deep track of blood could be seen running down to his chiseled chin. Even with the injury, he made the eight-second mark. This guy was the real deal.

That night, Renan's family cooked a delicious fish for us as we sat around chatting the night away. They called the dish "fish pizza." It consisted of a grilled fish fillet with vegetables, potatoes, and cheese on top. A delicious meal!

The next morning, Renan took us to see the town. We visited the local country store where I was forced to take a thousand selfies. I never imagined my journey would take on this magnitude. In some events and towns, I was a celebrity to the people and that meant that walking around became a hassle and sometimes even dangerous, something I learned very quickly when my first ride ended.

The year I arrived in Barretos, I was in the Brahma VIP section enjoying a show with some friends when someone recognized me and asked to take a selfie. I took the photo, and all of a sudden, I was caught in the middle of a tug-of-war between drunk men and women, wanting to be the next to get a picture with me.

My shirt was nearly ripped off, and thankfully, I was saved in the nick of time by a mammoth bodyguard who pulled me to safety and escorted me to a blocked-off area only for artists.

In Colorado, it didn't get that crazy. Only a few excited kids wanted selfies and autographs, nothing short of a humbling experience.

From the store, we went to meet the current president of the rodeo and then to help the local kids practice bull riding. As we walked toward the large wooden corral, Renan told me, "These are my bulls. I like to come here on weekends to help the kids out with their riding."

Unfortunately for Renan, he was off the bulls for a couple of months. A few weeks before our arrival, he had a bad wreck getting off a bull at a rodeo and dislocated his right knee. In good cowboy fashion, even with a boot cast, he was riding horses, jumping fences, and assisting with opening gates.

Though he had a big smile plastered on his tanned face, he also had a deathly, unblinking stare similar to a 2,000 pound bull. As he helped tie a cowboy's riding rope, he said, "I love this sport too much to sit still."

The last person to ride a bull that day wasn't tall enough to ride a roller coaster. At just nine-years-old *Palito* (Toothpick), as everyone called him, put his rope around a black calf. Renan held the young boy's vest tight, instructing him on how to place his hand in the rope. With a strong pat on the kid's back — he was so scrawny I worried bones might be broken — Renan told him to give it hell and threw the gate open.

Palito lasted about four jumps before he flew off, landing face-first in the dirt. He shot up to his feet with a smile full of pride on his face and a truckload of dirt in his mouth. He walked to Renan pretending the fall didn't hurt, limping a little every third step, before the injured bull rider gave the mini-bull rider a fist pump.

On the drive back to his house, Renan told me many stories about kids he taught. Sometimes their parents were in jail or out of work with no money. Sometimes, they were just gone. Kids lived in shacks with dirt floors. So many kids had it really tough and had little to hope for.

The tougher-than-nails cowboy softened his gaze for the first time since I'd met him. Even with all of his testosterone-fueled bravado, there was still room for love. "By teaching them to ride bulls, one day they could have a better life," Renan said.

It may seem brutal to us, but this was the way of most of the world. Life was very hard.

After a day's rest at Renan's ranch, it was time to hit the road once again. As I tacked up the mares on a cool morning, my new friend announced he would ride with me for the day. He took out his palomino gelding from his stall, saddled up the pony, and together we waved goodbye to his family and *Palito*.

What was meant to be a one-day ride turned into a three-day journey. Together Renan and I spent the day telling stories, laughing, and trying to rope bushes on the side of the road.

"You're pretty average," he would yell out with a smirk on his face after every loop I tossed.

Like many times before on my Long Rides, being up on our horses, riding south together, it seemed like we had been friends since childhood.

Like all good things, eventually, it came to an end. On a gray, rainy day, we arrived in Maringá. With a population of 385,753, it was the third-largest city in the state of Paraná. I had always heard how clean, organized, and modern the southern states in Brazil were compared to the north. I must say, after riding through Paraná, I had to agree. At times, it was as if I had entered another country. There was very little garbage on the sides of the roads, the cities were built in a grid, and the buildings were modern and clean. That was not the norm in my country.

In Maringá, we were welcomed by Rafael Tortolla, a local businessman with a love for team roping. As a light drizzle fell, I fed Life and Doll out in the pasture while Renan held his horse outside the gate. When the girls finished, he brought the palomino pony into the pasture.

As soon as the horse was released, he ran toward the mares in search of the feed they were eating seconds earlier. Doll lunged at him with her sharp teeth but missed the horse's neck. Angry, the palomino quickly turned his body around and shot off both back legs like a cannon.

Caught in between Life and Doll, I tried to turn around and jump, but there was no time. The horse's left hoof scraped my buttocks, but the right caught me on the outside of my left thigh. The impact was so strong, the kick threw me three meters back.

Landing in the cold mud on my ass, I quickly jumped up and ran toward the fence in fear of being hit again. When I arrived on the fence line and realized the chaos had eased, I almost dropped in pain. It felt as if someone was stabbing my thigh with a sharp knife. I couldn't put any weight on my left leg.

"You have to be quicker to get out of the way, cowboy," Renan said, laughing at my injury.

I wanted to be angry at him for his comment, but there was no time. Soon after, we realized Renan's palomino was in trouble.

The horse began showing signs of colic from fatigue. He laid down, rolled from one side to the other showing discomfort. He tried to use his head to rub his stomach. He had been living in a stall for months before Renan took him out and walked ninety kilometers.

"We need to get fluids into this horse quickly," I warned Renan.

Luckily, there was a very experienced vet at the ranch working with Rafael's horses. The vet treated the palomino all night, and the next morning he looked like a different horse. He saved the palomino's life.

Limping and still in intense pain, I said goodbye to Renan and thanked him for riding with me. It was a dramatic end to our three days together. I would miss his company.

WHEN IT RAINS IT POURS

After covering 613 kilometers in under two months, I rode out of Maringá with my left leg bruised in different shades of purple and yellow as heavy rain pummeled my blue poncho. I didn't mind riding in the rain, especially when wearing a rain poncho covering my entire body and saddle. However, when the rain was torrential, it was miserable.

In a few minutes, water began to creep down my neck and follow my spine all the way to my jeans. A freezing sliver shot through my body and left me shivering cold. Hypothermia was a real danger in low winter temperatures. When the rain was heavy, I was not the only one who dropped my head. The mares also hated it and tried to keep their eyes to the ground.

By the time we arrived in the town of Mamborê, three days after leaving Maringá, my beard was perma-soaked along with my soul. The rain accompanied us the entire time, but the warm reception from the Tiburcio family changed my gloomy mood.

Marcio Tiburcio was a short, bald horse vet with an egg-shaped head who only wanted to please those around him. He hosted us on his family ranch for two days. Before I could even dismount, Marcio greeted me with a wide smile on his light brown face. "Whatever you need, don't hesitate to ask."

Along with his wife, beautiful little boy, his brother, sister, and friends, we spent the first night getting to know one another over a delicious lamb he'd butchered that morning. "We raise these animals just for nights like this," Marcio told me.

The next morning, my face hurt from laughing so much. Marcio took me around to see his horses, lambs, cattle, and his long roping arena. In the southern part of Brazil, instead of roping like the American cowboys, people follow the Gaucho culture. Instead of using the shorter nylon ropes, twenty-eight to thirty-five feet long, they use a very long leather one, fifty-nine to sixty-five feet in length.

"Your loop must be eighteen to twenty meters long," Marcio explained to me as he played with his leather rope. Although his son was only three years old, Marcio already had him roping the dummy on horseback. The little boy could ride and rope better than most adults.

"I love this country life, and I hope my son will carry on our tradition," Marcio said after showing me a video of the young boy roping, tiny cowboy boots and all. His eyes glowed, and his chest seemed about to explode with pride.

Seeing the abundance of love the vet showered on his young son, and the smile on the boy's face when he was on a horse, made me think about having children. I would absolutely love to teach my child how to ride a horse one day. To swing a rope. To be a cowboy or cowgirl. Never in my life had I felt a stronger urge to have a kid. Being in the homes of so many families made me long to start my own family. But with whom?

Here I was, a lonely saddle tramp, traveling from town to town with his horses and best mate. No wife. No girlfriend. Not even a fling.

Of course, there were a couple of one-night stands. There was something romantic about a cowboy riding into town, I guess. My third night on the road, I had to escape a home by jumping over a tall gate when an angry father awoke to find me in his daughter's room. The twenty-two-year-old brunette had lied to me, saying she lived alone. In Presidente Prudente, a barrel racer made my heart race one night. In Paraná, a green-eyed, blonde flight attendant nearly made me give up my ride. However, those adventures ended just as quickly as they began. There was no substance, no love.

As a child, I had always imagined myself as a young father. Maybe it was because my old man was such a kid while I was growing up. I always saw myself having my first offspring before the age of twenty-seven. At that time I was twenty-nine and nowhere near beginning a family. A deep feeling of loneliness began to creep deep within my core. Even though I had Mark with me and met tons of people along the way, I couldn't help but yearn for the soft touch of a woman, one I loved. The smell of flowers in her hair. The warmth of a kiss. The desire to snuggle with her for hours. I felt so alone, a feeling that would ride with me all the way to southern Patagonia.

~

There was a saying in my country: Anything you plant in Brazil grows. In the state of Paraná, due to the high quality of the soil and the favorable weather, this statement couldn't be truer.

Every year, farmers managed to harvest soybeans in the summer, corn in the fall, and wheat in the winter. The soil was so rich in nutrients, and there was so much precipitation that there was no need to rest the land. This was unheard of in other countries and even other parts of Brazil.

From the moment I left Maringá, I started riding next to never-ending cornfields. In the city of Ubiratã, I got the first opportunity to share a roof with a family of real farmers. The Rosseta family had farmed the same piece of land since the patriarch of the family arrived there in the 1970s. It was during this period that people from all over Brazil started coming to this great state to cut down forests and work the fields. In those days, the land was cheap and opportunity was high.

"When my grandfather came here, he bought ten hectares of land and started farming. Today we farm 1,500 hectares," Wellington Rosseta told me as we drove around their property in his truck.

Although Wellington was only twenty-one, a pale kid with a patchy beard, he had already taken the reins of the farm's planting operation. His father dealt with the money, his two uncles ran the harvesting, and even his younger cousin who was only ten-years-old already knew how to work the machinery.

"This is easy!" Vinny Rosseta flashed a big smile that revealed his braces as he drove a gigantic John Deere combine through a field of corn. "I learned how to drive these when I was six."

Wearing baby blue skater shoes, dark fitted jeans, a bright red Burton T-shirt, and a green and red flat brim baseball hat sitting halfway on his head, he looked like most ten-year-olds I knew. Unlike most ten-year-olds I knew, he didn't spend his days sitting on a couch playing video games. Sitting next to Vinny as he piloted the colossal combine with ease and confidence, I couldn't help but feel proud. Kids who were raised on farms and ranches matured much earlier than city kids. In my opinion, they became much more valuable to society as adults.

While I was with the Rosseta family, I was able to see how hard they worked and how unified the family was. Everyone had a certain job within the farm, and they did it with passion. From sunrise until the job was done that day, no matter how late that might be, they didn't stop working. They didn't have weekends, holidays, or vacations, but they loved what they did so they did it with a smile on their faces, day in, day out.

Feeling inspired, I rode toward Cascavel, in the south of Paraná and discovered that a story filmed in Maringá about my efforts to raise funds for the Barretos Children's Cancer Hospital had hit the mainstream media. I was overwhelmed by people's solidarity.

Even before I arrived in Cascavel, a slim man passed me a $20 Real bill. "I watched you on the news last week, and I want to donate some money for the hospital."

Every time I neared a city, people would stop me regularly on the side of the road. Many told me stories of family members who had faced cancer, and how much my ride meant to them before taking out a bill and making a donation.

On a grim Saturday afternoon, I thanked the gray heavens above as

I rode into the rodeo grounds in Cascavel. I was ready for a cold beer and some real food. A barrel-racing competition was in full swing, and I was quickly swarmed by cowboys and cowgirls who wanted to take selfies and say hello. After untacking and feeding the mares, Adani Primo Triches, the president of the grounds, pulled me aside and offered heartwarming news.

"Filipe, we are so inspired by what you are doing we want to help you raise money for the Barretos Cancer Hospital," said the tall, kind-hearted president. He went on to explain how they would donate all of the proceeds from the last heat of the day to the hospital.

I was in awe of their kindness and initiative, but I never imagined they would raise as much money as they did. Together with the competitors and Quarter Horse breeders, they raised a whopping $1,500 USD!

With tears in my eyes, I thanked them for their help. Thanks to the horse and its ability to turn strangers into friends, I was slowly helping this tremendous hospital. This wasn't the only surprise the Universe held for me in Cascavel.

In the northern part of Paraná state, a family stopped me on the side of the road and asked to take some photos. They had been following me on social media since my first journey from Canada to Brazil.

"My kids love horses, and they are big fans of yours," smiled the blonde matriarch of three boys. The family, all blond with light eyes and skin, looked more Swiss than Brazilian. While I took photos of her youngest in my saddle, we talked about my motivation for this journey. I spoke about the cancer hospital.

I told them about some of the early signs of childhood cancer, information I shared throughout my ride. "To tell if a child has a life-threatening eye cancer called retinoblastoma, take a close-up photo of their face using a phone with the flash on. If one of the pupils reflects back as a white circle, that child must see a doctor."

It was my usual spiel. Thinking nothing of it, I said goodbye to the family and continued on.

Weeks later, while eating lunch in the city of Cascavel, I felt a tap on my shoulder. I was surprised to see the same gorgeous blonde woman with heavy tears running down her pale face. She was heading to the hospital with her youngest because he was diagnosed with retinoblastoma after she noticed a white circle in a cell phone photo. She was determined to save his vision and his life. She thanked me while we hugged tight.

In my heart, I thanked everything and everyone who put me on this journey. This was what would keep me trekking, no matter how difficult the journey got. On my first Long Ride, I was helped by hundreds of people every single day. Now, it was my turn to give back.

NEAR DEATH NEAR IGUAZÚ FALLS

I n the city of Cascavel, I gave the mares a much-needed break and drove to see Iguazú Falls, one of the New Seven Wonders of Nature. I had dreamed of seeing the falls my entire life! I'd never had the opportunity since they were located on the border with Argentina, more than 1,500 kilometers from my home.

To help those who had never visited Iguazú understand the magnitude of the falls, here were the words spoken by the United States First Lady, Eleanor Roosevelt, on her visit to Brazil in March 1944. Upon seeing the falls for the first time, she exclaimed, "Poor Niagara!"

It was impossible to convey the sheer size and spectacle that was Iguazú in words or photos. It must be seen, felt, and heard. Iguazú consisted of 275 separate falls.

The most impressive one was a U-shaped cataract nicknamed The Devil's Throat. It had fourteen falls plunging more than 350 feet, about the height of the Statue of Liberty. A metal platform allowed visitors to walk mere meters from The Devil's Throat. As that immense amount of white water hit the river beneath, a thick layer of freezing mist rose to leave you completely drenched. It was as if I were inside a curtain of water.

The sound of the rushing water pounding the rocks had the biggest impact on me. It was like rolling thunder, the kind that seemed to penetrate your bones. And it had no end, the thunder just kept on rolling forever.

On the one-kilometer trail to the falls, there were several lookouts with breathtaking views. Some displayed large, multicolored rainbows joining the deep blue sky to the dark green forest beneath. The fact that the falls emerged in the middle of a lush rain forest also made it unique and unforgettable. At times, it was as if I were looking at a painting wondering how nature could be this perfect and its painter so talented.

From the city of Cascavel, we trekked south toward the state of Santa Catarina. The once-flat terrain, bustling with corn and wheat plantations, transitioned into rolling hills and rugged mountains, home to beef and milk cattle farms.

As we climbed and climbed and climbed, the temperature plummeted lower and lower with each kilometer. Most mornings I swore in Portuguese and English as my fingers throbbed in pain from the piercing cold. Still early into the winter, I wasn't prepared for the temperature to hit such low numbers and found myself unprepared with no gloves.

The weather was not the only challenge we faced in the southern tip of Paraná. The roads also became unrideable. With twists and turns winding up and down the mountains, the mares and I faced off against our biggest rivals out here: massive transport trucks. Our lives were in danger every single day.

On one chilly, somber morning, my nightmare almost caught up with me. I swallowed hard as time stood still. Not a thought existed at that moment but one: *We are going to die.*

A massive, red Volkswagen transport truck roared up the mountain behind us snorting like an angry devil. It bore down as we hugged the jagged rock face to my right, nowhere to escape. With no shoulder, I was forced to ride in the right lane, the same as the truck that was traveling at one hundred-plus kilometers per hour. With a small red car traveling in the left lane next to the truck, death seemed inevitable. This was the end.

I tightened my muscles, bracing for impact. Everything went into slow motion. My mind went blank. Suddenly, in the far lane, the driver of the red car, seeing the disaster about to unfold, sped up, allowing the trucker to swerve over to the left lane at the last second. The truck's red grill missed us by centimeters.

I swore at the top of my lungs as the truck's engine drowned me out, the smell of exhaust permeating the air. My heart tried to punch its way out of my rib cage. My knees shook. Life and Doll, not missing a beat, trekked up the mountain as if nothing had happened.

During my travels on horseback from Calgary, Canada, to my eventual destination of Ushuaia, Patagonia, I had faced grizzly bears, drug lords, raging rivers, and rugged mountains. None posed a greater threat than Latin America's awful roads and its careless drivers.

On this long stretch of mountain ranges, more than 500 kilometers of rugged peaks would lead us all the way to the pampas of Rio Grande do Sul. We needed to find an alternate route if we wished to make it to Uruguay alive.

It was not just the lay of the land which changed upon entering the southern tip of Paraná. The closer we rode to the state of Santa Catarina, the official gateway into the south of Brazil, everything changed: the people, food, architecture, culture. What was once the land of cowboys slowly became the birthplace of the gaucho.

"You must always grab the *chimarao* (yerba mate) with your right hand," a gaucho reeking of horse manure said before passing me a *cuia* (calabash gourd) full of the warm mate. He went on to explain that I should suck the warm tea through the *bombinha* (a metal straw). I was to drink until I heard a slurping sound before passing it back to the *cebador* (person who prepares and pours the *chimarrao*). As it made its way around the circle, the *cuia* always returned to the *cebador* who was the only person who could pour the water and touch the *bombinha*.

In a horse barn sixty kilometers from the Santa Catarina state line, I sat in a circle with five gauchos passing the warm mate around. The tradition was so strong that people carry thermoses with warm water, their *cuia,* and yerba mate everywhere they go. While Life and Doll chewed some tasty alfalfa in a stall a few meters away, these *vaqueros* gave me a lesson on the Gaucho culture.

"The gaucho is the cowboy of Argentina, Uruguay, Paraguay, and southern Brazil," an elderly man with a big black felt hat told me, his face stern, his posture rigid.

All of the men wore ponchos and loose-fitting trousers called *bombachas* belted with a *tirador*. Each carried a large knife tucked into their belts at their backs. Everyone wore long-sleeve shirts. Some sported a silk bandana tied around their necks. On their feet, the only two options a true gaucho had: leather riding boots that rose up to just under the knee or *alpargatas,* a very light shoe made from thick fabric with a rubber sole that was worn with socks in the winter and bare feet in the summer.

While we passed the *cuia* around a circle, they explained how they drank mate every day in the early morning and late afternoon.

"The *mateina* in mate is like caffeine. It wakes you up and gives you energy," they explained.

The warm tea, which the natives of this region drank long before the Europeans arrived from the old world, was hot, almost too hot. It tasted bitter, old, and ancient, and made me think of old books whose pages hadn't been turned in years. But somehow, it also managed to be as fresh as a green maple leaf in early June.

Mate comes in different forms. It can be bitter or sweet (adding sugar or honey) and warm or cold. There were several varieties and brands of *yerba* which would also make a difference to the taste. The water temperature made a difference, too. To prevent the *yerba* from being burned and losing taste and quality, it must not be boiled.

My hosts told me that the most important detail of all was the person who prepares it: the *cebador*. Every person would prepare a different mate. Some said it was a reflection of their soul.

"I can use the same *bombinha* as my mother. The same *cuia*, the same mate, the same water, but my *chimarrao* will never taste as good as hers," one gaucho observed.

After learning about their traditional drink, it was time to get a lesson on the food. The men told me how the diet of a real gaucho was composed mainly of meat and more meat.

"The gaucho works hard all day, going out on horseback in the morning and returning at night oftentimes," one of the men told me. "He has to have a lot of energy. Meat in our culture can and should be eaten for breakfast, lunch, and dinner."

While we continued drinking mate, boiling liters and liters of water, they showed me photos of them long roping and *Jinetiando* (riding bucking broncos). These events made up the traditional gaucho rodeo. Just like in the American rodeo, they were invented by the workers who wanted to test each other and have fun while working on local ranches.

Before I laid out my saddle pads for the night, one of the gauchos, a polite man with a thick, bushy silver beard, pulled me aside. His long mustache covered his lips and was stained dark yellow from his many years of chain-smoking. "I want you to have my knife." He passed me a beautiful knife with a long blade, its handle was made from the shin-bone of an ostrich.

"Put it on your belt," he added. "You will immediately gain the respect of the true gauchos in the south of Brazil."

While I lay in my sleeping bag, I let the sound of the mares eating calm my heart down to the rhythm of their sluggish chewing. I realized this was my official welcome into the land of the gaucho, a stretch of land I would cross from Santa Catarina until the province of Buenos Aires in Argentina.

An excited smile spread across my face. I couldn't wait to meet more gauchos and learn from these men and their rich culture which for centuries had revolved around the horse, their god.

SANTA CATARINA

With the help of my new gaucho friends, we drew a route through small country roads leading into the state of Santa Catarina. The plan took me off the blind turns and truck-infested highways that nearly killed us.

However, this new route had its challenges. The stony dirt roads were slippery from recent rains. The mares struggled to climb steep mountain faces only to fight their way down the other side. I walked a lot to help the girls. By the end of most days, I was panting as hard as Life and Doll.

It also proved difficult for Mark. He got the van stuck during a muddy climb. As I arrived, Mark told me with a worried tone, "Sorry, bro! It slid into the ditch so quickly, there was nothing I could do!"

We were forced to ask a tractor operator for help.

After crossing the state of Paraná from north to south, we arrived in the city of Barracão, the last city we would cross before entering Santa Catarina. Here, three cities, three states, and two countries meet in one place. Barracão, Paraná is separated by one street from Dionísio Cerqueira, Santa Catarina, and General Manuel Belgrano, which sits in the state of Misiones, Argentina.

Brazilians and Argentinians, known for their hatred of one another because of their rivalry over soccer, are neighbors here. Our host, Pedro, a short man with swollen, frog-like eyes and a loud voice, acted as my guide as we walked through the streets of Argentina. "There are people who live in Brazil and work in Argentina and vice versa."

No river separated the two South American countries here. People roamed free through the dry border, entering one country and leaving the other all day. The situation gave a sense of how stupid these invisible lines people created really were.

On our first morning resting in Barracão, I made a horrible discovery while feeding the mares. Life had kicked Doll on her back left leg, leaving it swollen and her lame. With the only horse vet in town on bed rest due to a jaw operation, I was forced to deal with this problem myself.

I sent the recovering vet a video of the wound, and he prescribed the medication I was to use for the next four days. Every morning, I had to give Doll an intravenous anti-inflammatory injection. In the afternoon, she needed a shot of antibiotics in the muscle of her neck.

"When you are on a trip like this, I guess you have to be a bit of a vet as well," Pedro observed as I injected Doll's vein early one morning.

"For sure, I'm usually in the middle of nowhere with very few resources." I pulled the plunger of the syringe slowly, watching Doll's deep red blood mix with the clear liquid before pushing the mixture back in.

During the days I spent caring for Doll, Pedro, a rodeo announcer, took me to a cemetery on the border with Argentina. More than 200 soldiers who fought for the independence of Brazil's south were laid to rest there.

"The Ragamuffin War, or *Revolução Farroupilha,* was a Republican uprising that began in southern Brazil in the state of Rio Grande do Sul in 1835 and spread into Santa Catarina," Pedro explained as we walked among the many graves.

The war, considered the longest and third bloodiest in Brazil's history, was started by the state of Rio Grande do Sul in a bid to create its own independent country. After ten years of fighting and more than

20,000 soldiers killed on both sides, the war ended, and the South returned to the Republic of Brazil.

This war was so far removed from the rest of Brazil, I had only read about it in history textbooks in school. Being there, standing over these graves, put this war in an entirely new light. Seeing how culturally different the South Region of Brazil was from the rest of the country with my own eyes also helped me understand why they wanted to separate back then and why some still want to today.

After three days of treating Doll, the swelling on her leg went down, and she was walking much better. We said goodbye to Pedro and thanked him for all of his help before riding into the state of Santa Catarina. A gaucho and his little boy, Marcelinho, both dressed in traditional clothing, rode with me for the day as we followed small dirt roads south. Entering another Brazilian state gave me a feeling of great power.

Before leaving the city, we also rode into Argentina for a few seconds to take a photo. Sitting on our horses, next to a thick, white cement post which read Brazil on one side and Argentina on the other, I grinned next to my new friend Marcelinho.

Seeing him in his traditional black felt hat, black shirt, white silk bandanna tied tightly around his neck and black *bombachas* and sitting atop his little horse, for a second I wished he were my son.

Marcelo, the boy's father, had a firm handshake. "I don't think my son will ever forget this day as long as he lives, Filipe. I'm sure one day he will tell his grandchildren he rode with the cowboy who is traveling the world on horseback."

When I said goodbye to Marcelinho, I could see he wanted the heeling rope, used in team roping to rope the steers' heels, that I kept tied to my saddle horn. He had been eyeing it all day.

"Marcelinho, since you rode with me today, I want you to have this rope." I passed him the bright pink nylon rope. A big smile spread across his cute little face, and he gave me a tight hug. I melted in his embrace.

∼

During the First and Second World War, European immigrants flooded into the southern portion of Brazil. Leaving their war-torn homes and lives behind, families from Italy, Germany, Poland, and other countries of the Old World boarded large ships and sailed for a new life in the New World. When I entered the state of Santa Catarina, it became evident I was entering the Europe of Brazil: Wooden homes with curved roofs, and people with blue eyes, blond hair, and speaking German on the streets became the norm. While I rested the mares in the small town, the mayor of São João do Oeste, Sérgio Theisen told me, "In our town 93 percent of the population speaks German and 97.5 percent understands it."

With a population of just under 10,000 residents, the children learned German before they learned Portuguese. Symbolizing their deep roots with the European country, even the main street boasted German and Brazilian flags. It was there that one of Brazil's largest Oktoberfests was celebrated every year.

Over a delicious lunch which included *cuca*, a traditional German sweetbread, accompanied by meat and salad, I asked the mayor why the town was made up of only Brazilians of German descent.

"If you weren't German, you were not allowed to stay here. You had to find another town to settle in," the tall, pale man explained.

I found the towns in Santa Catarina to be safer, cleaner, and more organized than the rest of Brazil. It's literally a different country — a piece of Europe in Brazil.

On our final day in Santa Catarina, we climbed a mountain that seemed to have no end. Every time I thought we had reached the summit, the dirt road rose again. Dusk took over as we finally descended to a small village next to the Uruguay River.

My last hosts told me to look for a sign on the right side of the road to find the ferry that would take us into Rio Grande do Sul. They forgot to mention that the sign was the size of a notebook. I ended up riding right past it and trekking three kilometers out of the way.

Just before nine p.m., sore and stressed, we finally arrived at the ferry. The mares and I were exhausted and ready for a break, but first, we had to cross the Uruguay River.

The ferry's floor, made of metal, created a challenge to load the mares. When they stepped onto the platform and heard the noise their shoes made, they spooked and shot back.

"I don't know if they will go on," Mark said doubtfully as he watched me struggle.

It took some time to convince the girls the small ferry was safe to step on. With some patience and a little horsemanship, they walked on. Once we loaded the mares, and Mark drove the support van onto the ferry, it took ten minutes to cross the wide, brown river. I held the mares tightly as they eyed the darkness nervously. Only one bright light illuminated the river in front of the ferry.

When we stepped onto the shores of Rio Grande do Sul state, the ferry captain showed us a place where we could camp for the night. I tied the mares to a tree and gave them a bale of hay to munch. When I finished feeding them, the captain returned with ribs for us to barbecue and a bottle of *Cachaça* (Brazilian rum). The burly captain declared, "A man who arrives on horseback in the land of the gauchos deserves a celebration."

RIO GRANDE DO SUL

I awoke to a layer of frost covering my gray tent and thick fog floating atop the Uruguay River. We were 1,200 kilometers from Barretos after three months and one week on the road. While the mares munched on their feed, I observed the fog as it danced atop the murky, brown water. With the jungle coming to life, I couldn't help but feel like I was in the pages of *Heart of Darkness*.

After three months on the road, we were about to start riding through the final state of Brazil, Rio Grande do Sul. It felt good to be there.

We trekked through dirt roads in the middle of the jungle for most of the morning until we arrived in the one-street town of Pinheirinho do Vale, population 4,000 people. I rode into the center of the small town, tied the horses up to a street post, and walked into a one-room restaurant to purchase a coffee and ask for directions. By the time I walked back outside, half of the town was standing around the mares, along with the town's only two police officers.

"Good morning! Are you the man riding around the world on horseback?" one of the officers asked.

In minutes, I was taken to the local radio station for an interview and gained a riding partner for the day. One of the officer's sons, a fourteen-year-old boy, was allowed to skip class to show me the way south. Everything was going well until I looked back at the young boy and noticed he was whiter than a ghost. "Are you feeling okay, buddy?"

"Yes, I'm fine, just feeling a little sick." He looked down at the rocks in our path. Not five minutes passed before I heard what sounded like someone emptying a bucket full of water onto the road. When I looked back, my little friend was leaning off the side of his saddle spewing a thick, yellow liquid from his mouth. Tears ran down his face. I held his horse, Thunder, as he finished his business.

"Man, I needed to do that," he said and we both laughed.

After a few minutes resting under the shade of a *paineira* tree, he got back on his gray pony, and we continued our ride. His father met us for lunch and brought some delicious food. We ate together in front of an abandoned schoolhouse while the animals grazed nearby. After eating, I thanked the father and his son before the two returned to their town.

In the late afternoon, while crossing a bridge, Life nearly stepped on a spider the size of a dinner plate. It was black, hairy, and mean-looking! Life's right hoof landed right next to it and I panicked, worried the spider's defense would be to quickly climb the hoof and bite her leg. As the spider began to move toward Life, I put my right leg on her and neck-reined to the left. She quickly moved away from the spider, and it stopped in its tracks. I sighed in relief as I looked back at that monster in the middle of the road.

We finished the long day on the doorstep of a large rural church. I thanked the Lord we were safe and sound and fed the mares before setting up camp. Eating a bowl of ramen noodles, Mark and I shared a bottle of red wine.

Mark stared off into the abyss. "Can't wait to get to this town tomorrow and rest in a real bed."

My childhood friend had had enough. Life on the road was not for him. In the past few weeks, he talked less and less. When he did speak, he was always asking when we would arrive at the next resting point. I knew that when we arrived at the Uruguayan border, he would return to Canada. I could sense it by his demeanor. I began to stress about what I would do then, but I was too tired to think. Sleep was all I could do.

The following morning began with a mountain climb under heavy fog. It was so thick that my jacket was left soaked as if it were raining. I traversed small villages and farms on both sides of the narrow, winding road. In several of the small colorful wooden homes I passed, I saw smiling children hanging out of windows. I could hear the parents announcing, "Run, run! There are horses coming! Come see!"

Seconds later, more children would pop their heads out of the window to look out with wonder in their eyes.

I waved at them, yelling out, "Good morning!"

I also saw carts full of feed for the milk cattle pulled by teams of bulls. Here, instead of using tractors, many of the small milk farms run by families used these teams to do all of the work needed. It was as if, by crossing the Uruguay River, I had traveled back in time.

Just after lunch, I arrived in the town of Tenente Portela. The small town of 14,000 people seemed like a bustling metropolis compared to the villages and jungles we had ridden through the previous few days.

Our host, Andre, a long roper in his early twenties, met us in front of his family's pharmacy in the heart of town. Before we rode to his ranch, we took photos in front of a large tin statue of a native man with a bow and arrow.

As I snapped a photo standing on top of the saddle, Andre told me, "This area had a lot of indigenous people so this monument is here to honor them."

The monument, made from scrap metal parts, was raised to honor Chief Anastácio Fongue, a great warrior who was the first leader of the *Guarita* lands inhabited by the Kaingang and Guarani tribes.

About two kilometers before arriving at Andre's ranch, I could already smell the meat being barbecued.

"Welcome to our humble ranch, Filipe!" Andre's father gave me a strong bear hug before offering me copious amounts of meat. He looked just like Andre, just older. While I rested Life and Doll for two days in Tenente Portela, we went to see the *Salto do Yucuma*.

"You guys have to see the falls. It's spectacular," Andre said.

Salto do Yucuma was a waterfall in Rio Grande do Sul that ran 1,800 meters in length and was over twenty meters high at some points. Located in the middle of a natural reserve, it was rich in fauna and flora.

After driving for fifteen kilometers through thick jungle and trekking for another two, we finally arrived at the *Salto*. I looked right and left. The falls extended as far as I could see. We carefully maneuvered through the rocky terrain toward the falls.

"You guys are lucky. The river is low right now so the falls look even better," our host said. Standing next to the Uruguay River, only a few meters from the falls, I relished the beautiful view.

When we arrived back at Andre's ranch, his father surprised us with an unforgettable gift.

"A Long Ride like yours needs a rooster to wake you up early every morning," he said as he passed us the elegant bird. I inspected the small rooster in my right hand. He had a pointy yellow beak, a folded red comb that looked like Elvis Presley's hairdo, sharp spurs, and golden, red, and black feathers. Belonging to the *Garnize* breed, he was much smaller than a normal rooster.

"Thank you so much," I said, completely in shock at this bizarre gift. Andre's father, a huge fan of *cavalgadas*, the time-honored parades on horseback, explained how it's the tradition to have a rooster when a gaucho is traveling on the road. The animal acts as a natural alarm and — in case of emergency — dinner. After discussing what name to give our new traveling partner, we decided on Cluck Norris.

Traveling on horseback had awarded me the opportunity to live within rural communities all over the Americas. I had cut hay in Colorado, branded cattle in southern Alberta, and harvested corn in Brazil. As a lover of the land and the outdoors, I had enjoyed these moments immensely. One theme I had found in all of the countries I crossed was that more and more people were migrating from the farm to the city. In the twenty-first century, the farmer and rancher seemed to have no place, no value.

José Silva, a farmer from the northern part of Rio Grande do Sul said to me one night. "You know, I think one day people will have money to buy food, but there won't be any to be bought. Who will plant crops if everyone wants to move to the city?"

The town hall we stood in, in a small rural village, had a bocce court, barbecue, and several hundred stacked chairs. As I looked around at the cobwebs in the ceiling and the empty space, I could almost hear the laughter of children and the sound of an accordion being played as gauchos cut into succulent ribs. But these were only echoes of a memory of a time long gone.

"This place was full every weekend when my children were young," the elderly man told me with glazed eyes. "There were bocce tournaments, dances, and barbecues. Now this place is used once a month by a small women's group and that's it."

According to José, almost everyone from the small village left to live in the city, including his two sons. "No one wants to stay and work the land anymore. They all want office jobs," he added before kicking a rock with the tip of his knee-high rubber boot.

I couldn't say how many times I had heard this through my travels. Children who didn't want to learn how to ride horses, and sons and daughters who refused to carry on the tradition of the family farm, preferring to go off to university.

As a cowboy, all of this made me sad. It made me wonder what the future would look like. It made me scared to find out. Would my children and grandchildren ride horses? Would they know where their food came from? Would they be connected to the land like me? I truly hoped so, but with the direction the world was headed — fewer horses and more machines — it was doubtful.

As an eternal optimist, I would do everything in my power to continue inspiring people to live outdoors and to know the natural world. It was all I could do. If we wanted to preserve Nature, and actually have a shot at saving it, we must first know it.

It was in another small village, during my trek from Tenente Portela to Santa Rosa, Rio Grande do Sul where I received my first "no" of the trip.

After a long day in the saddle, I rode up to a church on the left side of the dirt road. A beautiful, trimmed yard of grass surrounded the quaint white building. Next to it, about twenty meters away, sat an old schoolhouse, no longer in use.

My hosts the previous night told me this would be the best place to set up camp and spend the night. I untacked the mares, offered them water, and let them graze on the short grass. While they munched away, I lay atop my saddle pads and stared up at the big, puffy, white clouds navigating the dark blue sky. The sun began to settle into the horizon in front of my dirty cowboy boots. Lost in time, daydreaming about eating a bagel with cream cheese and tomato from Tim Hortons in Canada, I felt the presence of someone watching me. When I turned my gaze to the side, a tall skinny man startled me. I shot up to my feet, embarrassed that I had not seen him walk up. I immediately began walking toward him with my right hand extended.

"Good afternoon, my name is Filipe. I'm riding my mares from Barretos to Patagonia and was hoping to camp here for the night," I told the cold-faced man.

"No, no, you're not!" he barked.

Completely in shock, I didn't really understand what he had just said.

"Sorry, what?" was all I was able to muster.

"You heard me, you are not staying here tonight," he said in a harsh tone. "You must leave."

Tired, I'd been ready to eat something and set up camp. All I wanted to do was rest, but next to God's house there was no place for a wandering fool. I would be forced to tack the mares again and continue riding south.

"I just want you to know that I have been on the road for three months and you, sir, are the first person to refuse me a place to sleep."

Swearing under my breath, I saddled Life and led the mares back to the dirt road. With dusk now swallowing us whole, I wondered where we would sleep that night. The skinny man simply watched me until I faded in the distance. Luckily, a couple of kilometers south, I managed to find a soccer field to spend the night.

The next afternoon, we arrived in Santa Rosa, and everyone was ready for a break. Friends from Tenente Portela put me in touch with a couple of long ropers in the city, and they were awaiting our arrival.

Just after six p.m., we rode into a ranch on the outskirts of the city. Several gauchos stood around a roping dummy, practicing their sport and drinking warm mate.

"Welcome to Santa Rosa!" one of the gauchos yelled out as I stepped down from Life's back.

I said hello to everyone and untacked the girls. Before they were done eating their feed, I was already roping the dummy and chatting with my new friends.

Cold beers were brought out, and a large amount of meat was put on the fire. We spent the late afternoon eating, drinking, and getting to know one another.

The meat in Rio Grande do Sul was penetrated by a long lance and cooked over charcoal, then placed right on top of the closest table. What I discovered is that the dirtier the table, the better! Everyone used the knife they carried on their belt to cut the piece they wished to eat. Plates and forks were nonexistent. I used a piece of bread to grab the meat of my choice and cut small pieces using my knife.

"Filipe, this is a poem that describes the life of a gaucho working on a ranch," one of my new friends said before reciting a gorgeous poem by Robinson Marques about Criollo horses, cattle, and the pampas. He spoke with great conviction.

I am gaucho!

Gaucho in tradition,
From the barbecue to the chimarrao.

From breaking wild horses,
Even though this doesn't pay very well.

This is the way I live,
I don't care about failure.

All I want is to celebrate this great tradition,
Inside my chest, my love for this ground beats with force.

Here in the state of Rio Grande do Sul, rich with culture, it was very common for someone to recite a poem in the middle of a barbecue. Everyone I met knew one or more poems by heart and acted them out with elegance and vigor. It was quite beautiful.

This was the first time in my life I had been in a place where grown men recited poetry at the drop of a hat. After the poem, someone pulled out a stunning black-and-white accordion. For the rest of the evening, traditional *Gauchesco* songs were played and sung.

At the end of the night, Ivan Carvalho, a small man with a thin mustache who looked like he should be in a *Three Musketeers* movie, took us to sleep at his family's house. "While you stay here in Santa Rosa, this is your home," he said as we entered his spacious house.

The next morning after feeding the mares, Ivan took us to the CTG (Centre of Gaucho Tradition) to watch a dance competition. Boys and girls from all over the state wore the traditional gaucho attire which consisted of a large black hat, *bombachas,* ponchos, and leather boots for the boys and colorful long dresses for the ladies matched with extravagant hairdos. They danced to traditional *Gauchesco* songs as stern-looking judges sitting on a wooden stage scored them in various categories. Over the loud music, Ivan told me, "Our culture is rich with poetry, dance, music, and horses. From very young, we are completely immersed in this world."

After spending nearly a week resting the mares and partying with my new friends in Santa Rosa, it was hard to say goodbye. On an extremely cold morning, with frost all around us, I tacked up the mares in silence as the guys watched. The grass was frozen white, and the tips of my fingers throbbed in pain. I said goodbye to everyone and climbed onto Life's back. The first day in the saddle after a few days off was always the hardest. The mares were off their rhythm, and I was off my game. Mixed with the low temperatures, the morning was a painful experience.

Luckily, by lunchtime, I was joined by a group of riders from Senador Salgado Filho. They warmed my day right up. We chatted the afternoon away as we rode south. They told me about their small community, their love for the Criollo, and asked questions.

"How many kilometers do you ride a day?"

"How did you cross the ocean into South America?"

"How do you pay for your trip?"

They asked the usual questions horsemen all over the Americas had asked me. I always found it funny how these men enjoyed bragging about their own adventures on horseback rather than asking about my travels. They asked three questions about my trip and then spent two hours telling me about the time they rode 150 kilometers to God knows where. I listened and laughed.

Just before four p.m., we were met on the road by even more riders. A group from Guarani das Missões, the town where I would rest that night, came to meet us on the road. The first two riders led the group holding the Brazilian and Rio Grande do Sul flags with pride.

"Welcome to our lost corner of the world!" one of the riders yelled out as he handed me a plastic Coke bottle full of *cachaça*.

I took a long sip of the clear alcohol which ran down my throat like a cat with sharp claws, much to everyone's amusement.

We said goodbye to the riders from Senador Salgado who returned to their town and continued south. Before sunset, we arrived at the CTG in Guarani.

I put the mares in separate stalls and gave each a mountain of hay. At the end of the barn, there was a wood oven which the gauchos were already tending to. They were preparing a delicious chicken broth that smelled heavenly. We shared mate while getting to know one another.

"We want to give you this poncho as a gift to keep you warm in these freezing temperatures," the mayor of the town said.

It was a gorgeous Uruguayan wool poncho, dark blue on the outside with a deep red lining. Heavy and warm beyond belief with a tall, Dracula-like collar, it hung down to my shins. Wearing my new poncho, I ate the chicken and yuca dinner while musicians played an out-of-tune song at the other end of the barn.

The horses could be heard neighing and eating. The thick smoke from the fire filled the low building, making it hard to breathe at times. The strong smell of horse manure, hay, smoke, and freshly cooked chicken wafted around us.

For a second, I put down my fork, looked around and simply took in the scene before me. Who else got to experience this? Being in a horse barn full of gauchos and Criollo horses eating a dish cooked in a wood stove while an accordion and guitar played? Quietly, I concluded there was no better way to see the world than from the back of a horse.

The following day, we arrived at Tinho's ranch at dusk. The thirty-three-year-old, built like a mighty oak tree, solid and wide, worked on his family's cattle ranch and raised Criollo and racehorses. The horseman's left eye was a light green and his right, a little lazy, a dark hazel. His face seemed to be stuck in a half-smile that revealed perfectly-aligned, white teeth.

That night, Tinho told me over dinner, "I pay my bills with the cattle, but my love is the horse." His father, a blue-eyed, messy-haired man in his sixties, who always had a beer or wine glass in hand, became good friends with Mark.

"This is my kind of guy," he said with his arm over Mark's shoulder while the two shared a cigarette and drank what seemed like their hundredth beer together.

The next day, we woke up early and drove with Tinho to another of his properties. Joined by ranchers from the community, we castrated and branded sixty calves and steers.

"Sure, today we could just load the animals into a chute and do the job in a few hours, but we want to keep this tradition going," Tinho told me as we stood in a large wooden corral. "We want to maintain and keep our culture alive. My grandfather branded this way, so did my father, now I'm doing it and hopefully one day, it will be my own children carrying the old ways forward."

In the south of Brazil, they didn't rope the head and heels of the animal from a horse like in Canada and the United States. Instead, they threw a *pialo* from the ground, which was a long loop at the animal's front legs. When the animal was caught, the rope tightened and caused the calf to flip over, both front legs roped. The men used their bodies, standing firm on the ground and leaning back, to tighten the rope with a ferocious grip.

Once the calf lay on the floor, other gauchos came to castrate, brand, and vaccinate the animal. The branding iron, a long metal rod with a wooden handle, sat atop a wooden fire until the brand at the end of the rod glowed orange. I tried their method of roping, but it was not easy.

After we finished the work, it was time to celebrate. A large table was set, and we ate and drank the afternoon away. This, I must say, reminded me a lot of my time branding in Western Canada on my first journey from Canada to Brazil. Although the method of roping the animals was different, the help from the community, and the feast afterward was identical. I was also forced to eat a testicle at both brandings. The meat was very spongy and — if you didn't overthink it — tasted great, especially grilled with some lemon juice squeezed on top.

~

In Rio Grande do Sul, I traveled back in time to the seventeenth century. A grand cathedral built by the Jesuits in 1635 still stood in the city of São Miguel das Missões. The ruins were declared a World Heritage Site by UNESCO in 1983 and were an architectural masterpiece.

I rode the mares up to the ruins and let them graze on the short grass as I watched the tall walls turn orange with the setting sun. The ruins had no ceiling and some of the walls had crumbled significantly, yet most of the structure had withstood nearly 400 years.

Left to the silence of my thoughts, I was taken back to all of the ruins I had seen during my life as a Long Rider: Teotihuacan, Chichén Itzá, Tulum, Tikal.

That night, we rested at the Center for Gaucho Traditions (CTG). Throughout Southern Brazil and Northern Argentina, traditional gaucho customs are celebrated and kept alive in these community centers. They may include buildings, stages, corrals, and barbecues. Some are as big as fairgrounds.

The next day, I visited the ruins. Walking through the old cathedral's doorway, about six feet wide by fifteen feet tall, made me feel so small. The walls were so tall, and the structure so grand. Every rock so colossal, some the size of an eighteen-inch television screen, with perfectly square edges, fitting onto one another like a giant puzzle.

And to think this place of worship was built in 1635! It was hard to fathom.

After visiting the ruins, I made my way to a small museum nearby that was run by a Guarani native man. "Welcome. Please let me start by blessing you on your long journey," the short fellow with dark skin and even darker hair said. He had read about my Long Ride in the local paper.

I was accompanied to the ceremony area of the museum where we stood around a large circle. He placed a wooden necklace around my neck and then hit a walking stick on the ground three times to commence the ceremony.

In the center of the circle, he grabbed a handful of powdered mate leaves from a wooden bowl and slowly released them onto a small cauldron of red coals.

"Here, I want you to ask for the protection of your god on your journey, for your life, and those around you." The thick white smoke coming from the burning mate leaves engulfed my body.

I knelt in front of the cauldron. After I finished my silent prayer, I stood and we walked to another cauldron where he threw more mate on the coals. "Here I want you to give thanks for all of the blessings in your life," he said in a quiet, hypnotic tone.

Again the smoke covered me while I knelt in front of the glowing coals. I said a silent prayer of thanks and rose feeling much lighter.

I couldn't help but think of the Canadian First Nations woman who had given me sage during my ride through southern Alberta. She instructed me to burn it and let the smoke cover my body when I felt afraid. She told me to pray to my god and ask for protection just as this man had.

That night at 3:30 am, Cluck Norris almost gave me a heart attack. Sleeping right near me in his cage, he began to crow like a mad man while flapping his wings. I don't know if he had a bad dream that he was on a KFC conveyor belt or what, but he scared the Jesus out of me. I awoke panting, ready to be brutally murdered. Then I realized it was just Cluck.

"Snooze! Snooze!" I said, hitting the top of the cage. I tried to go back to sleep but couldn't, so I boiled Cluck. Just kidding!

I boiled water, made a strong cup of coffee and, before the first light of day, saddled up my girls and rode south.

It was a terrible mistake. Just two kilometers into our ride, still in darkness, a pack of angry street dogs in an array of colors and sizes tore out of the shadows barking and growling. It seemed like a dozen but was more like four or five.

I tried to hold my mares, but couldn't. Both Life and Doll took off in an adrenaline-fueled gallop while the dogs chased us down a narrow winding road. I prayed for no cars or trucks to appear in front of us. We must have covered about two kilometers before the dogs finally lost interest in us, and I managed to stop my girls. With my knees shaking and my heart in overdrive, I stepped down from Life's back to let everyone take a breather.

"Easy, easy, girls." I held the mares while they pranced around searching for the loud pack of dogs. Luckily, it was just a scare. But out there, it took only two seconds for all hell to break loose.

ALONE

One day before arriving in Santiago, Rio Grande do Sul, my support driver and best friend, gave me the news that I knew was coming, but I didn't want to hear.

"I'm going back to Canada, brother. I'm sorry," Mark told me looking down at the floor, unable to look me in the eyes.

Our beards were both long and scraggly like NHL players during the late rounds of the playoffs. We'd come a long way, but I had a long way to go.

Boiling eggs, I stared at the simmering water in the small, silver pan. I wanted to cry, as if my own blood was bubbling with a mixture of anger and sadness. The thought of being on the road alone made me want to curl up into the fetal position and yell until my eardrums exploded. I swallowed my tears and asked him when he planned to leave.

"Tomorrow. I already looked up the bus schedule for São Paulo. My flight to Toronto leaves in a few days."

Mark's words hit me like a punch to the throat. How would I move the van ahead? Carry water and feed for the mares? How could I continue? Truth was, Mark was instrumental to our Long Ride to the end of the world. Without his help and friendship, this journey would be a million times harder. Every day it was thanks to his patience that I was able to offer my mares water, feed, and hay. After having to sleep countless nights on the last journey without having anything to offer my horses, I can't even begin to explain how much of a relief it was to have the support vehicle with me.

Mark also helped me film the journey, getting far-away shots I never would have gotten were it not for him. Not to mention his companionship and uplifting humor. There were times when he was the heart...Well, no, but definitely times when he was the belly of the journey. That was all about to come to an end.

Inside, I was fuming. He was my best friend. When he first offered to drive the support vehicle, I told him he had no obligation to continue on if he ever got tired of the gig. However, I begged that he give me at least a week or two notice so I could find someone else to help me. Instead, he gave me one night.

The next morning, watching Mark drive away, a light, cold drizzle fell. I was left with a lump in my throat. A great sadness took hold of my heart and soul. He would drive the van to Santiago, thirty-two kilometers south, leave it at the local CTG before getting a cab to the bus station.

I wanted to be angry at him, but I couldn't. After spending nearly the entire night awake, I realized all I could do was be thankful for the three months this selfless guy, my best friend in the world, took from his life to help me with this project. Later, he wrote me a beautiful letter essentially saying this was my journey, my dream, and now he had to find his. He was right and I would really miss him.

Long Riding was a lonely experience. Even though I met many amazing people and had Mark with me on this journey, I spent eight to ten hours alone riding every day, just the horses and me, without saying or hearing a word. Being left alone with only my thoughts for such long periods of time, often suffering, and away from my family and loved ones was difficult.

I often worried about the impact it could have on me in the long run. While riding that day, I did the math. With my two journeys, up to that point, I had spent two years and eight months living life as a saddle tramp. That's 974 days, 23,376 hours, 1,402,560 minutes. When you are traveling at four kilometers an hour, thirty kilometers a day, a minute can seem like a lifetime. There was nothing I could do about saving my sanity on the side of that road. The only choice I had was to continue trekking south.

I arrived in Santiago under cold rain, strong winds, and heavy fog. It was as if the world turned gray with me. My socks were drenched, and my toes were frozen. My hair was soaked, but worst of all, my soul was battered.

"Oh, my God, son! You must be freezing," an elderly gaucho wearing blue *bombachas*, leather boots, and a dark brown wool poncho exclaimed as he strode toward me. "You travel alone? Where are the other riders?"

I gave him a shy smile. "I ride alone, sir." He was perplexed, simply couldn't believe it.

"Wow, you are my hero." He offered his warm right hand. "You are freezing. Turn these horses out so we can get you out of these clothes and near a fire."

I dismounted in the shelter of a long shed and thanked the mares for all of their work. I found the keys to the van Mark had left next to the front left wheel. Then I fed the girls. With every bone in my body aching, especially my back, sleeping in my stinky tent was not what I wanted to do. Luckily, my new host offered me his spare apartment to rest. I couldn't thank him enough.

That night, I slept for fourteen hours straight. I was exhausted and felt a chill I could not shake from my bones. Being in a soft bed for the first time in days felt strange but wonderful.

Much better, I spent the next day with my new friends. They showed me photos of the *cavalgadas* they went on and told me about their love for the horse. Obviously, a lot of meat was barbecued.

To celebrate the end of the *Farroupilha* revolution, every year the *Criollo* flame is lit in a special location and carried on horseback to every single town in Rio Grande do Sul. From the fourteenth through the twentieth of September, the state stops to celebrate the men who fought in this long and bloody war.

"Every year we go get the *Criollo* flame and bring it to our community on horseback. To the Gaucho, this revolution is the most impor- tant event in history," the elderly man explained before passing me a warm mate.

That night, I presented my talk at the CTG to a room full of little gauchos, gauchas, and their parents. It was always such a gratifying experience to talk to young kids about my dream and my journey. I could see that it had an immediate effect on most of them. After the talk, many approached to thank me.

"Congratulations, Mr. Filipe," a twelve-year-old boy with bright eyes told me. "When I'm older, I want to ride my horse somewhere really far too."

As a present, they handed me an image of Our Lady of Aparecida. I placed her softly in the back of the support van with the other saints and rosaries I had been given on my journey south. It was starting to look like a shrine.

Before departing from the city of Santiago, I had to make plans to send the support vehicle ahead. Without Mark, I had to find a driver every day to help me move the cube van forward, thirty kilometers at a time.

My new friends from Santiago were the first to step up to the plate. "Don't worry. We will find a good place for you to spend the night and will leave the van there for you."

During the next four days on the road, a kind soul drove the van ahead for me every day. On this journey, I was constantly reminded of how kind my fellow humans were. That may have been one of the greatest lessons I took from Long Riding.

I arrived in Jaguari to an all-out horse parade. Juarez Bidinoto, the leader of the local horsemen, welcomed me from atop his mare just outside of town. The fifty-year-old had silver hair, blue eyes, and a wide face that looked like it sprang from his wide back, his neck nonexis- tent. He wore reading glasses that turned into sunglasses in the light and sported a five o'clock shadow. Alongside fourteen other riders, he led me into his beloved town. "The name Jaguari came from the large number of jaguars that lived in this area."

We paraded through the small town as people filled the sidewalks to take photos or simply wave us through. Shortly after four p.m., we arrived at Juarez's house. I fed the mares and turned them out in a picturesque pasture nearby. When we returned to his home, it was as if I had been a part of Juarez's family for decades. His father, an elderly man with snow-white hair, a pointy face, and a blind milky left eye, held Cluck Norris in his arms like a baby.

"I'm going to take care of this little rooster while you are here, no need to worry," he said, giving me a toothless smile.

Juarez's mother, a fiery woman with short caramel hair, came running from the bar she managed next door to give me a big hug. "Welcome to your home!" She held me tight like my own mother.

Her daughter, a skinny blonde who looked and dressed like Carrie from *Sex in the City* and ran a hair salon in the house across the street, bent her arm around my elbow, as if we were in the 1920s, and showed me where I would sleep while I rested in Jaguari.

I was in the middle of a big, crazy Italian family and I loved it! Just like the best parts of my own family, they gave me great comfort.

"Tomorrow I will take you to see the wineries in the area," Juarez told me over a traditional barbecue. "Jaguari is known for its great wine."

For the next two days, Juarez took me under his wing and showed me his beloved town. First, we drove to a local vineyard on the outskirts of Jaguari that was owned by one of his good friends.

The elderly gentleman, of Italian descent as well, showed me his grape plantation, holding his hands together behind his back. "My grandfather started the vineyard when he came from the old country. He passed it on to my father, and now it's in my hands."

From the vineyard, we drove to the Jaguari Wine Company, a co-op in the center of town that purchased grapes from local producers and made various types of wines. I was able to tour the large barrels that held the wine, the bottling plant, and their main store.

"We started in 1932 with the co-op and have been going strong ever since," the director told me.

Next, we visited the Grotto Our Mother of Fátima, which was built in one of the longest cave systems in South America, extending

400 meters in length. The dark labyrinth of caves led to a gorgeous waterfall named the Bride's Veil. Juarez and I sat on a rock nearby taking in its beauty. A light mist kissed my cheeks.

Leaving Jaguari wasn't easy. My new family wiped tears from their faces as I rode toward the edge of town.

"Anything you need, you call us okay, Filipe?" Juarez said before giving me a tight embrace. "You have inspired me so much with your ride. For the first time, I will go on the ride to get the Criollo flame this year."

~

A few months previously, the main bridge had collapsed under the weight of a large transport truck that was still half-submerged. Its broken pieces were still being hauled out of the green swirling water. I was forced to ride out following the train tracks. The narrow bridge, sitting high over the river with no guardrails, made it an intensely risky exit out of the small town. With nowhere to hide, I prayed the train would not appear. Luckily, it didn't and the mares navigated this obstacle with nothing but class.

Two days later, in the small town of Cacequi, I was welcomed like a king, just as I had in all of the other communities I crossed in the state of Rio Grande do Sul. Local ranchers and horsemen from the community gathered at the CTG, where the mares and I rested, to cook a feast and to get to know me.

We talked the night away sharing stories and drinks. After dinner, I was given a gift basket with products from their community and the tremendous opportunity to see a *trova galponeira* live for the first time.

"We will perform a *trova* for you, and the theme will be your journey," one of my hosts said.

The *trova* is a freestyle poetry competition where two competitors go head-to-head reciting improvised poems about a certain theme. The *trova* was born in the horse barns of Rio Grande do Sul where one gaucho would battle another to see who was the most creative at spinning unwritten verses under pressure. *Trova* competitions were held all over the South Region of Brazil.

With a guitar strumming in the background to a lively rhythm, two men went back and forth reciting poetry about me, the mares, and my van without a driver. I felt like a king. These guys were fast and full of wit. The gaucho was as sharp as the knife he carried at his waist.

WHISPERS FROM THE DEVIL

From Cacequi, we trekked south toward Rosário do Sul, the second to last city on Brazilian soil we would pass. We skirted giant potholes that looked like they were created by meteors. If a car hit one of these craters at full speed, it would most certainly kill someone.

On our third day, I found refuge at a cattle ranch. The farm was huge, but there was only a small house on the property where the worker lived alone. The house was simple, painted egg-yoke yellow with blue windows.

"You don't need to set up your tent tonight. You can sleep inside with me," the stout, bald worker said to me when I arrived in the midafternoon. I happily accepted his offer.

Because the home had recently run out of water, I carried my things to a stream nearby and bathed outdoors. The water was freezing, but I hadn't showered in two days. I was so stinky that I had to hold my breath as I jumped in.

After drying up and getting dressed, I returned to the small house. My host was tending to the cattle so I cooked myself a pot of noodles and, with the sun kissing the horizon, ate my dinner in the dirty kitchen alone. Piles of dirty dishes sat in the sink and were scattered about. A thick layer of dust coated everything, and the floor was slippery with grease.

With darkness taking over the world, the worker returned. He walked into the kitchen with a small Bible in hand. With the wide, wandering eyes of a wild animal, he told me he recently joined a church.

"Two weeks ago, the devil visited me during the night and didn't let me sleep at all," he told me, waving the pocket Bible around. "He whispered into my ear all night!"

A cold chill ran up and down my spine. My hands became clammy and my heart raced. Looking at the middle-aged man before me, I began to realize how scary this situation could get. I was in the middle of the boonies, alone, with no weapon, sleeping in the home of a complete lunatic. To top it all off, no one knew I was there.

"Why did you tell me this, brother? Now I'm not going to sleep a wink," I said, letting out a nervous laugh.

"You don't need to worry. He visited me because I was a bad man. I did bad things. But now I belong to the church. You will see Bibles everywhere in this home. We are safe."

His efforts to calm me did not work. He wasn't lying about the Bibles, either. I counted five pocket-size Bibles, opened in different corners around the house. One, near a couch that looked like a bomb had exploded inside of it, rusty springs and dark yellow foam pouring out of large tears, was opened to 2 Corinthians 11:3.

I started reading, "'But I am afraid that just as Eve was deceived by the serpent's cunning, your minds may somehow be led astray from your sincere and pure devotion to Christ.'"

I quickly wished I had never picked up that Bible. I also saw a shotgun standing up against the wall next to his bed. I'd caught a glance of the weapon on the way to my room. It drove my anxiety through the roof.

As I entered the room I was to sleep in, I took it in nervously. I saw a large space with white walls, a wooden double bed in the middle made some time in the early nineteen hundreds, a green armoire against the wall, a wooden desk, and chair. Scanning for escape routes in case this lunatic tried to kill me in the middle of the night, I spotted two windows I could jump out of. One was right behind the bed, and the other was behind the desk. I decided I could use the desk to block the door while using the chair as a weapon if need be. It wasn't a shotgun, but it was a pretty heavy chair.

"Look," my host said, passing me his small flip-phone. "This was my wife. Wasn't she beautiful?"

The photo displayed in the ancient, small screen showed his shirtless wife breastfeeding their child.

"Oh, yeah, she was a beauty."

This guy was absolutely smothered in sadness. He spent a half-hour showing me photos of his wife and kid and told me how she left him for another man. I felt really bad. It was obvious he was in a lot of pain. His eyes were red as if he had been crying nonstop for weeks. His pupils were dark black with a very small spark that was hard to see. There was a constant lump in his throat he tried to fight down every few minutes. If it weren't so scary, it would be depressing.

Eventually, he wished me goodnight. I was finally alone with my thoughts to keep me company in the darkness. As I lay there trying to tell myself I wasn't going to die, all I could imagine was the little bald man kicking the door down and shooting me to death.

I dozed off at some point. In the middle of the night, though it was freezing outside, I awoke drenched in my own sweat, as if it were a hot summer night. I checked my forehead for a fever, but there was no heat. The house was as silent as the inside of a coffin. It was an awful night.

From Rosário do Sul, after nearly four months on the road, we made our final push to the Uruguayan border. As I rode the final 105 kilometers on Brazilian soil, what should have been a week of celebration entered a realm of suffering.

On a chilly Friday morning, I woke up and looked at my phone. It was already 7:30 a.m. I was late. I jumped out of my sleeping bag only to discover that I was sick as a dog. My head was pounding, my nose stuffy and my body aching. I had the flu.

Every morning since Cluck Norris was given to me a month ago, the little rooster woke me up with his raspy crow at 4 a.m. With no snooze button, my natural alarm clock continued going off until I couldn't take it anymore and climbed out of my sleeping bag. On this cold morning, Cluck was silent.

I fed the mares and went to check on my rooster. When I arrived at the stall where I had placed his cage, my heart sank. Golden brown feathers were scattered all over the dirt floor. The door to his cage lay open. Cluck had been massacred by a wild dog during the night, and I was staring at the murder scene.

A deep sadness washed over me. Out here on the lonely road south, even a rooster can become your best friend. After losing Mark, a friend was all I wanted.

I whispered goodbye to Cluck and picked up one of his feathers to put on my felt cowboy hat. I thought about all of the times he had woken me in the early morning and the times he made me laugh with his funny antics and his curious eyes. I couldn't believe a wild dog had managed to unlock his cage, rip my little rooster out and eat him. I just wanted to sit there and cry. I couldn't. I had to ride 105 hard and desolate kilometers to the Uruguayan border. There was no eulogy for my murdered rooster. RIP, Cluck Norris.

With the flu making me feel like I had been run over by a bus, jumping into the saddle was the last thing I wanted to do. Like many times before, I only had one option: Cowboy up! In a state somewhere between grogginess and total fatigue, I began my four-day ride to the border city of Santana do Livramento.

On my first day, a strong wind screamed across the pampas. On both sides of the road stretched cattle pastures burned yellow from a harsh winter. Life and Doll enjoyed the chilly weather and trekked happily as if they hadn't just walked 2,000 kilometers. I was proud of them.

That afternoon, when I stepped down from the saddle, I felt like death. My head pounded from a severe sinus headache. Every muscle in my body ached. I felt like I was going to faint with each step.

After untacking, feeding both mares, and turning them out in a pasture behind the restaurant we would call home for the night, I set up the saddle blankets in the back of the van (which had been sent ahead by kind people who helped me out in Mark's stead). I soon passed out hard. I awoke two hours later feeling even worse. I ate a small dinner and went straight back to my makeshift bed.

The next morning when I awoke, I contemplated staying put for the day. I felt so weak that when I stood up, I had to immediately sit back down. The world turned dark and my head spun. I stayed put for ten minutes. When I regained some energy, I decided to keep trekking. The longer I took to reach Santana do Livramento, the longer it would be before I slept in a real bed.

Cold temperatures and strong winds accompanied us south. We rode thirty kilometers to a small cattle farm where I was welcomed by two workers. I only had enough energy to cook a pot of noodles. When I finished scraping the plate, I went straight to sleep. I felt as if I were a thousand years old.

On the third day, I rode thirty-five kilometers to our next stop in a deep fog. During the final hour, I had to push myself both mentally and physically. I was terribly ill at this point and began to wonder if this was just the flu or pneumonia.

The fourth and final day on the road was our hardest, by far. When I climbed into the saddle, I was so weak I contemplated tying myself to it, afraid I would doze off and fall from Doll's back. Every stride the fiery redhead took seemed like a hammer striking the middle of my forehead right above my eyebrows. A mild fever kept me sweating even though the temperature was extremely low. The strong flu medication I was taking made me extremely groggy, my eyes only half-open. I was in bad shape. When I arrived in Santana do Livramento, I was a zombie. Barely alive, it was painful to breathe, never mind ride.

I had contacted Thiago Lima, a horse trainer in Livramento weeks before while I was still in Santa Rosa. I needed to find a good place to rest the mares because I knew I would have to stay put at the border for a while figuring out how we would enter Uruguay. Thiago's training facility was the perfect spot.

The forty-year-old had the smile and energy of a child. Thiago met us a few kilometers outside of the city to make sure I was okay. He knew about my flu and wanted to ensure I would arrive alive. Although

I wasn't really sure I would actually find the strength to make it, I assured him all was under control. He guided me toward his barn.

When we arrived, just after one p.m., his workers were barbecuing to celebrate our arrival.

"Welcome to Santana do Livramento, Filipe, and congratulations on ending your ride through Brazil," Thiago said with a big smile on his round face.

I wished I felt like celebrating. We had every reason to. My mares and I had traveled 2,200 kilometers from our starting point, Barretos, São Paulo. We rode through cities and towns, up mountains, into valleys, and across bridges. We'd faced freezing temperatures, wind, torrential downpours, and scorching heat. Together, we worked hard and met our goal, but celebrating required energy and that was something I did not have. I was so sick and groggy, I wasn't even hungry. I ate a few pieces of meat but it just wasn't going down. I was dreaming of a bed, yearning to sleep to rest my tired body.

In the late afternoon, once the barbecue ended, and I had taken care of the mares, I finally got to rest. Thiago showed me to a cheap motel nearby and I died. That first night, after taking two nighttime Advil, I slept sixteen hours straight. I only woke up to feed the mares and then collapsed back into sleep again. Laying on a mattress with heavy blankets hugging my aching body felt exquisite. A warm shower? Orgasmic.

IMAGINARY LINES: REAL PROBLEMS

The moment I arrived in Santana do Livramento, I began working on getting my mares into Uruguay. I knew it would be a challenge from my experiences on the last journey from Canada to Brazil. However, I had no idea how bad it would actually get.

This was our first major challenge on this Long Ride, the first imaginary line to be crossed. Prior to embarking on my Long Ride Home, I spent months doing research and speaking to CuChullaine O'Reilly, the founder of the Long Riders' Guild. Having spent more than thirty years studying equestrian travel techniques on every continent and completing Long Rides across Pakistan and Afghanistan, he was the best mentor a would-be Long Rider could ever ask for.

"Borders and traffic will be your biggest obstacles," O'Reilly wrote to me in an email early on during our talks.

When I was stopped at the Panamanian border during that first journey, his words hit home. The horses were not allowed to enter, and I was forced to spend nearly three months looking for an alternative in order to continue. I was determined to finish the journey with Frenchie, Bruiser, and Dude. They had become my family and leaving them behind in Central America did not seem like an option.

In the end, I had to raise $30,000 Reais and fly them into Peru, the only country in South America which allowed the horses to enter from a Central American country. With the spread of new and deadly viruses amongst the global equine herd, countries were making it more difficult for horses to cross international borders. The new policies were turning Long Riding across continents — my life — into a bureaucratic nightmare. Unless I was prepared to switch mounts in every country I crossed, a mountain of money and a tone of patience was required.

Thiago Lima had imported horses into Uruguay from Brazil before. With my host's help, I spent two weeks trying to find a way to get my mares into the country. To do it legally was almost impossible. To begin, it used to cost at least $2,000 US dollars per mare in importation taxes, plus exam costs, and vet bills and a sixty-day quarantine period. Additionally, because of *mormo* (the glanders epidemic) Brazil had faced in the last few years, Uruguay made it even harder for Brazilian horses to enter the country.

According to the Brazilian Ministry of Agriculture, the highly contagious and incurable *mormo* disease saw 623 horses put down between 2013 and 2015. Uruguay was free of the virus.

It seemed that the only option was to cross the border illegally. This was common practice during my first journey due to the bureaucracy and lack of common sense found at all of Latin American borders.

An acquaintance set up the transaction with a Uruguayan friend who raised race horses and crossed equines illegally all of the time for different races. I paid $250 Reais, and we loaded the mares into a narrow, two-horse trailer.

The short, skinny driver looked like Joe Pesci. Before we took off, I asked him in Spanish, "Are you sure this is safe?"

"Yes, yes, no need to worry. It will take fifteen minutes," he responded, a half-burned cigarette hanging from his lip.

He wasn't lying. We drove them across the border into Uruguay. Easy peasy. In fifteen minutes, we were parked in front of a long dirt driveway in a sketchy neighborhood in Rivera, Uruguay.

Still, only three kilometers from the border, I was a nervous mess.

If the Uruguayan border patrol caught me entering their country illegally with the mares, I would be arrested and the animals could be put down immediately.

We unloaded the girls and walked them to two small, wooden stalls at the end of the driveway. Recent rains had left everything a muddy mess. On our way, we passed a malnourished boxer tied to a thick-metal chain, completely covered in mud. Straining at the end of his leash, only the whites of his eyes free of mud, the dog barked ferociously. I didn't feel good about this at all.

"Where are the horses' papers?" the owner of the house said to me before even saying hello.

Stunned, I shot back, "What papers?"

"The papers, their papers for entry into the country," he demanded.

The owner of the house seemed to think the driver told him the mares were entering Uruguay legally. The driver denied ever saying they had papers.

I didn't care who said what at this point, I was getting more and more paranoid by the second in the middle of this shanty town with my girls standing knee-deep in mud. The boxer's harsh barks along with the clanking chain in the background did not help my nerves.

"They will sacrifice these mares if they catch them here illegally," the bald man said to the driver. His words echoed in my mind. I was breaking international laws and putting my girls in danger. I had to put an end to this immediately. Interrupting the argument, I finally said to the driver, "Load them up! We're taking them back to Brazil!"

"You will not get your money back," he said to me immediately in an aggressive tone I did not appreciate.

"I don't want the money. I just want to get my mares back to Brazil and end this mess," I shot back.

After fifteen minutes, we were driving up to Thiago's barn again, much to the chubby horse trainer's confusion. He was a natural jokester. "You get tired of Uruguay already?"

"It went terribly wrong. The owner of the house where the mares were going to rest said they needed importation papers, that it was too dangerous to bring them in illegally."

"Don't worry, we will figure out another way." Thiago assured me.

After spending a half-hour inside Uruguay thinking I had crossed our first major hurdle, we were back to where we started, minus $250 Reais.

Back in Santana do Livramento, I tried to figure out a way to continue with my girls. After almost ripping my hair out speaking to Uruguayan politicians, the Ministry of Agriculture, and other officials, it became evident I would not be able to continue the journey with Life and Doll. *My girls. My family. My beautiful mares.*

They were fit, strong, and healthy. They had journeyed more than 2,000 kilometers with me. And now, an imaginary line would stop them from continuing on. It broke my heart. I became a very sad, horseless Long Rider. Useless.

How could I continue?

SEMANA FARROUPILHA

With no horses nor a support driver to continue on, things did not look good for me. But if there was one thing that growing up with a cowboy hat and spurs on has taught me, it was that quitting was never an option. No matter how hard that bronc, bull, or life pounded you into the ground, you picked up your hat, brushed the dirt off your Wrangler jeans, and got back on. That's what I did.

Even though my heart was broken at the thought of leaving Life and Doll behind, my mind fluttered with questions of who would drive the support vehicle and what animals I would ride. I immediately got to work and searched for a ranch where the mares could rest before they were hauled back to São Paulo. I needed two Uruguayan ponies.

The first problem was solved quickly when a new friend from Santana do Livramento, a medical student by the name of Mario Luna, offered his ranch to host the mares.

"When you arrived in Barretos in 2012, I was in the stands watching you finish your ride thinking, man, I would love to talk to that guy one day," the gaucho, always dressed in clothing that looked new and expensive, said before putting an arm around my shoulders. "Now you are in my hometown, and you have become my friend. It is an honor for me to tell my grandchildren one day that your mares rested on my property."

With a temporary home for Life and Doll secured, I tackled the second problem: finding new mounts. Luckily, there are some incredibly kind horsemen in the world. And the horse, as I had said many times, was a universal language.

After only two days talking to people in Rivera, Uruguay about my problem, Nicolas Lanfranco, a rancher and Quarter Horse breeder, offered to lend me two mares.

"I love horses and it will be a pleasure for me to help you, Filipe," he said running his fingers through his bushy silver mustache, like two wings above his lips. "We have been following you since you left on your first ride from Canada."

Nicolas was a rancher who looked like a painter. He wore his dark green beret pulled back like Che Guevara, and always seemed to be deep in thought, looking out at the horizon. He spoke eloquently. On a visit to his ranch an hour outside of Rivera, I met his beautiful family and learned that his son, Nico, following in his father's footsteps, had completed a Long Ride around Uruguay with one of his best friends a few years before. It was Nico's birthday, and he showed me photos of their ride while we drank Heineken.

"My favorite part of the journey was seeing how nice the people who hosted us were," Nico, a twenty-six-year-old, tall, and handsome gaucho, told me. I had to agree.

That afternoon, after eating a delicious *asado* (barbecue), we drove around the Lanfranco ranch in their gray Toyota Hilux. The Uruguayan family had 350 horses, 1,500 sheep, and more than 3,000 head of cattle on their property.

"This ranch has been in our family for four generations," Nico told me as he maneuvered his truck through a large inundated pasture. "I love this world."

After seeing the ranch, Nico introduced me to the two mares that would help me cross Uruguay. Cautiva and Andariega were two chestnut Quarter Horses fathered by the same stallion. With identical white stripes running down their reddish brown faces, they looked like twins. They stared at me from a wooden corral. I fell in love immediately. I walked into the corral and did the same ritual I had done with Life and Doll: introducing myself by blowing into their nostrils. They both perked their ears forward and took deep drags of the warm air.

Before letting them get back to their feed, I said, "I can't wait to get to know you girls."

~

What I had learned on my Long Rides was that the old cliché "it's not about the destination, it's the journey" was absolutely true! The richest experiences I had on my travels came at the most unexpected moments. It was not the tourist locations I visited or the days I planned that I remember most.

By far, it was the things I never imagined I would do or experience that have left the deepest impact on me: my days spent in Tegucigalpa, Honduras during my Long Ride Home treating a sore and stiff Bruiser, for example.

During my time in one of the most dangerous cities on Earth, I became really close with a horse handler and rider named Jairo. With a low gaze and dark eyes, the eighteen-year-old was a dreamer. He had jet-black hair and the athletic, strong body of a tennis player. A few years before, he began cleaning stalls in a prestigious jumping barn in the capital. Eventually, the owners let him exercise their horses and quickly noticed the boy was a natural rider.

"I love horses so much, and I worked really hard to learn everything I could about them," Jairo said as he helped me clean Frenchie's stall one day. The young man developed into an experienced rider and even got a chance to compete in endurance competitions, winning everything.

"An old man liked the way I rode and allowed me to compete on his horse. It was the best experience of my life," his eyes sparkled as he told me.

After that, a wealthy Honduran woman, who lived in Florida and competed in show jumping, flew Jairo to the USA where he lived for several months working and riding for her.

"Why did you come back?" I asked, baffled that he would give up such a tremendous opportunity.

"Because she made us work like slaves and paid us nothing. She took advantage of us because we didn't know how to speak English and didn't know anyone else in the country," Jairo explained.

I didn't think I had met a rider with a more perfect body, mind, and attitude than Jairo. When I watched him exercise those huge jumping horses in the Agafam arena, it was as if he were floating. He was one with the horse. He had so much potential to be a world-class athlete. Unfortunately, he didn't have the opportunity and was cleaning stalls to help his mother pay the bills.

I had never forgotten my days with Jairo in Tegucigalpa and, thanks to social media, we stayed in touch. The Honduran was now back in the USA training jumping horses and had a newborn baby girl.

Due to the month spent at the Brazilian-Uruguayan border dealing with bureaucracy and finding new mounts, just like in Tegucigalpa during my first ride, I made some of the strongest friendships of the entire journey.

I also lived some unforgettable moments. During my visit to Nicolas' ranch, I got a chance to *Jinetear* – ride a bronc – in the traditional gaucho style.

On a lazy morning, Nico showed me his herd of bucking horses. A worker from the ranch agreed to get on a mean stud to show me how the gauchos ride these devils bareback.

The stud was tied to the *palenque*, a tall wooden pole with a cloth over its eyes so he could not see. When the animal stopped freaking out, the tall, wide gaucho jumped on bareback. Wearing very long, metal spurs on his worn-out boots, he held his legs open so as to not prick the animal. The gaucho then tied a leather strap around the horse's neck and fastened it in between the fingers on his left hand and the stud's thick, muddy mane.

With a confident nod, his right arm lifted up high clutching the leather *rebenque* (whip). The cloth was removed from the stud's eyes, and his lead rope was untied from the *palenque*.

Like an angry devil, the stud took off, bucking hard as the gaucho tried to stay aboard. After two jumps, the stud's power was too much, and the young man was thrown and did a somersault midair before being hammered to the ground.

All of the workers laughed and yelled. I was hooked. I needed a go! "Can I try one?"

"Of course you can," Nico responded with a tricky smile.

The gauchos beamed with pride that I wanted to participate in their national sport. I also suspected some of them wanted to see this cowboy get tossed. They brought a big sorrel mare and, much to her dismay, tied her to the *palanque*. As the gaucho who had just ridden tied the long spurs to my ostrich-skin boots, I watched the other workers fight with the strong mare. Swallowing my fear, I wondered if this was a good idea.

When the spurs were tied on tight using a long, thin leather strap, the mare was finally blindfolded, I jumped on her dirty back.

She stood still, unable to see anything, but I could feel the adrenaline boiling within her. While a gaucho helped me tie my right hand to the mare's dark brown mane, Nico gave me some pointers on what to do. My heart began to beat faster and faster.

"If she spins, get off the opposite side she is moving so you don't get stepped on," he said from atop a chestnut mare.

Perfect, I thought to myself. *How the hell would I control what side I got off?*

Feeling 100 percent vulnerable, like I was completely exposed to disaster, I nodded and squeezed my legs hard into the mare. As soon as her blindfold was removed, she spun to her left and took off like a speeding train. She galloped for a full stride before throwing her front end up. She bucked and she bucked hard. On her third jump, I moved up to her withers.

Feeling my body going toward her neck, the sorrel quickly dropped her head. She then slammed on the brakes, turned the other way and left me in midair like a cartoon character for a full second. I slammed into the burned pasture.

"Good ride!" the gauchos yelled, smiling from ear to ear.

I loved it! Adrenaline pumping, I felt like I could take on the world.

~

My last week in Brazil was nothing short of spectacular. On a sunny Wednesday morning, I drove to the Rivera bus station to pick up my good friend, Victoria Hay.

"I can't believe you actually came!" I said, giving her a big hug.

Victoria was tall and beautiful. Her hair, a light brown, fell just below her wide shoulders, like a swimmer's, and her eyes were green, exploding with light. Her skin was smooth and pale and her chin pointy. Victoria grew up in Bolton, Ontario, just like me. Her father was heavily involved with the Bolton Wanderers Soccer Club where I spent most of my childhood. I became good friends with her brother and family. But what really brought us together was our love for horses. Victoria was a talented jumper and since I departed on my first journey, she had kept close tabs on my progress.

"I just had to come out and ride with you and the girls," she replied, putting down her heavy backpack.

Victoria arrived on the day the *Farroupilha* week commenced. Every year, the state of Rio Grande do Sul erupts in a party comparable to Carnaval to celebrate the end of the war in 1845.

"I don't know if you are ready for what's about to happen," my new friend Mario Luna said as we headed to the first CTG for dinner.

I hate to admit it, but he was right. I wasn't ready. For seven days, my new friends took Victoria and me to different CTGs at night where we drank and danced until the early hours of the morning.

In the afternoons, we would saddle our horses and ride to a bar called Barbeto, named after its owner and his prodigious beard. Alongside a hundred or so gauchos, we drank beer and told stories and lies. For horse lovers like Vic and myself, it was a once-in-a-lifetime opportunity. Neither of us had ever seen anything like this.

"I have never ridden a horse to a bar before, never mind with a hundred other people," Victoria said with a big smile on her pretty face.

The funniest part was watching the faces of the gauchos as they stared at our western tack and clothing. It was as if we were aliens. Everything on our horses and us was different, even the mares stood out. All of their horses were Criollos. The only two Quarter Horses in town were Life and Doll.

As exciting and fun as the week was, the icing on the cake came on the final day of the *Farroupilha* Week. Riding Life and with Victoria next to me riding Doll, we participated in one of Brazil's largest horse parades. More than 2,000 riders pranced down Santana do Livramento's downtown core as thousands of people watched from the sidewalks.

"Wow! This is amazing," I hollered to Victoria over the loud music and yelling.

"I can't believe this is legal!" she said as we laughed at how this would never be allowed in Canada. The parade was the perfect way to end our ride through Brazil together. Life and Doll looked so beautiful. Even with the loudspeakers, hundreds of people clapping, and other horses around, they maintained their cool. Atop Life, I smiled like a proud father as I carried the blue Barretos Children's Cancer Hospital flag.

When the parade ended, we followed a flatbed truck with a full band on the back toward the fairgrounds. Drinks continued being passed while meat was barbecued on open fires and music played until the late hours.

"We party this hard, and we lost the war," Mario said to me from atop his Criollo mare. "Can you imagine if we had won?"

We burst into laughter.

GOODBYE, BRAZIL

The day after the festivities came to an end, the first day of spring, Mario helped me trailer Life and Doll to his ranch. They would rest there before being sent back to São Paulo.

"Thank you for getting me this far," I whispered to Life and Doll, as tears rolled down my face. "I'm going to miss you two."

After 2,200 hard kilometers through Brazil and five long months on the road together, it was time to say goodbye to my girls. I took off their halters and let them go. They stood by me, confused. Eventually, they dropped their heads to eat.

Watching them graze in a stunningly bright green pasture in the middle of a grand valley, I reflected on my time in the south of Brazil. The Gaucho was a different breed, one near extinction in the twenty-first century. For the rest of Brazil, anyone from the state of Rio Grande do Sul is a gaucho. A true gaucho is a hard-working ranch hand cowboy with an almost mythical reputation. For them, the past cannot be forgotten, and their culture must be lived every day.

Even the smallest towns I crossed in the south of Brazil had a *Centro de Tradicoes Gauchas* (CTG), a kind of community center offering traditional dance, song, and poetry groups, even long roping arenas and spaces for large fundraising events.

"The *centro* is the heart of our community, and it ensures our culture remains alive," said Doeli Valente, the president of one of the three *centros* I visited in Rosário do Sul.

Many nights during the lively barbecues to welcome me in the south, a gaucho would stand and recite poetry to the soft sound of the accordion. Children performed traditional dances. Men strummed old, out-of-tune guitars and belted out *gauchesco* songs about love, land, and horses.

The gaucho's horse, the Criollo, the mustang of South America, originated in the pampas of Brazil, Uruguay, Argentina, and Chile. In these cold and desolate lands, the stocky, indefatigable Criollo, used for work, war, and sport for decades, became a god to these men. My own arrival on horseback was a revelation for them. Many were in shock that I had traveled so far in the twenty-first century. They were used to riding for several days, hundreds of kilometers at a time. But to see someone riding for years, across continents, made them euphoric.

"This cowboy is a Gaucho *Tche*," I heard many times during my ride through Rio Grande do Sul.

My favorite moments of this journey thus far were spent sitting with gauchos in old horse barns far from the tourist spots, drinking wine, talking politics, eating meat with our hands, and laughing. The barns were barely lit, reeking of horse manure and urine, filled with smoke from the woodstove, making it hard to breathe. But it was genuine. It was real.

"Don't worry, Filipe," Mario said, trying to comfort me and bringing me back to reality. "The mares will be taken care of really well until they return to São Paulo."

Before we left, with the help of one of Mario's ranch hands, we picked bushes of a poisonous plant that grows wild in the pampas, and rubbed the green foliage on both of the mares' front teeth. We also burned the plant and let the smoke enter their nostrils. This was a measure to ensure they didn't eat the poisonous weed. Horses born in the pampas knew not to touch the deadly plant. It would kill a full-grown horse that had eaten more than a pound of it. Horses who weren't born there were attracted to the plant's potent smell and unique taste.

From Mario's ranch, I drove over the border to a property two kilometers from the Uruguayan town where Nicolas Lanfranco had dropped off my new mares, Cautiva and Andariega.

My new girls had been living out with the herd so they were fit but a little skinny. The first thing I did was start them on feed, slowly so they wouldn't colic. I needed to beef them up.

While they ate their grain, I watched them closely. Born from the same stud, they looked almost identical. Cautiva was a little thicker, with four white socks. Andariega was leaner and had no markings on her other than the white stripe running down her face. For the next week, I trained my new mares in the art of Long Riding: ponying, carrying the packsaddle, and remaining calm near busy roads. Andariega and Cautiva were a little nervous but learned quickly.

Without a support driver, I planned on crossing Uruguay with the old, orange packsaddle lent to me by the Long Riders' Guild, the same I used to travel from Canada to Brazil. The thought of not having the van to carry feed and water for my new mares made me cringe with dismay. But, like many times before on this lonely road south, I remembered the words of my high school roping coach, farrier, and good friend, Jason Thomson. While joining me for a week out in Colorado during my ride from Canada to Brazil, Jason said, "Hope for the best, plan for the worst, take what comes."

Jason's advice pushed away some of my anxiety. With a heavy heart, the afternoon before my ride through Uruguay commenced, I packed essentials into the orange panniers: toiletries, ramen noodles, canned beans, four bottles of water, an extra pair of jeans, three long-sleeve shirts, two pairs of socks, five pairs of underwear, a horseshoe and some nails, the horses' first aid kit, and sleeping bag. It was unbelievable how little we actually needed to survive.

After organizing all of my things and feeding the mares, I drove to the immigration office to get my passport stamped. There was no turning back. After five months spent crossing my home country, it was time to say goodbye to Brazil. My stomach rumbled with nerves, while my mind raced. I just wanted to get back on the road. Driving toward the mares, my cell phone began to ring. It was Mario. I immediately asked if Life and Doll were okay, fearing something had happened to them.

"Yes, yes, they are great, brother," the medical student and rancher answered, laughing at my worried fatherly tone. "I'm calling to let you know I'm going to drive the support vehicle for you through Uruguay. You have suffered too much."

"What?" I was dumbfounded. Never in my wildest dreams did I ever imagine I would be getting this phone call from Mario.

"Are you deaf? I'm going to drive the support vehicle for you through Uruguay!" he yelled into the phone.

"I don't know how to thank you, brother! You have no idea what this means to me!"

We set a time to meet the following day and said goodbye. Once again, the Universe was conspiring in my favor, putting yet another angel in my path. I had arrived at the Uruguayan border a few weeks earlier in bad shape. With a terrible cold making it hard to live, I'd lost my pet rooster, my mares, and my support driver. A month later, here I was back to health with new mares and a new support driver, ready to continue my ride south.

With Nicolas Lanfranco and his wife Martha Marizcurrena taking photos, I waved goodbye to the Brazil-Uruguay border. I felt relieved to finally get back on the road after an entire month stuck at the border. Being back in the saddle made everything better, and entering the eleventh country I would cross felt tremendous.

Riding Andariega and packing Cautiva, I enjoyed the morning breeze while observing the beauty of the Uruguayan pampas. Both sides of the highway stretched out in green pastures with fat, Red Angus cattle grazing next to thick, Criollo horses.

At noon, an old Ford truck pulled up next to me, and a nice gentleman invited me to eat lunch at his ranch. "I am friends with Thiago Lima, and he told me you would be riding through here today."

My first day on the road, and I was already getting a taste of Uruguayan hospitality. In a small barn with four stalls, I untacked the mares and let them graze in the field nearby. Together with the workers, I ate a delicious pasta soup or *fideo*, as they call it there. While we ate, I spoke with the gentlemen who worked on the ranch about my journey, horses, and life in Uruguay.

"You are going to love this country," an elderly man with a red, worn-out beret said as he dunked a piece of bread into his soup. "Uruguayans love the horse, and I am sure you will be hosted like a hero all the way to Montevideo."

I continued on during the afternoon with a wide smile on my face. Green grass stretched out for several meters next to the highway on both sides, and every four or five kilometers, we crossed a fresh stream. So far, Uruguay was Long Riding heaven!

In the late afternoon, I arrived at the Cia del Norte Cabana. Pedro, the slim gaucho who ran the ranch, opened the front gate for me and welcomed us into his home. His face looked like the inside of a catcher's glove. He limped from a back spasm he had acquired several months earlier after falling off a young colt.

I rode next to a beautiful pond toward the main barn where I untacked the mares before giving them a bath. Walking past empty stalls, I asked Pedro where the horses were.

"This place used to be full of Criollo horses a few years ago, but the owner sold everything," the gaucho said with a crushed look.

Mario arrived just before the sun went down, and we began cooking dinner. "How was day one?" my new best friend asked, lifting the tip of his flat-brimmed, black felt hat from his dark eyes.

"It was amazing, brother," I said as I helped him set up our makeshift kitchen in the barn. Our first night on the road finished with an extremely salty plate of rice and beef jerky.

"Next time, remind me not to add any salt," Mario said as we tried to eat the dish. "The beef jerky is already salty enough."

Mario's thick Rio Grande do Sul accent was so strong it sounded like he was speaking Spanish at times. We laughed with Pedro until the time came to lay down my saddle blankets in front of the fireplace in the barn and stretch out my sleeping bag.

While I organized my bed, Mario pulled out a rolled-up king-size mattress from the van and laid it out on the dusty barn floor.

"No way! You brought a king-size mattress?"

"This is how I rough it, Filipe. In style!"

With the fire crackling in a white fireplace in front of us, I said goodnight to Mario and thanked the universe for another day on the road and a new friend.

URUGUAY

"Good morning, brother," I said to Mario as I slowly crawled out of my sleeping bag.

The crisp Uruguayan morning made me want to jump back into the cozy, dark blue nylon bag, but there was no sleeping in for a cowboy. After getting dressed, I walked out to the mare's pasture and was overwhelmed with the beauty I encountered.

The large pond that sat in the middle of the bright green pasture had a thick layer of mist dancing atop the sparkling water. With the sun rising just over the horizon, the pond's surface mirrored the pink and violet clouds that hung low in the light blue sky. I closed my eyes and took in a deep breath of the crisp air.

With only the sound of playful birds chirping, waking up to the new day, an explosion of joy warmed my chest, making its way through my limbs, hands, and feet. I walked toward the mares slowly as they grazed, the grass wet with morning dew.

Andariega (In English, her name means She Who Walks), the sassy pants of the team, started walking away when she noticed my presence. Cautiva, the curious and more loving of the two, pointed her brown ears toward me and stuck out her muzzle to smell me as I neared.

When I reached her, I put my hand on her white stripe, softly scratching her face before moving to her neck. I placed my left arm around the bottom of her neck and let my cheek land on her soft, full winter coat. With my nose touching her fur, I took in a deep breath, letting her strong aroma of wet grass and rich soil enter my soul.

Our second day in Uruguay couldn't have started better. Mario put our makeshift kitchen away while I fed and tacked the girls. Just after eight a.m., we said goodbye to our host Pedro and began riding south. Mario drove fifteen kilometers ahead and found a great place for us to cook lunch and rest the mares.

Just like the first day on the road, I was mesmerized by the scenery as I rode through the morning hours. Unlike the first day, after lunch, the pampas' green pastures turned into large pine and eucalyptus farms. On both sides of the road, trees lined the horizon. It would be a real problem to find a place to spend the night.

"There are no ranches or houses for at least forty kilometers from where we started this morning," Mario said to me over the phone that afternoon. He scouted ahead, looking for a place for us to spend the night. There was nothing nearby. Riding forty-plus kilometers on our second day out was not what I had in mind. There was nothing we could do but bite the bullet and ride on.

With dusk settling in, I rode past a burnt car on the side of the road and made a right down a dirt road leading to an old farmhouse. Mario waited for me with his mate in hand and a thermos of warm water under his armpit, something I grew used to seeing daily. Like every good gaucho, he was addicted to mate.

As I stepped off Cautiva, he asked, "How are you feeling, brother?"

"I'm sore as heck." The pain in my knees and lower back couldn't be denied. I untacked the mares and fed them before turning the girls out in the pasture in front of the concrete home.

The elderly man who owned the farm came out for a split-second to introduce himself before hiding back inside the house. He had kind eyes and a thin smile. With a strong handshake, he told me to feel at home.

Many people I met near the Brazilian border were very shy. They allowed us to set up our sleeping bags in an old garage but didn't mingle. We only spoke to the men for a few minutes, and the women stayed out of sight.

The journey took us on a long, beautiful road to Tacuarembó, the first town we would cross in Uruguay after leaving Rivera. It was a one-hundred kilometer trek over four days, sleeping in old barns, garages, and sheds with no bed or shower.

On our third day on the road, Mario found a stunning ranch for us to cook lunch in. I rode the horses up to an open barn with sheep hides hanging all over the place. The owner and his son greeted us with warm smiles.

"Thank you for allowing us to eat lunch here," I said as I stepped off Andariega. We shook hands and I untacked the girls. The mares dropped their heads and began munching away on the green grass.

While Mario finished cooking the pasta, we chatted with the rancher and his son about life in the pampas. "My grandfather raised cattle here," the elderly man said. "Now I'm working alongside my sons. I wouldn't trade this life for anything,"

Before chowing down on the pasta with Mario and my new friends, I placed my SpotGPS on the ground to let *Outwildtv* see my coordinates that day. Whenever I had a clear sky, I checked in so we had an exact route of the journey when I finished.

I didn't know if Mario was a tremendous cook or if I was starving, but I scarfed down two plates of the warm pasta in minutes. Our hosts ate with us inside the cluttered barn and brought out a dessert of chocolate mousse for everyone.

As with the rest of the houses we stayed in near the border, the matriarch never came out to say hello. When I went to get the mares to saddle them for the afternoon, they were fast asleep. Cautiva stood but Andariega lay on the soft grass. I walked up to her slowly, and when she finally heard my presence, tilted her head up unworried. I scratched her head for a little bit while she came back to life. When she was ready, she spread out her front legs and stood.

After thanking our hosts, Mario and I continued south. The afternoon brought with it heavy winds. About an hour down the road, I stepped down from Cautiva to take a whiz. While swinging my leg off the saddle, I saw a horse galloping over the hill from where we had just come. When the horse got closer, I recognized the rider. It was the son of the rancher. I wondered what he was doing galloping my way and guessed that he wanted to continue on to Patagonia with us.

"You forgot this," the teenager said when he finally reached me, handing me the orange GPS.

"Oh, my God, I'm so sorry! You didn't have to bring it all the way here," I said, turning red in embarrassment. I felt so bad.

"No worries. Can I take a selfie with you before I head back?" he asked with a shy smile on his wind-cracked lips and sunburned face.

We took the photo and I continued on, feeling terrible that the boy had to gallop five kilometers to find me.

That night, Mario made camp in an old barn at a ranch that hosted cattle sales. There were large pens set up all over the place and a beautiful pasture next to the barn. We turned out the mares and played soccer with a little boy while the sun made its way down.

Wearing boots and spurs, I played keep-ups with the nine-year-old for an hour. I love kids because it takes about ten seconds to become their best friend in the world, especially if you take the time to play with them.

After our game, his father, a worker at the ranch with a long, thin nose and sunken eyes, invited us to eat dinner in their home. As we entered the tiny house, the strong smell of barbecued meat almost knocked me out. Like all of the homes in Uruguayan ranches, there was a fireplace in the kitchen where there was always a large amount of lamb cooking twenty-four hours a day.

Before we ate dinner, the young boy let two baby sheep in the house to give them milk. Their mother had died, and he was now in charge of raising the cute little animals. They walked around the kitchen like two puppies while the boy prepared the warm milk formula.

He had brown hair, big dark eyes, and his skin was darker than his father's. He wore an orange T-shirt with a long sleeve blue fleece shirt underneath. His forest green *bombachas* were a little baggy, and his dark gray shoes had missing pieces and stitches.

"Relax. Your turn is coming," he said while one of the sheep tried to steal the bottle from his brother's mouth.

After the sheep had dinner, it was our turn. We cut into the succulent meat and placed it into small pieces of soft bread. The lamb chops tasted great and, after dinner, the young boy retired to bed.

Frederico was a skinny man in his early forties wearing a black beret tilted back on his head, revealing his black hair. His rough hands were stained with dirt. He opened his heart to us, explaining how his son was everything to him. "I have been raising my son by myself since he was two. His mother left us," he told us as he stared into his mate while we sat by the fire.

The proud father showed off a drawing his son had made of an orange horse. "Seeing a smile on his perfect little face makes everything worthwhile."

While he spoke about the hardships of raising a son alone, I looked around the small living room connected to the kitchen. There was a thick layer of dust on the corners of the floor and ceiling. Papers, crayons, and bread were spread out all over the table. It was a messy house but the love within those walls was evident.

Long Riding allowed one to enter people's homes and learn their inspiring and sometimes tragic stories. Traveling the world on horseback, there was no inauthenticity, only truth.

After our first four days in Uruguay, we finally arrived in Tacuarembó. I was hurting. After a month off the saddle dealing with the bureaucracy at the border, I was no longer used to the long days of riding. But deep inside, beneath the physical pain, I was smiling like a kid, finally chasing kilometers again.

Having Mario out there with me was also a real blessing. Cautiva and Andariega began gaining weight since I could give them feed every night, and I had a traveling partner, someone to cook with, talk, laugh, and yell with when things fell apart. That made all of the difference in the world.

Mario was a caring and selfless human with a bit of a troubled soul. He was self-conscious, but some read that as arrogance. He had both Uruguayan and Brazilian roots, a deep passion for ranching, the Criollo horse, and everything Gaucho. He also came from a lot — I mean a *lot* — of money. His father had several large department stores in Santana do Livramento.

Mario's parents' house, literally on the Brazilian and Uruguayan border, was a mansion like I'd never seen before. Marble was on everything. There was a large downstairs area with a beautiful barbecue inside the house. In the colossal garage, more like a hangar, sat a motorhome, a tour bus that looked like it belonged to the Rolling Stones, and a sleek, white yacht a drug lord would envy.

Since leaving Rivera, Mario and I spent a lot of time getting to know one another during our lunches and dinners together. "Sometimes I don't know if I want to finish medical school...or just focus on the ranch," he said.

One night while I opened up to him about how turbulent my life had become after I finished my first Long Ride, the short, pale gaucho with a dark, trimmed beard told me how, a few years back, he had gone into a deep depression.

"I was very sad and empty. Something was missing in my life." Mario explained how he reached an ultimate low. Cleaning his revolver, alone in his spacious beach house in Punta del Este, the twenty-six-year-old decided to shake things up planning a trip to climb Aconcagua in Argentina.

"I needed to push myself. I needed adventure in my life." Mario showed me a picture of him on the summit of the tallest mountain outside of Asia holding a small Brazilian flag. It had taken several tough days to fight his way up. Adventure liberated Mario from his depression. And now we were on our own adventure together, becoming closer friends with each kilometer.

Just after three p.m., I rode into Alvaro Indaburu's ranch in Tacuarembó. The stunning property sat on a hill with a large pond as a backdrop. On top of another hill behind the home was Alvaro's large outdoor riding arena with tall pine trees lining both sides.

"Welcome to your home for the next few days," Alvaro said as we shook hands. With broad shoulders, a prominent nose, chiseled jawline, and shaggy hair, Alvaro looked like every Argentinian polo player I had ever met. Only this Uruguayan didn't play polo. He was a reining competitor and instructor, considered one of the most renowned horsemen in the entire country. He not only won many prizes in Uruguay, he also competed in Argentina and Brazil. The Uruguayan even lived in Texas where he trained some of the best Quarter Horses in the world.

"I was going to move to the USA. After spending three months there, they liked my work so much I was offered a full-time job. Unfortunately, after getting everything ready for the move, they denied my work visa," Alvaro told me with a pained gaze.

It was his life's dream to work in the United States with the best reining trainers and horses in the world. Through his hard work and commitment to the sport, he gained the opportunity to turn that goal into a reality. Due to an invisible line filled with red tape, that dream was torn from his grasp when he was so close he could nearly touch it.

As an immigrant myself, I knew all too well what he felt. When you sell your home, tell all of your friends you are moving to a different country, get ready emotionally, and all of it falls apart last minute, it felt like someone had punched you in the stomach, removed the floor from beneath your feet, and shot you in the heart.

Alvaro's story reminded me of the many migrants I met in Mexico and Central America, walking and riding on top of trains for months to the United States in search of a better life. In a train yard in Tierra Blanca, Mexico, I sat with a group of migrants on the train tracks and asked if they would give me an interview.

A cute, round-faced young woman from Honduras who had been trekking for a month agreed to talk to me. Karla Marisela Amaya Rios told me about how she had already been robbed once and had seen a man fall off the train one night. He'd lost his right arm to the tracks.

"This trip is hard, but I need to get to America to make money and send it to my two daughters," she said with a frown.

When I asked Karla to talk about her daughters, her eyes lit up for the first time. "One is four and the other is turning seven next month. They are my reason to live, my happiness." Her lips spread into a pure smile on her dirt-stained face.

The risks people like Karla took in their search for a better life were immense. If she managed to find enough food and water, not fall off the moving trains, and pay off the cartels along the way, she still had to pay a coyote and walk across the Chihuahua Desert for days into the US — the most arduous part of their journey.

While in Marfa, Texas, I was told many stories by ranchers who run into illegal immigrants out in the middle of their pastures almost every day. All of the ranchers I spoke to told me stories of men and women who had walked up to their homes asking for food, water, and clothes on their illegal crossing into the United States. Many ranchers left a shed stacked with these resources so the immigrants could take what they need, without needing to approach the home.

One rancher named Brent told me a story that was hard to believe.

"I was out in the middle of the desert searching for some missing cattle when I came across a scene out of a movie," he told me before taking a gulp of his whiskey in a small country bar.

"There in the middle of the desert was a skeleton under a thin blanket, a cell phone in its right hand. I couldn't believe what I was seeing, I stepped off my horse and inspected the body. I ripped the phone out of the skeleton's hand, and to my surprise, it worked when I pressed the on button."

According to Brent, the coyotes give pay-as-you-go phones to the migrants to notify their contact in the US when they are far enough from the border.

"I felt so bad, there was an empty bottle of water next to the skeleton. I imagined how the person's family and friends must have felt not knowing the whereabouts of their loved one." The sadness in the rancher's eyes didn't fit the hard face tucked under his black felt cowboy hat.

I often wonder if Karla found her American dream or ended up like the skeleton Brent found in the middle of the desert.

From Karla's desert, I came back to Alvaro's Tacuarembó. After getting the sad news that his visa had been denied, the horse trainer began looking for a new place to train and found the stunning property in Tacuarembó. "Sometimes the universe works in mysterious ways," he said as we walked up to his magnificent riding arena.

On a gorgeous sorrel mare, Alvaro showed me some reining tricks and even invited me to get on. I grinned like a cowboy at the National Finals Rodeo.

For two days, Mario and I slept in an empty stall in Alvaro's ranch. Our neighbors were two noisy Criollos and a beautiful Quarter Horse stud. There was also a cute blue-heeler puppy who woke us up every morning by jumping on our heads and biting our hair. Needless to say, we didn't get much rest but at least the mares did. Cautiva and Andariega were out in a big pasture with a pond in the middle. For them, it was like a stay at a five-star hotel, and that's all that mattered.

On Sunday, the Lanfranco family drove to Tacuarembó for a barbecue. "Filipe, congratulations on covering the first one-hundred kilometers of Uruguayan soil," Nicolas said before showing me the lamb he'd brought for us to feast on.

We shared drinks and stories for several hours before driving to a *Criolla* – a Uruguayan Rodeo. When we arrived at the local park, it was packed with people and cars. We made our way to the arena and sat in the wooden bleachers to watch the action.

Three horses at a time were tied to the *palenque* at one end of the arena. The horse was then blindfolded, and a rider jumped on its back. When the blindfold was removed, the horse took off bucking as everyone clapped and yelled. When the ride ended, two singers with guitars improvised verses about how the horse bucked and the gaucho rode.

For a cowboy like myself who grew up rodeoing, this was an extraordinary opportunity! The smell of horse sweat, manure, and barbecued meat welcomed me. I loved every second of it, especially since Nicolas and his son Nico were there to explain exactly what was happening.

On Monday morning, celebrating four and a half months on the road, I awoke early and tacked the girls. We rode fifteen kilometers and found a beautiful hotel with a riding program to let the mares rest while we drove back to town for me to give a motivational talk. A school in Tacuarembó invited me to speak to their students about my journey and the importance of an early diagnosis of childhood cancer.

Okay, truth was, it wasn't the school that invited me, but a good-looking, young teacher with big blue eyes who I spent most of Saturday night making out with.

Mariela was soft-spoken, light-skinned, and had dirty-blonde, wavy hair down to her lower back. We met over beers at a local *boliche* (club) and while we talked about my journey, I explained to her why I was riding.

"Can you come to my school on Monday? My students will love your story."

I agreed and sealed the deal with a kiss.

Mario and I arrived at the school five minutes before my talk. The large white building in the center of town had a spacious play area in front where the kids were enjoying their lunch. As I watched a group of four boys kick a soccer ball around next to the buzzing playground, I was taken back to my childhood.

"You actually came," Mariela said, looking even more beautiful in the light of day. She opened the gate and gave me a kiss, this time on the cheek.

The school was bilingual, so the kids learned in English in the morning and Spanish in the afternoon. I gave my talk in English, and when they didn't understand something, I would transition into Spanish. I was surprised to see how well they spoke English at such an early age.

After taking a million photos and saying goodbye to Mariela, Mario and I drove back to the mares and I rode the last fifteen kilometers. Because of the talk, it turned out to be a very long day in the saddle. It was dark by the time I finally rode into the ranch where we would spend the night.

The elderly couple who owned the place had a little makeshift grocery store. We bought ham, cheese, and some bread. We cut everything up and made a nice entrée accompanied by a bottle of Johnny Walker Gold Mario had with him.

"Even in hard times, we live well," Mario said, adding another log to the fire.

It was a chilly night. The alcohol helped warm our bodies. We talked to the elderly couple for some time before they retired to bed and we did the same.

The next morning we continued south. It was a five-day ride to our next major city, Paso de los Toros. Every night we were hosted by a different ranch family.

On our third day on the road, the Universe helped us immensely. Mario arrived at Santa Eugenia, the only ranch in a radius of twenty kilometers, to ask to spend the night.

"If you had arrived one day earlier or later, you would have found a locked gate," the owner said. That time of year, the stocky gaucho, built like an Angus bull, only came one day a month to check on his cattle. We had arrived asking for help exactly on that day. Not only did this gaucho allow us to spend the night, he cooked us dinner and opened a bottle of wine to celebrate our arrival.

"I like horses so much that if I spend a week without riding, I literally get sick," he told us over the delicious pasta he had prepared.

The next night we were hosted in one of the most beautiful ranches I have ever ridden into. A dirt road snaked around tall trees toward a large house built next to a sparkling pond. Dotted sporadically by tall ombú trees, green pastures flanked the road on both sides all the way to the home. Big white puffy clouds, moving west slowly but surely, sat low over the ranch of my dreams.

"You know, I have worked here for two years and have never seen the owners spend a night here," one of the workers, a lanky, white fellow with a terrible sunglass tan, told me while we chatted over mate. It broke my heart. The family who owned the property lived in Montevideo and never came to this little piece of heaven. "If this was my place, I wouldn't leave — ever," I said.

The next morning, just after six a.m., our hosts butchered a lamb, something they did every morning for the ranch's internal consumption.

They gave us a piece to barbecue that night along with two wild ostrich eggs.

"There is the equivalent of twelve chicken eggs in here, so be careful how much you eat," one of the workers warned us.

Another worker, a clean-shaven kid in his early twenties who looked more like a computer coder than a gaucho, made everyone

laugh by adding, "Too much and you will need to find toilet paper —
quickly."

The pampas continued taking my breath away with its beauty.
However, as I neared Paso de los Toros, the landscape was altered by
large wind farms. Tall wind turbines cut through the air in unison, their
sharp blades the size of a bus. It made for an interesting sight, but it
changed the natural landscape I had enjoyed since leaving Rivera.

PASO DE LOS TOROS

I arrived in Paso de Los Toros under a light drizzle. A tanned man came to open the gate wearing a big brown poncho and a light gray beret. "Did you get wet or what?" he said, offering me a strong handshake.

Tito had a big smile and charisma! He was the kind of person you could immediately see through and what I saw was a kind and loving human being. I untacked the mares and let them go in a huge pasture with fifteen stocky Hereford bulls. With Tito, one of his friends, and Mario, we sat in the ranch's barn and drank mate. Passing the warm tea around in a circle, we began to get to know one another.

"There is a small museum here with some artifacts from this area. Would you like to see it?" Tito asked, widening his big brown eyes.

In a few minutes, we were all in his silver Toyota truck headed to town. We drove to an elderly gentleman's home that acted as the town's museum. He had bushy white sideburns, wore thick, round-framed reading glasses, and spoke with a slight lisp. A wide gap separated his two upper front teeth.

"I have been showing people my private collection of artifacts for over thirty years," the frail man in his late eighties said with pride. We learned about the indigenous people who lived in this region and saw their arrowheads.

"Historians believe that during pre-colonial times, Uruguay was inhabited by small tribes of nomadic Charrúa, Chaná, Arachán, and Guaraní peoples. These tribes survived by hunting, fishing, and gathering and are said to have had a population of about 20,000 people," he told us with excitement, spit flying out of his mouth with every third word.

Although the museum was built inside a home, there was nothing homemade about it. The artifacts sat in spacious display cases, the glass cleaned daily, with florescent lights above every shelf. Each item in the museum was carefully documented, and the arrowheads even had their number written on every piece with chalk. There were over 15,000 arrowheads on display.

I held the *boleadora*, a weapon made from leather straps with two or three rocks tied at the end. It was used to hunt wild ostrich. The gauchos would grind the rocks into perfect balls using larger stones. They would then chase wild ostrich on horseback, spinning the *boleadora* over their heads like a lasso. When they were close enough, they would cast the weapon, aiming for the animal's legs. In a perfect shot, the weapon would become entangled in the bird's legs. When thrown with enough force, it could also break bones and ultimately kill the prey. Although the *boleadora* is often associated with the gauchos, the weapon has also been found in excavations of pre-Columbian settlements, especially in Patagonia.

After we left the museum, Tito took us for a tour of his town. We visited the large statue — larger than a minivan — of a muscular black bull. It symbolized the town's name: Paso de los Toros.

"This is the ugliest statue on earth," Tito declared. We laughed together as Tito added that though the statue was supposed to be a bull, to him, it looked more like an elephant.

While I tried to see the elephant in the bull, the gaucho told me that the town was famous around Uruguay and Argentina because of a popular soft drink made here. The logo was the exact bull we were looking at, called *Paso de los Toros*. I later bought a can and sipped the milky-yellow liquid. It tasted like pomegranate mixed with elephant piss. I finally understood what Tito meant!

We drove by the main church, Santa Isabel, one of the first buildings built in the town, founded in 1903. We finished on the shores of the Río Negro, a beautiful river that divides the country in half from north to south. Early settlers were forced to cross its waters using rafts to transport animals and goods from one side of Uruguay to the other. The Spaniards who worked at this river crossing were called "bulls" due to their extraordinary courage and strength. That's how the town got the name Paso de los Toros, meaning "Crossing of the Bulls."

Watching the sunset over the sparkling water gave me a great feeling of peace. An old iron railway bridge sat silhouetted against the blazing orange sky directly in front of me. To my left, a second bridge used for car traffic glowed in rays of the setting sun. Small waves crashed on the shore nearby. We sat in silence, taking in this glorious event, each man engulfed by his own thoughts.

I couldn't say what the others were thinking, but for my part, I thanked the Universe. We were halfway through Uruguay and only 250 kilometers from Argentina.

Leaving Paso de los Toros on a cool Tuesday morning, Andariega and Cautiva were feeling as fresh as the weather. With three days off, the ladies were acting like feisty fillies, nervous at everything in their path. Every four kilometers in Uruguay, there was a stream that crossed underneath the highway. Since I rode on the grassy patch next to the road, sometimes I crossed the stream. If it was too muddy or deep, I rode on the highway next to the guardrail.

When we came up to the first stream that morning, I was riding next to the fence line. When Cautiva stepped into the water, she sunk up to her chest in mud.

"Oh, no!" was all I managed to get out before she shot back and began backing up. Because the fence was right next to her, she became flustered. She backed up until she hit Andariega, who was carrying the pack to her left, freaked out, and went to spin to her right.

Not a great choice. Both her front hooves went into the fence. When she felt the wire touch her front legs, she went crazy. She fought to get her legs out while I struggled to stay on. She freaked out so much, she fell on her left side nearly squishing my leg. Luckily, I took my foot out of the stirrup before she hit the grass and ejected myself from the saddle.

Standing next to her, I tried to calm her down, but she shot straight back up. Thankfully, her legs came free from the fence.

I shook off the accident, thanked the heavens we were okay, and climbed back into the saddle. Four kilometers later, at the next stream we reached, I thought, *I'm not going to take any chances, let's go up on the highway.*

As we began to ride up the small hill toward the road, I saw a large truck speeding up. I tried to hold the mares to allow it to pass before we got on the shoulder, but the rattling truck spooked Andariega. She took off at a gallop. On instinct, Cautiva did the same.

I fought to stop Andariega by yanking on her lead rope with my right hand and Cautiva by pulling back on the reins with my left. All the while, a large brown container truck flew by, inches from my galloping ponies, like a train robbery scene out of a John Wayne movie. The sinister wind from the truck's back wheels made my soul scream with horror.

Just as the girls began to slow down, the right box of the pack-saddle hit Cautiva's right shoulder and flew off Andariega's back. I watched the bright orange pannier do a full slow-motion flip in midair as the mares both hit fifth gear.

With the thud of the clunky box hitting the shoulder's rough asphalt, they turned their heads left and ran onto the highway. We missed the back of the truck by meters, but when I shot my head back toward oncoming traffic, I discovered a white van headed straight for us. I pushed my left spur into Cautiva's ribs and neck-reined her hard to the right. She moved her body sideways swiftly and in a split second, my right leg was squished between both mares as we pushed Andariega off the road.

"Oh, God!" I said shakily.

I stepped down from the saddle with rubbery legs and led the mares toward the orange pannier, some thirty meters back. They snorted and twitched freakishly, still convinced something was out to kill them. Luckily, the mares calmed down, and that night we arrived safe and sound at the home of a ranch hand.

A friend of Alvaro from Taquarenbó, Jorge looked like a Polo Ralph Lauren model yet to be discovered. He was tall and lean, with an intense gaze that matched his face. When I arrived, Jorge was cutting the lawn. He had kept this ranch looking sharp for over fifteen years for the owner, a doctor from Montevideo.

"Filipe, we have been waiting for you to arrive," he said, removing his dark green beret and releasing his silky, black, shaggy hair.

I untacked the mares. While he finished his job, I sat near a large barn to rest my legs. After about twenty minutes, he returned with a jar of cold lemonade and two glasses.

"I am writing a book," Jorge said. "My son is helping me because I never went to school and am just learning how to read and write now."

Jorge was a simple man, but he was also a great man. A few years before, while watching a fundraiser on television, he was inspired to raise money for a Uruguayan clinic that helped kids with mental disabilities. It took him years to come up with a plan and organize the right people to help him. He did not give up on the idea and eventually his plans came to life. Last year, Jorge put on a rodeo that raised more than $10,000 US dollars for the organization.

"I know it's not a lot of money, but if everyone helps a little, it will go a long way," he said with a wide smile that showed off his crowded, crooked teeth.

I was incredibly inspired by Jorge. A ranch hand who made a simple man's wage, worked hard every day caring for cattle and sheep, yet had the desire to help others and found a way to do it!

The book he was writing with the help of his fourteen-year-old son would also raise funds for the clinic. "I will donate 100 percent of my earnings from the book sales," he told me over dinner.

After we finished eating a delicious plate of lamb and pasta, we drove to Jorge's sister's home and helped celebrate her son's birthday. We sang happy birthday and ate a delicious piece of *dulce de leche* cake.

~

With the weather going from rain to sunshine at the drop of a hat, I continued trekking toward Durazno (meaning *peach* in English). We arrived after three days on the road and were welcomed by a chef who was the president of the local *Criolla* (Rodeo) Association.

"Welcome to Durazno! Tonight you will eat a delicious barbecue at my restaurant," Eduardo, a short man with a full head of dark hair and a bit of an arrogant air said as he shook my hand.

We turned out the mares in a spacious pasture north of town and drove to his home. After a much-needed shower, Mario and I drove to Eduardo's restaurant for dinner. Everything was absolutely delicious.

The following morning, we were interviewed by every media outlet in Durazno. From nine a.m. to lunchtime, I answered questions about the journey. As hard as it was to tell the same story over and over again, these moments were extremely important for me to talk about the Barretos Children's Cancer Hospital, the early signs of childhood cancer, and the importance of an early diagnosis.

Once the question period was over, we drove to the field where the mares were resting. I had a ten-kilometer ride ahead of me to get to Eduardo's home. When we arrived, I made a terrible discovery. Andariega was lame on her front right leg. Really lame.

"Oh, man, this is not good," I told Mario as we inspected her leg for any cuts or swelling.

I detected nothing—no cuts, no swelling, no heat. When we fed the mares that morning, she was walking fine. We tried to understand how this could have happened, but had to quickly move on to figuring out what the heck to do next.

Luckily, like many times on this journey, when you need an angel, they appear. Javier, a gaucho and a close friend of Eduardo's, offered to haul Andariega the ten kilometers to Eduardo's home while I rode Cautiva. I thanked him and began my half-day in the saddle. Every stride Cautiva took, I worried about what would happen to her sister. How would I continue with only one horse? It was the worst three hours ever. Even though I rode next to a gorgeous river and beautiful green park, on the outskirts of town, worrying was all I did.

When I finally arrived at Eduardo's home, Andariega was already there, still extremely lame and calling out for Cautiva. I untacked Cautiva and began inspecting Andariega's leg and hoof again. She was in a lot of pain and put very little weight on it, but there were still no signs of what it could be. We called a local horse vet and waited for him to arrive.

Just before dusk, the white-haired vet showed up with his tack box filled with medicine and syringes. I told him what had happened, and he inspected Andariega's leg and hoof. After about fifteen minutes, he told me he believed she had hurt the tendon in her hoof and that she would need some time off.

"By the way she is walking right now, it looks serious, a four out of five," he said, rubbing his stubbly chin. He prescribed four days of intravenous anti-inflammatory injections and told me to place her leg in a bucket of ice water for thirty minutes daily.

After we injected her with the first dose of anti-inflammatories and soaked her leg in the icy water, I gave her a couple of pats on her neck, telling her things were going to be okay. I was lying. I had no idea what was going to happen.

My new friend, Javier, a tall, light-skinned, blue-eyed Uruguayan who looked more like a German, not only trailered Andariega to Eduardo's home for me, he also rode out of Durazno by my side. As his light brown poncho flew in the wind, Javier said, "I can't let you ride out of my hometown alone."

Riding his blue roan Viejo and ponying another blue roan colt, he kept me laughing the entire time, sharing tales of his wild youth and riding crazy broncs. In a matter of minutes, the saddle made old friends out of Javier and me. When we arrived at the farm, Mario had organized for lunch, Javier got a serious look in his blue eyes.

"The truth is, I wish I could continue on with you. This is a dream for me, but unfortunately, I have my family and work to care for. It would be an honor for me if you would take my horse Viejo with you until your mare has recovered."

"Oh, my God, thank you so much, Javier! Are you sure?"

"I'm sure. When you arrive in Florida, call me, and I will trailer your mare there for you and pick up Viejo."

I didn't even know what to say. Here was yet another man I had just met a day ago lending me his favorite horse and helping me with the logistics of the journey. I felt blessed. Andariega was in good hands with the vet and Eduardo in Durazno. For the first time since leaving Canada, I would be riding a Criollo south.

For lunch, Mario and I cooked rice and beans at a milk farm while the kids hung around us. One of the boys, a four-year-old, had a runny nose and a bad cough. He was standing outside with no shirt on and bare feet.

With a cool wind blowing, Mario, a medical student, couldn't hold back and jumped into action. "You need to cover him up," he told the child's mother while she held her baby in her arms. "If this turns into pneumonia, it could be extremely dangerous for him and for your newborn baby."

This simple family, one of many I met along the way, told me about how far the closest hospital was — over an hour's drive. They usually had to wait for hours for medical attention after they arrived and when they received it, the service was terrible.

"One time my son broke his arm," the father told us while he smoked a hand-rolled cigarette. "They made us wait all day in the emergency room while he cried in pain. It was only when I rushed past the door and started yelling that they finally treated him."

Under the shade of a tall tree, Mario and I spoke to them about the early signs of childhood cancer and the importance of an early diagnosis. For a second, watching Mario examine the children, I felt as if I had taken a page out of Che Guevara's book, *The Motorcycle Diaries*.

Ever since I was a little kid, I have trembled with indignation at the sight of injustice. Maybe it was because I read so much of Guevara's early writings. Or it could be the fact that, at the age of nine, I moved from the socioeconomic dichotomy that was Brazil to Canada's almost perfect equality.

Whatever the reason, this deep feeling had fueled most of my life decisions. At the end of high school, I decided to study journalism because I felt it was the perfect weapon in the fight for a more just world. Maybe it was naive of me, but I felt that if I was able to show people the suffering of the forgotten, giving the voiceless a chance to tell their stories, maybe things would one day change for the better.

Being with that family at that moment, traveling with a medical student, and raising funds and awareness for a children's cancer hospital in the middle of rural Uruguay made me feel I was on the right path.

MONTEVIDEO

When I arrived in Florida, Javier trailered Andariega to the small town and picked up his horse Viejo. As we met on the town's rodeo grounds, he asked, "How was the ride?"

I told him about the last few days on the road and thanked him for lending me his fine horse. Viejo was a great mount, both a powerhouse and a calm, cool, and collected beast. Javier and I shared a tight hug before he drove off.

Andarieja had been resting in Durazno for the past three days, treated by the kind vet. Much to my relief, the treatment had worked. She walked normally again. I trotted her around, and the mare moved as if she had never even been injured.

Feeling a million times better, Mario and I rested in Florida for two days. On our first night, a Criollo group invited us for a barbecue in their headquarters. We talked, drank wine, and ate succulent meat before talking to the local media. At the end of the get-together, Mario and I were presented with two plaques.

"As horsemen, we appreciate the hard work you two are doing," announced the group's president, a big man with squinty eyes who looked like the Uruguayan version of Buddha.

The following day, a local tour guide took us around the historic town to show us the sights. We went to *Piedra Alta de la Florida*, a rock by the Santa Lucía Chico River, where the country's independence from Spain was announced in 1825.

"Florida was an extremely important town in the making of Uruguay," Manuel, our energetic tour guide and history teacher, told us. We continued on to a spacious museum and a beautiful church.

After two days of resting and learning, we were ready to make the final push to Montevideo, the capital of Uruguay. There I would bid farewell to this great country before entering Argentina.

However, while trekking toward the town of Canelones, tragedy nearly struck once again. I was riding Cautiva when suddenly I felt the lead rope go tight in my right hand. When I looked back, Andariega, had dropped to her belly in a wet grassy patch and was about to roll.

My instinct was to pull on the lead rope. In doing so, I put all of my weight on my right stirrup. Riding with a loose cinch, the saddle slid sideways. In seconds, I was falling off my mare. Noticing the saddle slip, Cautiva panicked and began to gallop in frantic circles. I fought to push the saddle into the middle of her back with all of my might, but it was not enough. Eventually, I tried to bail off her right side but my right foot remained caught in the stirrup. That was one of the most dangerous things that could happen to a rider.

I managed to bend Cautiva's neck by pulling on the right rein as she twisted her back end away from me. Hitting the pasture with my shoulder, she pulled her body away, ripping the reins out of my grip, and my boot clean off my foot.

I collapsed in the short grass, one boot on, watching her gallop in circles to the right with the saddle dangling off her side. Andariega now stood right behind me, as still as a statue.

"Whoa, whoa!" I yelled, eventually getting the mare to stop. After quickly putting my boot back on, I walked toward her and fixed the saddle. She shook as if staring at a ghost. Thankfully, it was just a scare, but things could have gotten very ugly had my boot not slipped off my foot.

Two days later, after a month riding through Uruguay, I entered Montevideo. What a feeling it was! Alongside the *Blandengues*, the

Military Mounted Unit, the Lanfrancos, and friends from across the entire country, I rode toward the country's Kilometer Zero.

Mario drove the support van ahead as the riders followed close behind. Everyone smiled with joy. I was so happy to be finishing my journey through another country, yet extremely sad to be ending my time with Andariega and Cautiva and Mario.

"We made it, brother!" Mario gave me a big hug when we arrived at the Balisco. What could I say to this remarkable gaucho at that moment? A medical student and rancher who dropped everything to help a stranger with a dream, a stranger who became a brother. I would never be able to thank him enough. For the past month, Mario not only drove the support vehicle for me, he helped me cook lunch and dinner and aided in raising awareness about the importance of early diagnosis in childhood cancer.

"You have a brother for life," I said to him when we finally let go from our fierce embrace. After all the photos were taken, we made our way to a children's cancer hospital a block away.

The staff was waiting for us. Since I was riding for the Barretos Children's Cancer Hospital, I gave them the hospital's flag I was carrying. The staff took me for a tour of the hospital and told me how the foundation had managed to raise their success rate of saving children diagnosed with cancer to 80 percent, exceptionally high for Latin America.

When I came out of the hospital, I received the greatest news possible. A friend of Nicolas Lanfranco and a well-known equine journalist, Vasco Echevarne, had spoken to the Solanet family in Argentina moments earlier.

"Filipe, you will cross Argentina on two Criollos with the same origins as Mancha and Gato from the estancia *El Cardal*," Vasco, a strong man in his late fifties with the body of a wrestler, said in his raspy voice.

Everyone applauded. I couldn't believe it! I looked down at the card Vasco had handed me with the word Solanet written on it in blue ink with a phone number next to it. I spent my entire childhood dreaming of one day going on a Long Ride like Aime Tschiffely, Mancha, and Gato had in 1925 from Buenos Aires to New York!

The last name, Solanet, belonged to the esteemed vet Emilio Solanet. He had singlehandedly begun the Criollo breed and lent Tschiffely his mounts. I'd spoken his name silently hundreds of times while I read and reread the book *Tschiffely's Ride*. And now, after living that dream and then some, our two Long Rides, separated by nearly a century, were about to connect in a way I had never dreamed. I was ecstatic. It was the greatest way to end my ride through Uruguay.

After trailering Andariega and Cautiva to La Baguala, a ranch turned posh hotel that offered to host the mares before they returned to northern Uruguay, Mario and I met the Lanfrancos to celebrate. As our glasses clinked and we yelled, "Salud!"

Martha, a gaucha with the heart and air of a hippie who had become my mother in Uruguay, toasted me. "Filipe, we are so proud of you!" We hugged.

After celebrating with my new family, Nico and his cousin Santiago took Mario and me out to a club called *El Rancho*. The tight club, frequented by young Uruguayans, who had come to the capital to study agriculture and veterinary medicine, was packed that Thursday night.

Out of all of the beauties in that place, there was one who made this Long Rider's heart beat faster. She had long, straight, brown hair past her shoulders and pale skin. Her eyes were a sparkling light brown and her full, perky lips were painted with a deep red lipstick. She wore a black see-through shirt with a black lacy bra underneath, leather pants, and tall platform shoes. Petite in stature, but mighty in spirit, she stood out from the rest of the girls in that place. I didn't know why, but something told me I needed to speak to her. I told Santiago about my desire to talk to that beautiful girl.

"She is in my class. Wait here!" He dashed off toward her before I could protest. Blushing with embarrassment, I pretended as if I didn't see him pointing my way.

When Santiago returned, he said, "Okay, she is waiting for you to go talk to her, but I told her you were a Canadian cowboy and that you don't speak a lot of Spanish, so you have to talk in English."

I didn't want to start my relationship with the new love of my life with a lie, but I trusted Santiago, so I went with the flow. Walking up to this Uruguayan goddess, I was as nervous as the first time I got on the back of a bull. My heart accelerated with the adrenaline coming from the butterfly wings fluttering in my stomach and a Bud in my hand. I tried to hide my nerves by taking a long swig of the cold beer. Just like in bull riding, pretending to be confident was extremely important. I didn't think it worked on her.

"Hello, nice to meet you," I said before giving her a kiss on the cheek, the customary Latin American greeting. When my right cheek met hers, I took in the sweet aroma of her perfume. Soft, yet strong, like the ocean breeze.

"Nice to meet you, I'm Carolina. Sorry, my English is terrible," she said before showing me her beautiful smile, her eyes squinting.

Her English wasn't terrible. It was actually quite good, and with a thick Spanish accent like Sofia Vergara's, every word she spoke sounded way more sexy than it should have. We talked for about half an hour, and I discovered Carolina loved horses as much as I did. Her father bred, trained, and raced endurance horses, and she competed as well. *What were the chances?*

"I love the series *Heartland*," she said. "I want to visit Canada so bad."

After getting her number, I gave her a goodbye kiss on the cheek and returned to my comrades with a smile stretching from ear-to-ear.

Later, back at Santiago's apartment, I sent Caroline a message so she had my number as well. She responded with a heart right away. I wished her goodnight and fought my urge to tell her how much I loved her. Being on the road, traveling on horseback, I hardly ever met women that I was truly attracted to. Finally, I had met someone I could see myself dating! I couldn't believe my luck on that magnificent Thursday in late October, only two days before my thirtieth birthday. Meeting her was certainly a gift of good fortune from the Universe.

The next morning, hungover and in love, I drove to La Baguala hotel with Mario to check on the mares and talk to the local media. We fed the girls and spent the entire day answering questions for newspapers, magazines, and televisions.

The most memorable interview was a famous radio host who would ask a question and then, as I began to answer, he would begin to doze off into a deep sleep. Mario and I tried not to burst into laughter. Just as I finished my answer, his recorder held loosely by his bear-sized hands slowly dipped farther and farther from my mouth. He would snap back to life and ask another one, only to begin sleeping again. At one point, he started snoring so bad that we couldn't contain our laughter. We later discovered the elderly gentleman had a disorder that kept oxygen from getting to his brain. I had no idea how he managed to drive.

That night, the hotel threw a special dinner to celebrate my birthday. They invited horsemen from the community, prominent media personnel, and the owner of the hotel. We ate a delicious *asado,* and I was given a Uruguayan flag as a gift. That night, after spending the last month sleeping in barns, garages, and the smelly van, Mario and I were given the presidential suite.

"Can you believe this?" I yelled to Mario while we ran around the posh apartment looking at the full kitchen, three bedrooms, living room, and bathrooms. It was nicer than my house. The bed was like sleeping on a cloud. The mattress made me feel like I was floating while the heavy duvet hugged my body.

On November 1, nine days away from celebrating seven months on the road and my birthday, Mario and I drove to his beach house in Punta del Este to celebrate in style. When we arrived at his beautiful home, we took his yellow Camaro out of the garage and went for a drive so I could see Uruguay's Miami.

"Wow, this place is gorgeous, brother!"

Everyone stared at us in the flashy and loud—very loud—sports car. As fate would have it, Carolina's father's ranch was just outside of Punta del Este, and she invited me to come by to meet their horses and my "future father-in-law," as I put it to Mario. (That made him spit out his coffee in laughter.)

Only a thirty-minute drive from the beach town, Javier Garcia showed me their Arabian and Criollo horses and explained how they trained their animals for endurance races.

"We start them when they are around three to four years old and ride every day to get them in shape for the races," the trainer told me while we looked at his herd of more than one hundred horses.

Endurance racing was a big deal in Uruguay, and Javier had even sold horses to a sheik in Dubai.

"Last year, a sheik invited us to race, and I had a chance to compete alongside my daughters. It was an extraordinary feeling," Javier told me as he saddled his best animal.

He was built like an athlete, lean, tall, and in way better shape than most men in their forties. Unlike all of the other horsemen I had ever met, he wore spandex pants and running shoes, just like his daughter, the way all professional endurance racers dress.

The saddle they used was also very different from anything I had ever seen. Light, small, and plastic, it had a space in the middle that ran from the pommel to the back of the seat.

When the tall bay Arabian was saddled, Javier invited me to go for a ride. Knowing the temperament of these warm-blooded horses, I was more than a little nervous. I couldn't back down, not in front of my new love. I jumped atop the prancing horse and followed Javier's instructions.

"Don't touch his mouth and just let him move forward. These horses want to go, go, go!" he yelled out while I let the Arabian trot ahead.

To my surprise, Carolina jumped on another pony and took me for a gallop down a winding dirt road. It was magical. I left Carolina's father's ranch with one desire: to kiss this goddess. Hell, I wanted it more than I wanted to arrive in Ushuaia on horseback. I *needed* her.

When I returned to Montevideo, I said a painful goodbye to Mario who returned to Brazil. "Brother, thank you for all of your help and your friendship this past month."

"Thank you for allowing me to share this journey with you."

Just like that I was once again alone in a completely foreign land. The good news was that I had to wait for the Solanet family to organize the horses I would ride before crossing the border. This allowed me to spend a week in the city my new love called home.

Only twenty years old, Carolina worked as a babysitter and studied to be a vet. That week, she saw me every day.

The kiss finally came on our first night together in Montevideo, and it was powerful enough to set off fireworks. Her lips against mine.

Her petite body against my own. Her fingernails on the back of my neck. It was a week in paradise.

As they say, all good things must come to an end, especially for a Long Rider. It was with a heavy heart and a lump in my throat that I gave Carolina a kiss and a photo in a pretty wooden frame. The image was of a gorgeous Uruguayan sunset I had taken the day we met.

Atop the ferry that would take me across the Río de la Plata and into Argentina, with a strong wind blowing ferociously, I whispered, "*Adios, amor.* Goodbye, Uruguay."

BIENVENIDO A ARGENTINA

I arrived in the tango capital of the world at eleven p.m. following a rocky and expensive ferry ride. After driving through immigration, I said to my Canon video camera, "I can't believe I am finally in Argentina!"

From the dock, I drove into the city in search of a bed. Every hotel and hostel I tried was full, and I hadn't made reservations anywhere. Driving through the dark streets of Buenos Aires, trying to find my bearings on the GPS was a hectic experience.

Finally, at one a.m., I found a cheap motel and got a room for the night. The small space reeked of cigarette smoke, sex, and cheap perfume. When I locked the door, a red light turned on along with the radio. Adele's *Someone Like You* blared over the speakers beside the bed.

I didn't know whether to laugh or cry. Loneliness swallowed me. I lay back on the double bed and stared at my reflection in the large mirror on the ceiling until I finally dozed off.

The next morning, I managed to find a cheap hotel near the Casa Rosada. While I waited for the Solanet family to give me the green light to go to their ranch, I got to know this important Latin American capital.

I played tourist and visited museums for a week. I saw the pink executive mansion and office of the president of Argentina. I listened to live tango played in spacious and stunning parks while elderly tourists from around the globe tried to master the sexy dance. I ate incredibly succulent steak and drank smooth Malbec wine.

This lively capital made me feel as if I were in Europe. And it never fell asleep — literally. There were bars and clubs open twenty-four hours a day, seven days a week. Buenos Aires felt like the Las Vegas of Latin America, with more class, of course. I loved it!

That is, I loved it until a pickpocket stole my iPhone 7 Plus as I browsed a busy street market.

It was a beautiful Sunday afternoon. The sun shone with all its power, bringing downtown Buenos Aires to life. Birds chirped in the treetops while tourists yelled in excitement to one another in various languages. Walking down the narrow cobblestone street of San Telmo, stopping to look at antique cameras, precious stones, and intricate keys from the seventeenth century, I fought to maneuver through the crowd.

At one stand, a beautiful map of the Americas burned onto a rectangular piece of leather caught my eye. When I went to pull out my phone to snap a photo of the art, it was nowhere to be found.

"Damn," I murmured at the realization a thief had snatched the phone from my pocket without me even noticing it.

Surrounded by thousands of people, I felt so helpless, so stupid. I rushed back to the hotel to check if my photos were backed up onto my iCloud. They were not. All 30,000 plus images from my journey gone. I was indescribably heartbroken.

After having my phone stolen and still waiting on the Solanet family, I decided to drive to Luján and take a journey back in time.

In the quaint town, only ninety kilometers from the capital and known for its neo-gothic Basilica, Mancha and Gato are on display. The two Criollos that served as my childhood inspiration were stuffed after their deaths and housed in the country's Museum of Transportation.

In the stuffy museum, squished between the popemobile and a large boat that sailed around the world, I met my four-legged heroes for the first time. I spent an hour simply analyzing their paint and buckskin fur. Housed in a large glass case, they were just as I'd imagined them, just as Tschiffely had described them in his book. In the middle of my Long Ride, it was astounding to stand in front of Mancha and Gato, ninety-one years after they rode out of Buenos Aires.

From Luján, I drove to Ayacucho, only forty kilometers from El Cardal, the ranch belonging to the Solanet family, where a statue of Tschiffely, Mancha, and Gato was erected. In the town square, I told bronze Tschiffely about my own ride, how the Brazilians had also raised a monument of my horses and me. I wished that I could have met him. I felt inspired anew.

That night, Don Carlos Solanet invited me to visit him at the famous El Cardal ranch the next morning. I would finally get to meet the Criollos I would ride to Patagonia — Criollos with the same origins as Mancha and Gato. Raised in the same pastures those two majestic animals were retired in. I felt like I was dreaming.

The next morning, I awoke early and made the much anticipated thirty minute drive to the ranch.

When I arrived, Juan, a soft-spoken ranch hand who lived with his wife and two daughters, took me to my new horses. In his late thirties, he was a helpful gaucho in great shape. His forearms were thick, with wide veins running down to his calloused hands. I was to learn that Juan laughed often and rested little.

I was as excited as when I met my first horse at age four. Juan pointed to the two Criollos I would ride to Tierra del Fuego. "Meet Picasso and Sapo (the frog)!"

My excitement quickly soured. Sapo, a cute little buckskin, the same color as Gato, had a bite wound in the middle of his back that would clearly prevent me from riding him for weeks. And Picasso, a gorgeous, tall, dark bay with wild eyes like Mancha, pranced nervously, tied to a post and hobbled.

"Sapo is sixteen-years-old and very quiet, but Picasso is only four and a little crazy. You will need to saddle him hobbled until he gets used to you," Juan warned.

I approached the horses, and Picasso reared up at the sight of me. I swallowed a lump of fear. As soon as I saw Picasso standing there like a ball of nerves, I was taken back to my nightmare. The thought immediately entered my mind: *This is the dark horse that will kill me.*

I tried to push that foreboding feeling away and got to work. I started by brushing Picasso to get him used to me. It was touch and go. He was skittish as the soft brush glided down his dark fur, but I kept at it. The first time I climbed onto his back, I held my breath, waiting for him to blow up. Luckily, I held the left rein tight, and before he could start bucking, I pulled his nose in toward the tip of my boot and flexed his neck, making him turn in tight circles. He calmed down and I straightened him out so he trotted forward.

After my first ride on Picasso, I rested under the shade of a tall *Jacaranda* tree (which in *Guarani* means fragrance). Its flowers were a stunning bright-purple, releasing a subtly sweet and pleasant aroma. I let the smell, a mixture of honey and freshly-cut grass, calm my nerves while analyzing my two new steeds.

Sapo was short, standing at only 14.2 on his tippy-toes, with a great big belly and the eyes of a frog. I guessed that was where his name came from. His fur was a dark golden color and his neck was thick, really thick. Sapo's forelock and his mane contained a mixture of dark black and dirty-blond hairs. He had a white star and a thin interrupted stripe that ran down the right side of his Roman nose. On all four legs, from the knee down, his dirty-golden coat turned black with three partial fetlocks. His demeanor was calm, his eyes always soft, and not much appeared to bother him.

Picasso was the complete opposite. He flinched at flies and moved when the wind changed speeds. He pawed at the ground before moving over. He stood at 15.2 with long legs. His fur, jet-black, or *Picazo* as they say in Argentina. That was where his name came from. He had a black mane, but his forelock was red! It didn't make any sense. Picasso had three white stockings, and on his front right leg, a partial fetlock. He was a more modern style of Criollo, with a smaller head and a longer, not so thick, neck. The only thing the two horses had in common, apart from their breed, was the fact that their manes were cut super short atop their neck, the norm in Argentina.

That afternoon, Don Carlos Solanet, a sweet man in his late seventies, arrived to meet me. "So you are the crazy Brazilian," he said as we shook hands. Don Carlos had snow-white hair, a slight figure, a large aquiline nose, and kind eyes.

He showed me where I could sleep while training the horses. Then he walked me around the home to see photos of the Solanet family growing up around the retired Mancha and Gato.

"Don Emilio loved horses more than anyone I have ever met," he said of his uncle, the veterinarian who lent Tschiffely his prized horses, Mancha and Gato. There was one photo that nearly made my heart explode with joy: A black and white photograph of five Solanet children atop Mancha's back. His coat was much lighter, showing his elevated age when the image was captured.

After lunch, Don Carlos drove me to meet Emilio's son, Oscar Solanet, and to see the home where the vet had lived and written his books. Surrounded by sepia photos of Tschiffely, Mancha, and Gato, Don Oscar sat in his father's old office with hundreds of books.

"The first time Tschiffely came to try out the horses, he tried to saddle Mancha without tying him. When he tightened the cinch, the Criollo took off bucking and threw everything off his back," he said, as if trying to remember exactly how his father had told him this tale.

"Emilio never thought the crazy Swiss would make it," he added, leafing through a book his father wrote. He showed me a signed copy of *Tschiffely's Ride*, with a dedication from Tschiffely to Don Emilio written in black ink.

His handwriting was messy and hard to make out, reminding me of my own. He had written a traditional saying he learned in Panama which I could not decipher. It was signed: *A.F. Tschiffely* and then his first name, *Aime*.

I was so impacted by seeing Tschiffely's handwriting on the front page of his book. It was like I was getting to meet a little part of the legendary Swedish Long Rider, as if fate had knitted our lives together. My dream was to ride from Canada to Brazil. Never in my wildest dreams did I imagine I would one day be riding through Argentina, let alone with two Criollos from the Solanet family herd.

From Emilio's office, Oscar and Carlos accompanied me to the tomb containing the bones of Mancha and Gato and Tschiffely's ashes. It was like visiting a shrine. I said a prayer to my three heroes and asked for their protection on this ride.

Before I left Don Oscar's stunning nineteenth-century home that looked like it belonged in Switzerland, Don Carlos asked him, "You think the kid will make it?"

Don Oscar gave me the once over before answering, "We'll have to wait and see now, won't we?"

I flashed a fake smile and put my head down, both angered and saddened by his comment. *Make it where? I already rode from Canada to Brazil! From Brazil to Montevideo! Where did I need to make it to?*

At that moment, I realized that unless I arrived in Ushuaia, the capital of Tierra del Fuego, my story meant nothing to this traditional Argentinian horse family. To them, I hadn't ridden a single kilometer yet.

For the next four days, I spent hours riding Picasso and structured a saddle pad out of foam for Sapo to carry the packsaddle so it didn't rub the sore on his back. Because I had no support driver, I would have to resort to carrying all of my belongings on my second mount. The thought made my stomach hurt.

Slowly, I began to see signs of trust from Picasso and decided it was time to tango. The morning I departed El Cardal, a strange wind started to blow. As I slowly tacked Sapo and Picasso, I wondered where I would sleep that night.

Neither Don Carlos nor Don Oscar had arranged for anyone to receive me down the trail. And Juan, the kind ranch hand who had been my only host since Don Carlos left a few hours after arriving, was from the north of the country. He didn't know anyone outside of the property. To say this was a weird send-off by the Solanet family was an understatement.

"Thank you so much for inviting me over for dinner every night and hosting me so well," I said to Juan before jumping into the saddle.

"Good luck on your travels, Filipe. I will keep the van safe until you return for it. Tell them I broke Picasso."

I wanted to feel excited about starting my ride through Argentina, but all I felt was fear. Fear that Picasso would not calm down and in one of his panic tantrums leave him or me seriously injured. Or worse, dead.

I feared the Argentinians would not welcome me into their homes like the other eleven nations I had crossed. I worried that the bite on Sapo´s back would rub with the packsaddle and leave me without a packhorse. But like John Wayne always said, "Courage is being scared half to death but saddling up anyways." So that's what I did.

My plan was to ride a week to Benito Juárez before returning by bus for the van. Making my way out of the ranch, a strong wind picked up. I ducked my head to prevent my cowboy hat from flying all the way back to Uruguay.

All day I fought to keep Picasso calm while he spooked at anything and everything that crossed our path: Bridges, tractors, cows. Everything made him want to take off at a gallop the other way. Luckily, we were following a dirt road toward Tandil which had very little traffic.

Not knowing what was in front of us, we rode forty kilometers before we arrived at a large cattle ranch. The gorgeous property looked like the perfect place to rest the ponies that first night.

I stepped off the saddle and led Sapo and Picasso toward a worker on a green John Deere tractor cutting the grass. The dirty man covered in dust and freshly cut grass spotted me approaching and turned off the machine as he waited for me to arrive. I explained my journey to him and asked to spend the night. He said he would ask the manager and return with an answer.

As I thanked him, he turned the tractor back on, and in a split-second, all hell broke loose. Picasso freaked out and pulled back, nearly ripping the lead rope out of my hand. His back end hit Sapo with force, driving the buckskin to buck like a rodeo bronco. I tried to hold on, but the rope burned a deep welt into my palm, and I had to let go. Picasso held steady, but Sapo galloped and bucked in circles.

The lid of the right pannier flew off, and my belongings began to fly as well.

When Sapo finally stopped, I grabbed him and began to collect my things from the tall grass: camera, batteries, sunglasses, food, water bottles. It was a mess. While I gathered my shaky mounts and myself, the manager returned to say I could not stay. No owners. No permission. Swallowing back tears, I thanked him anyway.

All my fears from the morning hit me like a wrecking ball. I wanted to cry. I wanted to quit. Instead, I kept going.

We made it about three kilometers down the road when a white Ford stopped next to us. A tall man with a crooked nose and smile and yellow teeth jumped out. Javier Bianco gave us the once over. "Looks like you could use a place to stay. I have a ranch three kilometers from here."

I looked up and thanked the Universe. When I rode up to the small ranch home, Javier told me, "I have gone on my own pilgrimages, you know."

I guess he must have understood something of my struggle. I untacked Picasso and Sapo and thanked them for this first day on the road. With the sunset giving everything a golden tinge, I gave the boys a bath and turned them out in a pasture with tall grass. They dropped their heads and munched away. A chiming windmill glowed behind them.

Outside Javier's home, we sat on the floor with his two ranch hands and drank mate. I told them about my long journey, and they told me about their life on the Pampas of Argentina. After a few rounds of the warm tea, we drove to a nearby clogged water trough to fix it.

"This is life on the ranch," Javier said, smoking a wooden pipe. "The work never ends."

It took us about half an hour to unclog the pipe. After the trough was filled, we drove back to the house and showered before driving to Tandil, a city forty kilometers south.

"I'm going to take you out for dinner and introduce you to one of your cousins," he said with a big yellow smile.

Javier was a nice fellow, but he was very socially awkward. He had several tics that controlled the muscles on his sunken face. He laughed at all of the wrong times. I sensed craziness in his wide, wondering eyes, but he was a nice man with an extremely kind soul.

"My cousin" ended up being a Brazilian coder who now lived in Argentina. We chatted about our country and the food we missed. Dinner was delicious. We drank local beer and talked until two a.m. when I reminded my new friends I had to start my forty kilometer day in only four hours.

We drove back to Javier's ranch where I slept on the floor with two massive greyhounds using me as a mattress. I tried to shoo them, but I was too tired and eventually accepted my fate as a temporary dog bed.

When my alarm went off at six a.m. I wanted to shoot my phone or myself. Tired and hungover, I dug myself out of my sleeping bag and made my way to the kitchen. Javier was sitting at the dining room table where he had a clear view of my makeshift bed. He had coffee ready, and I got the feeling he hadn't slept at all.

Before I departed, he drew a map on lined paper of the route I should follow south. Rubbing his pointy chin in deep thought, he said, "I am a Reiki master and would like to check your energy before you ride out this morning."

Following his instructions, I signed my name on a white piece of paper. Javier then used a crystal tied to a string to measure my energy. He held the string with the dangling crystal just over my name while moving the stone in circles. All the while, he whispered words I could not make out and rubbed his temples with the thumb and index finger of his right hand.

Javier looked worried. "Someone really close to you doesn't want you to make it. This is putting a lot of bad energy on your being," he finally announced when the ritual came to an end.

I swallowed dry. This was the last thing I wanted to hear.

"But don't worry! I will clean this negative energy off you during the next few days with prayer."

He then gave me a piece of a meteor he found near his home for good luck. I thanked this mystical man and rode off into the unknown.

TANDIL

From Javier's ranch, I rode hard to Tandil. It was yet another windy day in Argentina, but at least the clouds kept the sun's powerful rays off my skin. My lips were already badly burned and cracked. We followed a dirt road the entire day, snaking through the forty-five kilometers of trail, but we stayed on track thanks to Javier's map.

Water was another story. All day I searched for a place to give the ponies water. There was nothing. We rode by dry creeks and locked gates left and right. I had entered Argentina in the middle of a horrible drought, something I had encountered in nearly all of the twelve countries I had crossed on horseback, a true sign of the climate change we were experiencing globally. That area of the country had not seen any precipitation in more than forty days.

With no support driver, I couldn't carry water for Picasso and Sapo as I had for my mares in Brazil and Uruguay. It's terrible to harbor anxiety all day, wondering if I would find water for my boys, worrying one of them would colic if deprived of water for too long.

Luckily, in the early afternoon, I found a pasture with an unlocked gate. I walked the horses in and found a blue water trough. Both Sapo and Picasso dropped their heads and began gulping forcefully. They were thirsty. I accompanied them and drank my last water bottle dry. With the wind up, my mouth got dryer than the Sahara Desert.

That night, I rested at a ranch that offered equine therapy for children and teens. Rotxo, a friend of Javier's, was waiting for me along with eight kids. He was a big guy who looked and acted a lot like the comedian Ricky Gervais.

The kids had just finished riding. When I arrived, they began shooting off questions like an AK-47. Where did you come from? What are your horses' names? What do you eat? Where do you sleep? How do you go to the bathroom?

I tried to answer with enthusiasm, but I was dead tired. After untacking the horses and giving them a bath, I sat with the kids under the shade of a *Fresno Dorado* tree for about an hour. I could tell many were on the spectrum, but they interacted well. After they left, Rotxo told me some of their stories.

"The boy in the red hat has autism. Before he started riding here a few months ago, he was extremely antisocial. He never wanted to be around people or play with other children. Now he is a completely different kid, and it's all thanks to the horse."

Rotxo had a look of contentment in his eyes. For him, seeing the kids' transitions made his work the greatest job in the world. "I mean, I get paid to help kids, and I get to be outdoors with horses all day! It doesn't get much better than this!"

I had seen and heard about the benefits of equine therapy for many years, but riding into that ranch and meeting those kids had a big impact on me. As I lay in my stinky tent that night, listening to the horses eat their hay close by, I dreamt about having my own ranch one day and helping children as Rotxo did. It was another dream I hoped to live out someday.

The next morning, I took down my tent, saddled the boys, and prepared to leave Rotxo's ranch. Just before I jumped into the saddle, I spotted an elderly gentleman riding by on a big chestnut mare.

"Luis! Stop! Stop for a second!" Rotxo yelled down the driveway. The old man pulled back on the reins and turned his horse's nose down the driveway. He squeezed his legs and trotted up toward us with a leather *rebenque* (gaucho's whip) hanging from his right wrist.

After my host explained to him who I was and what I was up to, Luis agreed to accompany me out of Tandil, a bustling city of 110,000 people. With Picasso still afraid of his own shadow, I worried about narrow roads roaring with traffic. This was the first time the high-strung bay would be near a city of this size. Luckily, Luis had been riding these roads since he was a child. He promised Rotxo to guide me down small country roads until we reached the main highway south.

"My three brothers and I used to ride the same horse to school every day and back," the elderly gentleman told me as we rode side by side.

I absolutely love talking to old-timers like Luis. These men and women whose hands feel like tree bark and whose minds host an abundance of knowledge about the natural world have so much to share. Their wisdom was worth gold and all they asked was for a friendly ear. Luis talked the entire three hours we rode together. He told me about how his grandfather used to train horses in his youth, and how he has a grandson with Down's syndrome who loves horses.

"I take him out for a ride every weekend. He loves it so much. This is his mare," the elderly man said as his eyes filled with tears.

According to Luis, his grandson had improved significantly in many different ways thanks to his close contact with these majestic animals. His speaking, movement, and mood had all gotten better since his loving grandfather put him in the saddle.

Eventually, it was time to bid Luis farewell. We embraced from atop our steeds, and I thanked him for his help. He thanked me for the company, turned his horse around, and rode off.

I continued on alone for a few kilometers before a gray Volkswagen truck pulled over in front of me. A big man wearing a straw fedora and his beautiful wife jumped out and walked toward me.

"Filipe! Pleasure to meet you," Rodrigo said, giving me a firm hand-shake. It's funny how sometimes you just know that you would get along with people extremely well the second you met them. Both Rodrigo and his wife had big, loving smiles. He had the body of a linebacker with shaggy brown hair, and she had the figure of a ballerina with blonde curls.

"We are friends of Rotxo," Rodrigo said. "You will rest your horses at our ranch today."

I accepted their offer gratefully and continued on through a beautiful area of rolling hills. Pastures with tall, burned grass stretched out on both sides of the road, and I enjoyed the view.

Just after noon, I saw a woman waving her arms on the left side of the road next to an Argentinian flag flapping in the wind. It was Rodrigo's wife. I rode into their ranch as she snapped photos. I met their two daughters, and we turned Sapo and Picasso out in a gorgeous pasture. We then moved a long wooden table outside and sat around drinking beer, eating cheese, and chatting.

"We have so many questions, I don't know where to start!" the youngest daughter, a cute fifteen-year-old with brown hair, said. Her excitement was so evident, we all laughed.

It was a perfect afternoon. I felt like I was with my own family in mere seconds. This transformation happened so many times on my journey. You met complete strangers, and in no time, they felt like old friends. I didn't know if it was because I was so lonely or because I rode in on horseback. Maybe I just took on new friends easily. I had no idea why this happened, I was just happy it did.

After eating a delicious lunch, the family showed me their beautiful Criollo horses.

"We have over 200 horses," Rodrigo told me as one of his mares nibbled at his shoulder. "To me, these animals are everything."

Rodrigo competed in *Paleteada* competitions all around the country. Argentina's national rodeo competition, *Paleteada* involved a paired team of horses and riders that approached a steer from both sides at full gallop.

The steer was sandwiched between the two horses that leaned onto the bovine, practically carrying it down a sixty-meter long path until it finally stopped and turned around. Both riders must then turn their horses also and perform the same ritual heading down the same way they came. It was an astonishing demonstration of control that was born out in the Pampas from the gaucho's need to literally pick up a steer and place it wherever it needed to be.

After spending the afternoon at the ranch, Rodrigo invited me back to his home in the city to shower and eat dinner. While eating some delicious empanadas with the family in their gorgeous home, his daughter, Valentina, a tall blonde in her late teens with an intense gaze, asked me if I wanted to go out with her and her friends for a drink. I was tired and sore from the long days in the saddle and dreaming of a bed to pass out hard. I still had two more long days before I arrived in Benito Juarez where we would rest for a day. I wanted to say no, I really did. But what came out was inevitable and excited, "Yes!"

Have you watched the movie *Yes Man* with Jim Carrey? The one where he goes to a seminar and was left saying yes to everything people asked of him? Well, that was me, folks. I was born with the inability to say no. Although sometimes this could be a good thing, oftentimes, it was not.

We went to the local Tandil Sunday night scene. I thought it was going to be a laid-back bar, drinks until midnight and everything closes type of thing. Boy, was I wrong! We danced in a packed nightclub until finally, at three-thirty a.m., I begged Valentina to go home.

By this point in the night, I had already learned about how the drink of choice in Argentina is Fernet with Coke. I had downed too many of those bitter concoctions. By the time we arrived back at her house, it was four a.m.

At 6:15 a.m., my alarm went off. I tried to open my eyes. They burned as if I had rubbed them with gasoline. Rodrigo drove me to his ranch where I saddled up the boys and bid farewell to my new friend. With my head low and the bitter taste of Fernet lodged in the roof of my mouth, I trekked south.

By eleven a.m., I was nearly falling asleep in the saddle. My eyes got heavier and heavier with each stride. Unable to continue, I entered a milk farm and asked if we could rest for a couple of hours. I tied the boys up to a tree and untacked them.

Sitting on one of the panniers, I slowly ate a tuna sandwich I made by opening a can of tuna and slapping the oily fish on a stale slice of bread. It wasn't anything special, but it was what I had. After lunch, I laid the saddle blankets out under a tree and slept deeply for two hours. I awoke to a puddle of drool.

Feeling groggy, but better, I tacked the boys back up and continued on. In the late afternoon, with no ranches in sight, I found a river and set up camp. Eating a pot of warm ramen noodles, I thought about what tomorrow would bring as the boys grazed on tall green grass nearby. Accompanied by only the sound of the blowing wind, I sat in front of my tent and watched the sunset.

Eventually, I tied the boys to the fence behind my tent and climbed into my sleeping bag. When I tied up the horses at night and slept in my tent, I never really slept. I tried to, but the fear that they would get loose was too great. This was especially true since I'd had bad experiences in the past. Once, while crossing a Wyoming mountain, I awoke at two a.m. to the sound of wood breaking followed by horses galloping. It was terrible. My heart almost stopped. I jumped out of my tent in my underwear and boots to find that my three horses had broken the pole they were tied to, and two of them were gone. One stood shaking, staring at the broken pole he was still tied to. It had taken me an hour to find the other two.

In Mexico, Frenchie untied himself from a fence post one night and was run over by a truck. That was by far the worst experience of my life. Everything went into slow motion as I watched the truck hit him. I thought I was watching my boy die. Luckily he survived, but the traumatic experience left deep wounds on both man and beast. I still had nightmares about that night.

Needless to say, I woke up every thirty minutes worried, unzipped the tent' door, and used my flashlight to make sure the horses were still there. With every little noise, my heart jumped to my throat and my eyes shot open.

At five-thirty a.m., dead tired but unable to sleep any longer and wrapped in anxiety, I started my day. When I opened the tent's door, I nearly yelled. Picasso was standing wide-eyed with his left front hoof stuck on the bottom wire of the fence line. I quickly put my boots on and ran to his side. When I arrived, I tried to calm the big bay down as he pulled back on instinct, trying to free his hoof.

I inspected the problem and realized he had been pawing at the ground and got the wire caught between the back of his shoe and the bottom of his hoof. When he pulled back the first time, the wire moved forward up to the last nail, and the shoe closed behind it. Bending over, with my right foot on the wire, I used all of my strength to push his leg forward, trying to get the wire to come out the same way it went in. Impossible!

I tried and tried and tried, but it would not release. There was no way but to cut the wire, and I didn't have pliers on me. I was screwed. I tried to figure out a way to get the hoof out but nearly exhausted myself trying. Luckily, Picasso stood still and didn't freak out, so he didn't get injured any further.

The only way would be to borrow a set of pliers from someone who was driving by. That early in the morning, there was no one on the country road I was next to. Standing in the middle of the dirt road, I prayed for a vehicle to appear in the distance. I prayed for half an hour until a white truck finally roared up. I waved my arms and begged for the driver to pull over. He was skeptical at first, only slowing down at the last minute, when I could see his face and he mine. Thankfully, he did stop.

He rolled down his window, and I explained my predicament. An elderly gentleman with a full head of silver hair got out of the vehicle and reached into a tool box in the truck bed. When he handed me a rusty set of pliers, I wanted to kiss him.

I ran to Picasso's side and began working on cutting the wire. It was not easy. The pliers were old, and it took me several minutes to cut the metal. Eventually, it gave way, and I was able to slip Picasso's front left hoof free at last.

As I stood, I let out a huge sigh of relief and patted my pony's neck. He licked his lips and chewed, a sign he was finally relaxed.

After five long days in the saddle and seven and a half months since starting the journey, we finally arrived in Benito Juarez, our first resting point in Argentina.

Rodrigo, my host in Tandil, put me in touch with Rodolfo Tula, a horseman and agriculture technician who had a small farm outside of the small town. I wasn't sure exactly where the property was and when I neared the small town, my cell ran out of battery. *Perfect,* I thought.

Unsure of what to do next, I spotted a family drinking mate outside of their home. I rode up to them and asked if I could charge my phone in their house. They graciously allowed me to charge it and offered me some mate. When the phone turned back on, and I told them my host's name, I didn't even have to call Rodolfo! As it turned out, his farm was right next door! Once we realized how close I was to my destination, we all had a good laugh, and I bid my new friends farewell.

Rodolfo, like the rest of the Argentinians I had met thus far, welcomed me with open arms and, of course, an *asado*.

"I'm going to sing a traditional Argentinian folk song that talks about a horse the same color as yours, a Picazo," my new friend said to me, cradling his wooden guitar next to the fire.

As he strummed the chords and belted the sweet melody, I felt like I was in a movie. His face was lit orange from the fire, the fat dripping from the meat making the fire sizzle and change colors, the moonlight illuminating the scene. It was too perfect. I was in the heart of Argentina, drinking red wine with a gaucho singing a song that seemed as if it was written about the horse I rode in on! Too good to be true!

That night, I slept very well in a child's bed with stuffed animals staring at me. My feet hung off the end. I didn't mind. I was exhausted.

The next morning, there was no time to rest. I was first interviewed by the local radio station. Then Rodrigo picked me up in his truck and drove me all the way to Ayacucho to get the support van. Another angel on my path, he drove me 160 kilometers. By the time I arrived back in Benito Juarez, it was already dark.

When I got to Rodolfo's home, seven gauchos were waiting for me with a platter of cheese, chorizo, ham, and a lot of wine. I was excited to see their smiling faces under multicolored berets, but I must admit a little part of me deep inside thought, *No!* I'd been hoping to sleep early for the next day's ride. That wasn't an option. We drank and shared stories until two a.m. when I finally crashed.

At six a.m., my alarm clock went off. I wanted to disappear to *a galaxy far, far away*. All I could do was brush my teeth, get dressed, saddle my steeds, and use *the force* to continue south.

"You're burning the candle at both ends, young man." Mark Maw's mom was Mary, and that was her favorite line as we were growing up. The memory made me smile.

ROAD TO BAHÍA BLANCA

Riding out of Benito Juarez was not an easy task. Still fresh on the road, everything scared my Criollos: bicycles, cars, cats, colorful houses, large gates. To them, everything was the devil, and the devil was out to kill them. We danced down the road, going from left to right, moving to the frightful rhythm of their hooves.

The radio interview I'd done the day prior also made leaving a difficult process. At the end of the interview, the host welcomed everyone in the small town to come out of their homes and bid me farewell as I rode out. Obviously, they did. I was shaking hands, holding babies, and taking photos with grandmothers. It was a circus. All of this, while trying to keep my Criollos, especially Picasso, calm.

To make my departure even harder, two dogs began following us as if they had been traveling with me since I left Barretos. They were beautiful, big dogs. One looked like a Golden Retriever crossed with a smaller breed, and the other was a German Shepherd.

However, both dogs were really stupid. Instead of walking next to the horses on the side of the road, they wandered in the middle of the highway and crossed from one side to the other as if there were no traffic. They were nearly hit on more than one occasion. Trucks and cars had to slam on the brakes or swerve at the last second, coming inches from striking the animals.

Figuring the crazy canines were mine, angry drivers would hit the horn and curse at me. It was an extremely stressful situation. Those dogs came close to dying several times as I rode, wincing each time they nearly caused an accident.

Just before I got on the main highway, I rode into a police checkpoint and begged them to tie the dogs for an hour or two before releasing them again. The officers reluctantly agreed to help me and, relieved, I continued on.

I stopped at a gas station a few kilometers down the road and went in to put credit on my phone. I knew I had a two-day ride before the next town and my pay-as-you-go tab was running low. The clerk told me they didn't work with my phone company. I thanked her and headed outside.

"Are you on some kind of journey?" a tall man asked with a big smile as he analyzed my mounts. He was tall, handsome and wide, built like a retired NFL quarterback.

"Yes, sir, I'm riding to Ushuaia."

"That's so cool. My son is riding his bicycle with a friend through Africa." He told me about his son's adventures, and his wife shared her worries. Asking me how my own mother felt about my journey, I admitted that she was also worried.

"So many people help my son out on the road, we need to do something for you. What do you need? Food? Water? Just tell me," the father said with enthusiasm.

"No, no, I'm fine, thank you," I responded, laughing with his wife.

"There has to be something we can do, man. This is good karma for us. Please," he urged.

That's when I remembered I didn't have credit for my phone! "Okay, you can actually do me a huge favor. If I give you my number and money, will you please drive to a store that puts credit on a *Claro* phone?" I asked shyly.

Not only did he agree immediately, he did not accept my money.

"Be safe out there, okay?" the mother said. The slender brunette hugged me tightly as if she had her arms around her own son. I thanked them and continued south.

Just a kilometer down the road, my luck continued to soar. A gaucho in his early seventies wearing rectangular reading glasses and driving a white Toyota pickup stopped and asked me what I was up to. I told him about my journey and he said he had a friend with a ranch thirty kilometers down the road. I could spend the night there.

With a place to stay and credit on my phone, I rode south with a smile on my sunburned face. We arrived at the ranch in the afternoon as the worker was about to head to town in his rusty-red truck. He told me to make myself at home and that he would return in a few hours.

I let the boys out in a green pasture and went into an old, dusty home that seemed like it hadn't been used in years. Wide cracks ran up the walls and big chunks of painted cement sat on the floor. It was where the owner stayed when he spent the night at his ranch. By the looks of it, he didn't visit very often.

I picked a room, cleaned the cobwebs off the bed, blew the dust off, and laid out my sleeping bag. With the sun still shining, I closed my eyes to rest for a bit. The next thing I knew, it was morning.

While riding toward Adolfo Gonzales Chavez, we ran into a major scare. Following a narrow dirt road right next to the fence line, we came to a small stream. Riding Picasso, I inspected the water to see how deep it was. It didn't look very deep. Only a few feet wide, I decided to cross it and allow the horses to get a drink in the process.

When I kicked Picasso up, he took a full stride into the water and immediately sank up to his belly. In a second, my legs were drenched up to my knees. I went into a panic as I tried to turn him around and back out the way we came in. The bay turned. As he moved to get out of the stream, he struggled to find his footing and fell onto his right side. Luckily, I removed my right leg just as the side of the saddle made contact with the tall grass. I half stood while he tried to get his balance back. As he stood up, I grabbed hold of the saddle horn. In a flash, we were back on dry ground.

I sighed with relief as Sapo stood frozen, watching us with wide eyes. I stepped down from the saddle, took my boots off, and poured three liters of water out of each one. Laughing at myself, I picked up my Ray-Bans, which had flown off into the grass, and got back into the saddle.

We continued south with caution, and just before arriving in the small town of Chavez, a young man stopped on the side of the road to welcome me. In his early twenties, the young gaucho had the nose of a toucan and the long, thin body of a eucalyptus tree. "I follow you on Instagram, Filipe! We have been waiting for you with a barbecue," Joséma said as he shook my hand.

Driving slowly ahead in his truck, he led me to a ranch where I could rest the horses for a few hours. Then he drove me to his house. Just as he'd said, his parents and friends were waiting to meet me with cold beer and bright smiles. We spent the afternoon sharing stories.

After eating way too much meat, it was time for Argentina's siesta, the period after lunch where every resident of that great nation naps anywhere between one hour to five hours. It's insane. When you drove through a small town between the hours of one p.m. to five p.m., it would look like a ghost town: no cars or people on the streets, all businesses closed, everyone out cold. Even the street dogs!

Feeling groggy after my siesta, Joséma drove me to the ponies so I could continue my journey. On the way, he told me he would pick me up in the afternoon from the ranch where the horses would rest to eat a lamb barbecue with him and his friends.

I rode another ten kilometers on Sapo. As the sun began to sink over the horizon, we arrived at the ranch. A few minutes later, Joséma showed up, and we drove back to his house for a quick shower. When we got to his friend's house, I couldn't believe what I was seeing. They made — yes, *made* — a Canadian flag and tied it next to Brazilian and Argentinian flags to welcome me.

"We want you to feel at home," my host said, greeting me as males do in Argentina and in Uruguay with a kiss on the cheek.

"Tomorrow, we rest. The following day, I will ride out with you," Joséma announced after we had downed three Fernets each.

I had heard this all over the Americas while out drinking. However, when the time comes to do the riding, no one shows up. I pretended to believe the young man. However, my new friend was a man of his word.

"Told you I would ride with you, brother," he said with a smile on his face while we made our way out to the ranch where the horses were resting. Alongside Joséma and Mariano (another friend from Chavez) we rode forty kilometers toward Tres Arroyos. It was a great day. We laughed the entire time, told jokes, stories, and enjoyed each other's company.

"Have you ever seen a drunk armadillo?" Joséma asked as he stepped down from his horse.

He ran toward an armadillo walking in the grass and grabbed the animal by the tail. Holding the tail with his right hand, he began spinning it around and around clockwise. After a few seconds, he let it go. The armadillo ran off in zigzags, jumping every few feet. Laughing, Joséma said, "Now you have!"

In the early afternoon, we crossed a beautiful river and rode into Tres Arroyo. We made our way to the rodeo grounds where the horses were allowed to rest that afternoon. I got a ride back to Chavez with Joséma's father. He then drove me to Juarez to pick up the support van I had left at Rodolfo's house a few days earlier.

"Thank you so much for all of your help and for riding out with me," I said to Joséma before saying goodbye.

He took off his straw hat and gave it to me. "I want you to have this hat to remember me by," he said as he handed me the dark beige hat.

"Okay, then, here, you take mine," I said, giving him the hat I had worn since Barretos. The young Argentinian glowed with happiness.

I arrived back in Tres Arroyos at night and got everything ready to ride out the next morning. When I woke up and went to move the van to a location where I could leave it while I rode toward Coronel Dorrego, it wouldn't start. The starter was broken.

On a Long Ride, there was never an easy day. I wondered how many days we would be stuck in Tres Arroyos.

~

It took two days to fix the old van, and it ended up costing me an arm and a leg. While waiting for the starter to be fixed, I also received some terrible news from Brazil.

My paternal grandmother had passed away from pneumonia. In her late eighties, her fragile body was not able to fight off the disease. I was so sad I wasn't able to see her one last time and felt even worse for not being at her funeral. I prayed for her in my tent that night.

From Tres Arroyos, I rode south toward the town of Coronel Dorrego, a 102-kilometer stretch of nothing. Every night, I was forced to camp on the side of the road and fend for myself. With the wind still blowing forcefully and the heat rising, every day became a mental and physical battle.

On our first day out, after forty kilometers, I finally found a windmill to give the horses water. I untacked the boys and tied them to two fence posts. As always, the gate was locked. Dying of thirst, I jumped it and walked 500 meters to the windmill with my foldable canvas bucket.

When I arrived, I took a long drink from the fresh water pumped out of the iron pipe. After filling the bucket, I trekked back. When I arrived at the ponies with the first bucket of water, I realized my GoPro, which I always carried in my chest pocket, was gone.

Panicked, I looked all over my tack, the ground, and the way to the windmill — nothing. I knew where it was, but I didn't want to face it.

I took off my clothes and went into the tank that held the water from the windmill. It was freezing. I walked to where the pipe pumped the water into the tank and began feeling around with my foot. I cursed as my foot touched the little square camera and snagged the device with my toes. The GoPro I had carried from Brazil to Argentina was done, soaked and broken.

When I bent over to drink the water, tired and thirsty, I didn't notice it slip out of my shirt pocket and plunge into the dark water. I wanted to cry. I used it several times a day to document my journey. One of the most important tools I carried was gone.

I made the same trip with the full water bucket three more times for the horses to drink and let them graze while I put up the tent. Fighting the forceful wind that never let up, I was tired, sore, sad, and frustrated.

The next morning, I rose with the glowing sun and continued south. We trekked until noon when I rode into a small village. I found water for the boys and sat next to a tall, white wall to shelter myself from the wind for fifteen minutes. It felt heavenly to escape that beast blowing me into insanity for a few minutes, a gigantic relief. The wind blew with such force, it was hard to think, never mind ride.

While I rested, a clean-shaven gaucho in the filthy clothes only a man who works the land would wear, stopped his truck. He had seen me trekking and wanted to know where I was going. After I explained the journey to him, he told me that I would have no water for the horses that night.

"I will bring you some jugs of water for the *pingos* (horses) in the afternoon," the friendly man offered. I thanked him profusely and continued on.

After four p.m., I arrived at a small gathering of trees where he instructed me to camp. I waited for the water to arrive while the ponies filled their bellies. As two hours passed, I wondered if the man would show up. Just when I was about to lose faith, his truck arrived. We filled up a plastic bucket he brought, and Sapo and Picasso drank ferociously. They were thirsty. I thanked my new friend and he left.

After a few minutes, another truck pulled up. A man from Coronel Dorrego jumped out with a smile on his face. Tilting his head so as not to lose his fedora to the harsh wind, he said, "I brought alfalfa for your horses and food for you."

I couldn't believe it. We went from having nothing to having everything we needed in a few minutes. The ponies and I filled our bellies as the sun went down and by nine p.m., I was snoring in my tent.

The following day, my new friend drove to Tres Arroyos and picked up the van for me before I arrived in Coronel Dorrego. From there, I began my final trek before the holidays. It was a three-day ride that once again left me feeling like I was riding in a wind tunnel meant to test airplanes. The first night I rode thirty kilometers to a feedlot. The owner welcomed me and allowed me to pitch my tent next to the horse corral. After he left, I spent the late afternoon chatting with his worker, a thin man in his mid-thirties.

Carlitos told me about how he almost died a few years back. "I was working at a farm, and a wildfire began burning all of our fields," he said. "I went out in a tractor to try to put out the fire but got caught up in the flames."

He got out of the tractor and began running, trying to find a way out. Passing out in the heavy smoke, he didn't remember anything else. "Apparently, I fainted in the tall grass. When my friends came looking for me, they didn't see me and ran me over with the truck." He showed me scars on his chest, shoulders, and arms.

It took the worker a year to walk again, and he was fortunate to be alive. "This experience made me realize how important it is to enjoy life. Before the accident, all I did was work. I hardly saw my family. Now, I make sure I am always with them and only work enough to make a living."

The next day saw me ride a hard forty kilometers to my next resting point. A long bridge with trucks roaring over it nonstop was unavoidable. I stopped before the colossal structure to analyze how I would get over this obstacle safely. Riding Picasso, the crazy Criollo, it didn't seem possible.

Luckily, the owner of the feedlot was driving by while I sat pondering what to do and offered to help. "I'll drive behind you with my four-ways on," he offered.

We took the panniers off of Sapo's back, and I trotted the ponies across the long bridge while my new friend escorted me safely.

In the afternoon, following a small dirt road next to train tracks, I came across a baby armadillo. This area of Argentina was crawling with these cute animals. Every day, I saw one or two or three. When they heard the horses coming, they would roll into a little ball and hide their heads in their shell. It was so funny, they were clearly still visible but felt like they had entered invisible mode.

I stopped, got off Picasso, and grabbed the little armadillo. It was so cute, I wanted to take it with me. Before I let him go, I snapped some photos of my new friend, its little face and ears, hard shell, and tiny feet!

That night, I arrived at a small farm and was welcomed by a sweet elderly gentleman and his son. We drank mate and chatted the afternoon away while the horses filled their bellies around the house.

The old man was as skinny as a marathon runner, his face sunken in. His gray hair, balding from his forehead to the middle of his head, was combed back and gelled like a mobster.

He showed me his 1960s tractor and told me about how much the world had changed. "What we used to do in a day, a new tractor does in an hour," he told me as he ran his fingers over the old machine.

We spent a great afternoon and night together with another gracious host.

The following afternoon, after a stressful ride through Bahía Blanca, a major city in the province of Buenos Aires, we finally arrived at the fairgrounds where the ponies would rest over Christmas.

With my shirt drenched with sweat from the heat, I patted the boys and thanked them for their hard work this first month on the road. Together, we had covered 500 windy and dry kilometers.

As I watched them eat their hay, I told them, "Now you boys get to rest for a few days."

Knowing the desolate stretch that awaited me upon leaving Bahía Blanca, I made plans to spend the holidays in the coastal city. Bahía Blanca translates to White Bay. While staring at the name on my map of Argentina before starting the ride from El Cardal, I imagined white sandy beaches, a stunning turquoise blue ocean, coconut trees, beach bars and bikinis — basically I imagined I was riding toward Cancún.

Boy, was I wrong! Bahía Blanca was a scorching metropolis where smog and terrible car traffic was about all you'll find. The ocean was a polluted bay with no beaches for bathing. It was more like downtown São Paulo! I wasn't resting in paradise, but at least I was resting.

With the horses installed at the local fairgrounds, I wrote blogs and got to know the city. Pachi, a friend of Joséma from Chavez, took me under his wing during my time in Bahía.

For Christmas, Pachi, who looked like the cool kid from high school, took me to a friend's house for a major barbecue celebration. After a delicious dinner, we danced the night away in their neatly trimmed yard. At one point, much to everyone's amusement, one of my new friends lifted me up in the air and danced with me in his arms for five minutes.

"Argentina loves you, Filipe!" he yelled up at me as I tried to contain my laughter.

While in the city, I also met a group of gauchos who became great friends. Roberto Millán and Luis, two horsemen with much wisdom, told me many stories from their travels on horseback, gave me gifts, and helped me make connections for my route south.

"Don't worry. We have contacts no matter what route you choose south," Luis, a skyscraper of a man with terrible teeth, told me.

Roberto, a pint-sized man with a shy gaze and a high-pitched voice, ran a mechanic shop in Bahía Blanca. He ended up helping me out tremendously. The support van broke down again, and he fixed it for me, charging the bare minimum. It ended up costing $700 dollars. It was a lot, but if it had been any other mechanic, the bill would have been double that or more.

For New Year's Eve, I decided to drive to a beach town forty kilometers from Bahía called Monte Hermoso. I loved the ocean and thought it would be good to take in some of its powerful energy before taking on this next stage of the journey: Patagonia, the most arduous stretch.

Monte Hermoso had more than thirty-two kilometers of beach overlooking the Atlantic Ocean. Because of its unique shape, the sun rose and set over the sea. It was a stunning town that attracted Argentinians and tourists from around the world every summer.

I spent the day sitting in the sand, watching the waves crash, and thinking about life. It ended up being lonelier than I imagined. There were so many families and groups of friends around me, laughing, drinking, and playing. I couldn't help but yearn for someone to share this moment.

"Life is meant to be shared," I whispered into the ocean breeze.

I wondered what my family was up to in Brazil. What were my friends in Canada doing? Probably all getting ready to celebrate the New Year. Putting on their nicest outfits...taking perfectly basted turkeys out of the oven...driving to extravagant parties in white dresses and shirts.

I was one miserable cowboy. I drank my *Quilmes* and tried to wash away my sorrow. After a lonely dinner of dry chicken and vegetables, I watched fireworks paint the sky various shades of green, red, purple, and blue. The smell of gunpowder mixed with sea salt permeated the air while Argentinians hugged and kissed all around me.

It was 12:01 a.m., January 1, 2017. I was surrounded by thousands of families and their abundant love, yet at that moment, I felt like the only human being on earth. I swallowed my tears. With loud *cumbia* music blaring from a stage 300 meters away, I stretched out on the sand to stare at the starry sky above.

I missed my family. I missed my mom. She drove me crazy with her love, but she only dreamed of helping me to be the best person I could be. I missed my dad. Desperate to protect me, he was so proud of all I did right and silently forgiving of all I did wrong. I missed celebrating a new year full of hope, dreams, and happiness with people who loved me unconditionally. I was so sad they were so far away.

The stars twinkled at me through the smoke of fireworks. This was a new year. I grabbed fistfuls of sand and wondered what to do next. I had been on the road for eight long months and covered more than 3,000 kilometers.

I had to make a difficult decision. Ride south on Highway 3 following the coast toward Tierra del Fuego, a two-month ride, and finish the journey in March or May? Or head due west toward Bariloche and follow Highway 40 south, adding three months or more to my Long Ride? Finishing the journey sometime in June or July, I'd be in the heart of winter in the south.

I closed my eyes tightly and squeezed the sand through my hands as I asked the Universe for a sign, any sign. I opened my eyes and saw nothing. No falling star. No meteor streaking across the dark sky. No cloud-shaped mountain top. But deep in my heart, I already knew the answer. Like always, my instincts told me what to do. I just didn't want to listen. For weeks now, something deep in my core was telling me to ride my horses the extra 1,000 kilometers to the Andes.

I didn't yet know why, but in a few months, I would discover that the tremendous suffering it took would be well worth it.

THE SUFFERING

On January 3 at 5:30 a.m. with the sun still hidden under the horizon, I mounted Picasso and ponied Sapo with the packsaddle on his back. Saddling the horses in the dark had left me drenched. We were now in the middle of the Argentinian summer. In this region, that meant temperatures would soar above 30°C constantly.

Luis and Roberto organized a group of riders to accompany me out of Bahía Blanca. "If you need anything, don't be afraid to call," Luis said, giving me a strong hug from atop his gray steed.

Roberto gave me two books as a gift before we parted ways. One was the story of an Argentinian female Long Rider who made an unbelievable journey from Argentina to Canada in the 1960s. The other was Tschiffely's book about his car trip to Tierra del Fuego years after riding to the United States.

"I hope these books make your nights in the tent more enjoyable," Roberto said as I shoved the books into the orange panniers.

The boys and I continued south alone. At lunchtime, I rode into a little town called Argerich, where a Uruguayan woman awaited my arrival. "I'm so happy to be hosting you for lunch," she said with a smile on her round face.

I unsaddled the boys and allowed them to graze while we entered her house and western store. It was a stunning building made of wood and bricks. Pictures of horses galloping in open fields plastered the walls. In between rustic tables and leather chairs, I felt as if I was in a *Country Homes Magazine* spread.

My host poured me a cold glass of water and cut up some fresh ham and cheese for me to eat. "Lunch has to be light when you are riding all day," she said.

I agreed. We talked about dreams, life, and Uruguay. I loved sharing that moment with her. Our time together was food for the soul.

After resting for two hours, I saddled the boys back up and continued toward Médanos, only ten kilometers south. My host had warned me of horrible fires ahead. Smoke filled the air, and the sky glowed a weird shade of orange. I knew that wildfires had been burning up the province of La Pampa since Christmas, but I didn't know they had entered the province of Buenos Aires.

When I arrived in Médanos, it was as if I had entered an apocalyptic film. Breathing became a battle as gray smoke choked the horses and me. Ash blew into our faces. The sky looked like it was on fire.

"At this point, we don't know if you will be able to ride out tomorrow, son," a big gaucho who was friends with Luis from Bahía told me. "The highway has been closed because the fire is burning on both sides."

As I untacked the boys, sirens screamed, calling all volunteer firefighters to the fire station. The sirens were loud and piercing, like those used to warn island residents of a possible tsunami. My heart moved to my throat. I worried for my ponies and my life. Had I made the wrong decision to ride west to Bariloche?

A journalist who came to take photos of us told the gauchos who were hosting me, "Two women burned alive in their car an hour ago. They tried to turn around on the highway because they couldn't see anything with the heavy smoke. A truck hit them as they made the U-turn."

We looked at the ominous sky in silence, in sadness, and in fear.

That night, my host, an elderly horseman in his early seventies with silver prickly hair like a porcupine, had me over for a barbecue and a couple of bottles of wine.

In that region of Argentina, they drank their red wine with a few ice cubes and tonic water. I found it weird at first. However, after drinking the concoction on several occasions I learned to appreciate it, especially during those scorching days in the saddle. The next morning we rose early, and my host drove me to the horses.

"I called my friend, the police chief," my host said. "He told me the fire has burned up everything up ahead. There is nothing left to burn, so it's safe for you to ride."

I wasn't sure if that was good news or bad news. I rode out of Médanos with heavy smoke filling the air and my lungs as the wind blew ashes everywhere. The police chief was right, the fire had completely burned the terrain ahead, and there was nothing else to light on fire. But the suffering and desolation were immense.

The scene was of an apocalypse. Swollen, blackened carcasses of cows, wildcats, and armadillos dotted the roadside. Their rotten, bitter, nauseating smell forced me to hold my breath to stop myself from vomiting. Their frozen expressions of suffering made my heart break. Tongues out. Mouths open. Eyes wide.

Many cows had tried to escape the flames and became entangled. They were stuck to the fence. Officials estimated more than 80,000 head of cattle were killed and over two million hectares of land burned. Horses, dogs, and houses were also lost in the fires lit by electrical storms.

"I tried to release my horses in time, but when I got to my farm, it was too late," one gaucho told me. A single tear left a clear track down his dusty face.

For 170 kilometers, smoke blocked the sky, the sun only seeping through, a deep orange above us. The ponies and I fought to breathe as strong winds blew smoke and ash into our faces all day. My eyes stung and the back of my throat burned. On both sides of the highway, what was once tall green, yellow, and brown grass was now black tar and gray ash.

The night before arriving in Río Colorado, I had only one 500-ml bottle of water left. I found an unlocked corral where I set up my tent and sipped my water slowly. With parched lips and a dry throat, I wanted to chug the bottle, but I knew I would need it the next day.

Feeling completely vulnerable and dirtier than a chimney cleaner, I watched as an old truck drove up and parked in front of the gate. A tall, grimacing man jumped out.

"Who allowed you to enter?" he demanded as I approached him.

"No one, sir," I answered. "I saw the gate wasn't locked and let myself in." As I explained my journey to him, he looked me up and down in silence.

"Okay, I guess you can spend the night, but if the owner comes, you tell him you spoke to me."

Relieved, the tension in my shoulders eased. I asked if I could drink the water from the nearby windmill. He said no because of sulfate levels.

We shook hands and he walked toward his truck as I headed to my tent, my head hanging low. Staring at the rocky soil, I heard a yell. When I looked up, the man who minutes earlier I expected to swallow me alive was holding a liter bottle of frozen water in his hand. I ran up, grabbed the bottle, and thanked him.

Later, alone and sitting in my tent watching the horses graze, I cried silently, holding that cold bottle against my left cheek. The icy plastic gave my burned skin momentary relief.

It was just water. It seemed ridiculous for someone to cry over a liter of frozen water, but I had been so desperate moments earlier. When you felt thirst, when you suffered its repercussions, you learned that water was the most important resource on the planet. Water was life.

I was a sad sight by the time I arrived in Río Colorado. I knew the road out of Bahía Blanca would be hard, but I didn't think it was going to be as difficult as it became. The wind, ash, smoke, and fire made me suffer like few times on this Long Ride.

Pro football player Alex Karras once said, "Toughness is in the soul and spirit, not in muscles."

On that first Long Ride from Canada to Brazil, while my horses and I were struggling up a humid and muddy mountain in Honduras, a drug lord had quoted him to me. Now, after starting 2017 with such intense suffering, those words carried much more weight than they did when I first heard them.

My limits were tested that week. Every day, I realized I had the power to go further than I ever imagined. In the end, we made it through the fire and walked out alive. Filthy, exhausted, and in pain, I rode over the Río Negro and into Patagonia.

I wish I could have been excited to enter this majestic and rugged land I would ride through to Tierra del Fuego. All I felt at that moment was fatigue.

A police officer stopped me in town to snap a selfie and chat. I put on a fake smile on my dirty face and answered his questions before continuing to Hector and Caro Molina's ranch.

"Filipe, welcome to Río Colorado!" Hector Molina said as I rode toward the one-room home at the center of the ranch. The two brothers were raised in the saddle, one with short hair, the other with hair down to his shoulders. Otherwise, they looked identical.

They welcomed me to Patagonia with so much generosity. We shared a delicious barbecue and cold beer on my first night in their town. They asked many questions about the journey and told me stories of their own trips on horseback.

"We love riding off for weeks straight, hunting and fishing along the way and sleeping in the woods," Hector told me as he ran his fingers through his long hair.

The next morning, I took a bus back to Bahía Blanca to pick up the support vehicle. I looked out the window, imagining myself riding through this exact scorched land a few days earlier. What took me five days on horseback amounted to four hours on a bus.

The van was in the shop being fixed, so I was forced to sleep in Bahía Blanca before driving back to Río Colorado.

When I returned to the Molina brothers' ranch, they gave me great news. Caro Molina's son-in-law, Luca, would drive the support van for me during the next stretch to Choele Choel.

"There is literally no water in the next 120 kilometers, Filipe. You will have to carry water in the support van for your horses," Caro warned me with worried eyes.

Luca was a nineteen-year-old with a baby face and short dark hair. He could fix anything with a pair of pliers and a piece of wire.

On our first day out, the sun burned bright early in the morning. By noon, riding became unbearable. I found a *ñire* tree to hide under and ate a light lunch followed by an Argentinian siesta atop the saddle pads. Sapo and Picasso had their own siesta under a taller *coihue de magallanes* tree nearby.

Thanks to my new support driver, the horses had water and alfalfa to keep them busy and happy while waiting for the heat to ease.

Just before we were about to ride out again, a couple with a small child pulled over and asked for help. Their car had broken down, and they needed someone to tow them back to town. I had received so much support every day, I felt it was my obligation to offer a friendly hand and return all of the favors I had received on the road. I asked Luca if he didn't mind, and he happily towed the family's car to Río Colorado using a piece of rope.

With the day feeling a little cooler, I continued south alone. I rode and rode and rode as the sun made its way down the sky. When it was about to dive under the horizon, with no sign of Luca, I decided it was time to stop. I found a fence line to tie the horses and sat on the side of the road staring at nothing as dusk began to swallow us.

I was in the middle of nowhere and began to worry that Luca would not be able to see me. I grabbed my headlamp and put it on flicker mode. Luckily, he arrived shortly and spotted the light.

"Man, I'm so sorry, but they made me drive them from one mechanic to another looking for a better price," he said, worried he had let me down on our first day together.

"No worries, brother," I responded with a smile to calm him. We cooked sausages over hot coals using a little grill Luca had donated to the journey and ate them with bread. While we munched on our *choripan*, the silence of Patagonia was only interrupted by our crackling fire.

We talked about life. Luca was only nineteen years old but already had a two-year-old daughter to care for. "It's not easy, you know," he told me, staring far off to the horizon. "Life changes completely after you have a child."

He told me how he used to love partying, but when his girlfriend told him she was pregnant, that all ended. Unfortunately, when his daughter was born he was fired from his job as a ranch hand.

With worry in his eyes, he added, "I'm hoping to work picking fruit this season. I need to make some money to support my family."

Staring at the fire, I tried to imagine a life with kids. If I had been a father at an early age like Luca, would I be entering Patagonia on horseback? Probably not. One second, one decision can change the trajectory of your life forever.

For the next couple of days, we rode hard through the dry, dry north of Patagonia. The vegetation became semi-arid with short bushes like *neneo, la llareta, and Coirón* alongside a lot of small rocks and dust.

Having Luca with me made all of the difference in the world. Without the van, the horses would have gone days without drinking. As Caro had warned, there wasn't any water in sight, and all of the gates we passed had chains and locks.

On our second-to-last night, we rode up to a small house on the right side of the road. It was the only building we'd seen in the 120 kilometers. The elderly couple who lived there had run a small bar and restaurant out of their house for the past forty years.

"People on bicycles, motorcycles, and cars have stopped to sleep here, but you are the first to come on horseback," the frail lady said through her one-tooth smile. She had a strong nose and dark skin that looked like leather. She wore a colorful, flower-patterned silk handkerchief around her neck. Her hair was a mixture of black, white, and silver, short and coarse. It stood up like an Afro.

Living in the middle of nowhere had clear effects on the old couple. Lonely, they had a deep desire to chat and share stories. Both had the look of people who spent too much time alone. We spent an hour chatting with the pair while the elderly man, with pale blue eyes and harsh lines running down his face, chain-smoked.

He showed us the bruises and cuts he had sustained on his arm, hands, and face a day earlier. "I fell down coming out of the house and almost broke my arm," he told us with embarrassment before taking a long drag of his cigarette.

His wife added she worried that one day he would fall down the well and die. She laughed out loud after, so I wasn't sure how worried she really was. They were both in their late seventies or mid-eighties, and it was hard to imagine how they lived in this lost corner of the world in such utter isolation.

After four days, Luca and I rode into Choele Choel with dusty smiles. It had been another rough stretch of road but thanks to his kindness, we made it. After we wet our dry throats with a cold Miller by the wide, gorgeous Río Negro, I thanked Luca.

Before saying goodbye to my new friend, I paid him for his time helping me. "Filipe, I can't accept this," he said.

I didn't give him an option. He had helped me tremendously and needed the money for his little girl. We both had our own journeys to continue.

LAND OF SAINTS

I rode out of Choele Choel before four a.m. With the heat reaching into the forties Celsius, I needed to ride as much as possible before noon. Atop Picasso and with the packsaddle on Sapito, I once again headed south alone.

The road was littered with large rocks and sharp stones ranging from the size of a golf ball to a tennis ball. They made every step the horses took a painful endeavor. The edges of the rocks would more often than not poke the sole of their hoof and frog. The shoe protected the outside of their hoof but left the center exposed to jabs.

After only a few days, Sapo especially began to limp once in a while when he got poked badly by these rocks. I lost sleep to worry and flinched every time the ponies missed a step.

Because my horses came from the Buenos Aires Province, they were not used to walking over such rocky terrain. In the *Estancia* where they were born, pastures were grassy and sandy. There were very few rocks if any. Their hooves were not strong enough to take this stress all day. They were becoming increasingly sore as each day passed.

I needed to do something, and I needed to do it fast. When we arrived in Chichinales, I knew the boys needed to rest their feet. They weren't lame and didn't have any abscesses, but the soles of their feet, especially the front, were sensitive.

The night we rode into town, a big, loud, and fun family hosted me with a barbecue. I met their cousins, uncles, and friends as we chowed down on mounds of delicious pork and lamb. They took photos with me and asked to hear stories from the road. With one too many Fernets, I slept like a baby and managed to forget my troubles for a night.

~

"Patagonia is the farthest place to which man walked from his place of origin," Bruce Chatwin wrote in his book, *In Patagonia*, published in 1977. At more than 20,000 kilometers from where I was raised in the Great White North, I couldn't agree more.

Both Chatwin and I made it to the ends of the Earth not just by determination, but by kindness. During both of our journeys, we slept in strangers' sheds and homes. The people who welcomed me from the city of Chichinales southward were simple folk, living in dirt-floor homes in the middle of the desert. The little they had, they shared with me.

"Filipe, we have butchered a lamb to welcome you," I heard from my hosts night after night.

In the small town of Chimpay, the birthplace of Ceferino Namuncurá, South America's first indigenous saint, beatified by Pope Benedict in 2007, I made a friend for life: Ramon Bastias. He was a fifty-eight-year-old Secretary of Employment in the province of Neuquén. Ramon, with his short, snow-white hair, squinty eyes, and strong nose from his indigenous roots, was soft-spoken and loved to listen.

He not only hosted me like family, but two days after I rode away from his home, he surprised me with some unbelievable news. "Filipe," he said over the phone, "I have been losing sleep worrying about your and Sapito's feet. I'm going to drive the support vehicle for you. I don't want you to have to travel with the packsaddle anymore."

Clearly, Chimpay had the edge on saintly people. I nearly jumped with joy at the news! Sapito was still struggling with the rocky terrain. From what I had heard, the way was only going to get worse as I neared the Andes cordillera. It was an immense relief to take the pack-saddle off his back and have him walk without the extra weight.

This selfless Argentinian took his vacation days early to help me cover the 400 kilometers that separated the city of Neuquén from San Carlos de Bariloche. The day Ramon arrived to officially join me on the trail, he brought a gift from his daughter Daiana who had accompanied me on horseback the day I entered her hometown. We had hit it off and had become good friends in the short time I spent in her home. She was a petite girl with long, dark hair, almost always tied in a single braid.

"Daiana sent this bracelet of hers for you as a present," Ramon said, handing me the shiny silver woman's bracelet. I stared at it, confused as to why she had sent me one of her bracelets. It was beautiful, had an intricate flower on it, and looked like an antique that had been passed down in her family.

That night, thanking her over the phone, she told me why she chose that present. "I want you to have this bracelet for when you find your *flor del pago* (flower of the desert). Give it to her," Daiana said in her raspy voice. She explained *flor del pago* was the Argentinian way of saying woman of your dreams or soulmate.

I laughed. "Daiana, I am in Patagonia, traveling on horseback and not showering often! I'm never going to find a girlfriend."

I hung up the phone and stared at the little white flower on the silver bracelet. Hoping that somehow, some way, the strong, little Argentinian was right. "Flor del pago," I repeated the words in my head like the chorus of a song. I liked the sound of it.

Ramón was one of the nicest humans I had ever met. The first night he slept in the van, he nearly pissed himself because, in the darkness, he couldn't figure out how to open the back door. I was out cold in the front.

When I asked him why the hell he hadn't woken me up, he responded, "I didn't want to bother you. When I was about to piss my pants, I remembered we had empty water bottles in the back! They saved my life!"

Every morning, we drank warm mate while the horses grazed on alfalfa. In the evenings when I rode into camp, it was already set up with a place to tie the horses. Water waited in buckets and meat sizzled atop a neatly made fire. At night, we discussed politics, philosophy, and women. We never arrived at any answers, but during our two weeks in the heart of Patagonia, we became brothers.

In Villa el Chocón, we took an afternoon to visit the Ernesto Bachmann Museum where I discovered that I was riding through a land of giants. This part of Patagonia was one of the world's richest areas for finding dinosaur bones and fossils. The skeleton of one of the largest carnivorous dinosaurs ever, *Giganotosaurus carolinii*, was discovered here. Looking at the skeleton of this monster that roamed these parts some ninety-eight million years ago, it was hard to fathom how big the dinosaur actually was. Scientists estimate the *Giganotosaurus carolinii* measured between twelve and thirteen meters in length and weighed around 13.8 tons. It was massive.

Later, on the shores of Lake Ezequiel Ramos Mexía only a few kilometers away, we saw the actual tracks left by dinosaurs on their journeys millions of years ago.

Staring down at the marks left in the hardened mud, I couldn't help but question our existence. Who created all of this and why? These tracks were the size of a Smart Car. How could an animal this large have roamed the Earth? And why did they all die off? I had no answers, but I felt inspired to continue riding, to keep learning.

A few days later in Piedra del Águila, Ramon pointed to the horizon wide-eyed. "Oh, my goodness! That is the cutest thing I have ever seen," he said.

Riding toward us was a little gaucho, about seven years old, atop a feisty miniature paint pony. My heart melted.

Luis, a caramel-skinned gaucho with a silver goatee, stood next to his son, a miniature version of himself. "Filipe, it is so nice to finally meet you!" We rode into Piedra del Águila together. We made our way toward the rodeo grounds where the horses would rest the following day.

The little paint horse was the devil. Every three strides he hopped and began to buck, but the miniature gaucho controlled his mount and continued by my side without falling off.

He wore a lime green polo shirt, black *bombachas* covered from the knee down by black leather boots, and a dark red beret covering his messy, dark brown hair. Around his neck, he wore a black silk bandanna with details in red and beige. I wanted to steal him!

Luis hosted Ramon and me in his home where I fell deeper in love with his young son. At night, over a pizza made atop a juicy steak (the meat acted like the dough while cheese, potatoes, and tomatoes sat on top), the little gaucho showed us how he could play the guitar, accordion, dance to folk music, and recite poetry. He was an all-round gaucho!

The next morning, Ramon and I marveled at the large rock formations around the town. They were so intricate and interesting, like nothing I had seen before. A bright red, they rose out of the middle of the desert in varied shapes. Some looked like faces while others resembled small buildings.

"Millions of years ago, this was the ocean floor. That's why the rocks have those round shapes," Ramon explained.

The only place I had ever seen that looked a little like Piedra del Águila was the Nevada desert. Separated by thousands of kilometers, both had similar rock formations, mainly because both were once upon a time covered with seawater. It was in these large stone formations that many eagles established nests when early settlers arrived. That was where the town got its name. *Piedra del Águila* translates to The Eagle's Stone. From the small town of 3,000 people, we traveled southward for 200 kilometers.

The Andes pre-cordillera sprung up around us as the vegetation transitioned from burned grass, low bushes, and sand to green fields and pine trees. The droughts of northern Patagonia and Argentina came to an abrupt end as bright blue, sparkling glacial rivers and lakes emerged on both sides of the road.

Ramon was ecstatic. Like most men who live in Patagonia, he loved fly fishing. He'd brought his gear along for the journey and, as soon as we arrived in this bountiful region, he began casting his rod. Unfortunately, it was the wrong time of the year to catch trout, but I thoroughly enjoyed my late afternoon fly-fishing lessons. I felt like Brad Pitt in *A River Runs Through It* (minus his boyish good looks)!

The Andes showed off its majesty daily with the mountains getting larger and larger the further west we trekked. One afternoon, we camped in a field that had a clear view of the Lanín volcano. The ice-clad, cone-shaped stratovolcano glowed in the golden hour of Patagonia's sunsets.

"These are the moments when I know there is really a god," Ramon said while we passed Mate back and forth, staring at the magnificent natural painting in front of us.

"Amen, brother," I said, keeping my gaze riveted on the volcano.

The mountains also brought new dangers in the blind turns and twisty narrow roads sandwiched between rivers and jagged rock faces. Trucks and buses roared past us at one hundred kilometers an hour. My sturdy steeds kept going without missing a beat.

Picasso and Sapo had matured from fearful ponies to brave horses in these past three months. My boys had earned new aliases that became their *nom de guerre*: Sapito Gonzales and Pablo Picasso!

Ramon also took on a new, quiet power. When we were five kilometers from Bariloche, an old friend of Ramon's took over driving the van so that we could enter the city together. I rode Pablo Picasso while he rode Sapito Gonzales next to me.

With the Andes glowing under the midday sun and Lake Nahuel Huapi giving everything a sparkling blue glow, it was the perfect ending to our time together.

"I will never forget this beautiful adventure," Ramon said, wrapping his right arm around my shoulder.

I smiled at the white-haired saint as I wrapped my left arm around his waist.

"I have learned a great deal from you, Filipe, especially to give thanks." Ramon stopped for a second, rearranging Sapito's mane before continuing. "You thank everyone you meet after every small thing they do for you. This is a beautiful thing I will incorporate into my life."

"Ramon, are you kidding me? I have learned an abundance from you, sir!"

He laughed and shook his head.

Arriving in Bariloche was a huge milestone on the journey. Looking at Google maps when I was planning the trip months before, the city of gorgeous mountains and supreme lakes looked so distant, so impossible to reach on horseback. Yet here I was, only 2,000 kilometers from my end goal in one of the most beautiful cities in the world. The mountains' magnetism had pulled me there, and I would soon understand why.

EL TOTEIRO DAS AMÉRICAS

In Bariloche, celebrating our tenth month on the road, I was hosted by a lovely Brazilian family. "It feels good not to be the only cowboy in Bariloche," Ronaldo Pucci, a Brazilian horse trainer with a thick black mustache and wicked humor said, shaking my hand.

The cowboy, who roped and trained reining and cutting horses, had been chatting with me via WhatsApp since I left Tandil. Some friends who hosted me in that city knew Ronaldo and put me in touch with him. After nearly a year on the road, being able to speak Portuguese again made me feel as if I were home momentarily.

"While you are in Bariloche, you will stay with my family. Your horses can rest at my ranch," he said before we ate a delicious feast in a local restaurant.

When I arrived at Ronaldo's ranch, forty-five minutes from Bariloche, I felt like I was in Montana or Colorado. It was like nothing I had ever seen in Latin America before. The barn was huge and made of thick wooden logs. The stalls were spacious and .... the horses? The horses were from the best Quarter Horse lineage on the planet. Constructed in the foothills of the Andes, Ronaldo's riding arena had the most spectacular view of Lake Nahuel Huapi and the majestic mountains beyond.

"This was a dream of mine for a long time," the Brazilian cowboy said, showing me his stunning stallion. Looking up at the mountain that climbed toward the heavens behind his ranch, he made an invitation I couldn't refuse. "We should take a pack trip up to the summit of this mountain together."

Sure, I was tired and sore from the past ten months on the road and ready to rest for a week. Still, I couldn't say no. While I trekked toward Bariloche in the weeks prior, I imagined myself eating sushi and drinking cold beer while sleeping in a comfortable bed for hours on end. But like many times before on this journey, resting was only an option served to Sapito Gonzales and Pablo Picasso. For me, it was more riding and even more adventure.

On a gloomy day, Ronaldo, two Argentinian horsemen, and I began climbing the beast of a mountain behind the ranch. We used Criollos and Quarter Horses to ride and carry our packsaddles. Only a few hours up the harrowing trail, we were hit with heavy rains and worse — hail. Large white pebbles fell from the sky and landed on our heads and our mounts with force. Their manes quickly turned white.

We trekked silently through slippery trails while the trees cracked and creaked above us in the strong winds. Silently, I prayed none of these ancient beasts would snap in half on top of my head. Wet and cold, we rode up to an old hunting cabin with no roof and made camp.

Over succulent meat and fiery whiskey, we found warmth and comfort while telling fibs. Everything was going to plan until the next morning's disaster. I had just had my morning coffee when nature came calling. Out there on the lonely road south, the only bathroom available was in the woods. I dropped my jeans to my ankles and squatted behind a colossal pine tree.

In a daze, staring at the snow-tipped mountains and the sparkling blue lake far beneath in the horizon, I was startled when the ground started shaking.

Oh no, I thought. *Thundering hooves!*

I quickly whipped my head around just in time to catch a glimpse of three of our horses galloping down the mountain. They were running all-out down the same trail we had fought our way up the previous day. I didn't know if I should start running or pull my jeans up. We were 1,000 meters above sea level in the middle of the Andes cordillera and horseless. Things were not looking good.

After two hours walking down the mountain following the horses' hoof prints in the deep mud, we found our ponies happily grazing in a gorgeous meadow. We slowly approached them, and carefully captured the sweaty beasts, only to discover that one of the horses had broken his lead rope on the way down.

"Someone will have to ride this horse back up the mountain bareback and with no lead rope," Ronaldo announced.

Everyone turned their gaze to me. *Bastards.*

Minutes later, I held the chestnut's red mane as we trotted up the slippery and steep mountain. It was a hairy trail that took us past jagged rock faces, shallow rivers, and scary cliffs. All the while, I fought to stay on my horse's back, slipping farther and farther back as we trekked up 45-degree angles. With no lead rope, I had no steering. I kept his head close to Ronaldo's horse's ass, hoping he would follow the palomino without taking any detours.

Hours later, we finally stepped upon the summit of the mountain. "Wow, I don't even know what to say. This is one of the most spectacular views I have ever seen," I said.

"You are one of a few humans who have ever stepped up here before, my friend," Ronaldo said with a strong slap on my back.

I sat down in the tall green grass and took in the gorgeous vista. The bowl we were in had jagged rock faces all around and opened up in a V in front of me to show the Andes cordillera as far as one could see. A few stratus clouds hung low just above the mountaintops. Otherwise, it was a light blue sky. A few feet from me, a natural spring offered pure freezing water from the gut of this monstrous mountain. The air was fresh and smelled of wildflowers. We spent several hours up there chatting and enjoying the view while our horses grazed.

～

During my week off in Bariloche, I spoke to my mom about how sad I was to continue the journey alone now that Ramon Bastias had returned home. She suggested posting my need for a support driver on my Facebook page since I had more than 15,000 followers. I was skeptical at first. It was hard enough having a friend out here on the road, living intensely with that person every day, never mind a complete stranger. Worst of all, what if the stranger turned out to be an annoying crazed serial killer? I put those negative thoughts aside and created the post.

In less than twenty-four hours, I received many messages from Brazilians, Uruguayans, and a twenty-six-year-old gaucho from Buenos Aires province who had stopped me on the side of the highway a month before to ask if I needed anything. He sent me his resume.

"Filipe, I spent four months traveling on horseback from Buenos Aires to Salta a couple of years ago and would love to drive the support van for you," wrote Sebastián Cichero, or Toti, as his friends called him.

He included photos of his journey and explained that driving the support vehicle was important to him. I called him and the next day he was in Bariloche.

The moment I met Toti, I had a feeling we would get along. Even though we were from different countries, we spoke the same language: the horse. After a few minutes chatting, it was as if we had grown up together.

Toti had a medium build, shaggy, light brown hair, a pointy nose, tanned skin, and thick dark eyebrows. When he flashed his warm smile, which was often, two dimples appeared on his cheeks, making him look more innocent than he really was. He had a small gap in between his top middle teeth and was blind in his left eye. When he was a little kid, he was playing the now inappropriately named gauchos and Indians with his cousin and got hit in the eye by an arrow fired from a homemade bow. Toti was a workhorse who moved with a thousand peps in his step as if he had chugged three Red Bulls minutes earlier.

While a farrier worked on the ponies' feet, we organized the van and got everything ready to ride out toward El Bolsón, our first resting spot. We knew the road would not be easy the next few days. A lot of switchbacks would guide us through the cordillera.

Secretly, I worried if Toti and I would get along in the face of adversity. After all, through hard times, even the best of friends fight. I wondered if Toti worried as well. With only one afternoon to get to know one another, we started our trip together through Patagonia.

Happy to be back on the road and rested, I bid farewell to Bariloche, Ronaldo and his family, and Flavio Ferrari.

Flavio was a good friend and also my boot sponsor. The fifty-year-old cowboy flew down from Brazil to spend a few days with me and to bring me a new pair of boots. Due to the large amount of time I spent on my feet and walking next to the horses, I went through several pairs. It took seven different pairs of boots to trek from Canada to Brazil. On this journey, I was already on pair number three!

"I'm so relieved Toti is going to drive the support van for you. I was worried," Flavio said before he made his way to the airport. I knew he was still worried.

~

From Bariloche, Toti and I trekked south toward the town of El Bolsón, a 120 kilometer, four-day ride through divine mountains. By the first afternoon, it was already like we were old high school friends.

He always wore a blue checkered shirt that sat baggy on his body, rolled up at the sleeves, a dark blue beret, gray *bombachas,* and dark blue *alpargatas.* The high-spirited gaucho seemed to have the stamina of the Energizer bunny. He woke up with a smile on his face, organized the van five times a day, had water for the horses ready when I arrived, helped me feed the ponies, and carried saddles. If there was one person in the world who I could choose to drive the support vehicle for me, it would be this guy. His energy was refreshing, and his knowledge was a great addition to the journey.

Toti knew a lot about horses. Like myself, he was raised around these majestic creatures. He even spent four months riding 2,000 kilometers with his cousin from Buenos Aires to Salta. To top it off, Toti spent two seasons working with polo horses in England and Spain. While we ate lunch by a beautiful lake on our first day out, he told me, "The horse is everything to me."

That night, with few places to camp, he found a home for us to rest. A *Mapuche* family allowed us to sleep in their cabin and even invited us to a delicious barbecue. Their cabin, used for weekend trips, was built in the middle of a dense forest. Cypresses, radal, lenga, coihue, and pine trees towered over us.

"I was born on this land, as were my ancestors. I feel a deep love for this Earth and a desire to always protect it," the matriarch of the family said to me while she made *torta fritas*, a traditional Argentinian bread that was fried instead of baked. In her late fifties, she had a broad face that hid nothing. She went on to tell me how the mountains with a round top were considered females in their culture, and the ones with prominent tips were the males.

Then she explained how Patagonia earned its name. "When the Spanish arrived in this area, the indigenous people who lived here, *Tehuelches*, were very tall with large feet. The Spanish named them the Patagon people because of the large footprints their *patas* (feet) left behind," she explained, passing me a warm *torta frita*. Early Spanish explorers soon began calling this land Patagonia.

Eventually, a *boot* (a canister made out of goat hide full of red wine) was passed around. We played a traditional Argentinian game where the drinker must yell out, "Gregorio!" while spraying the wine into their mouth. Whoever took longer to say the word, drinking the largest gulp of wine, won. Extra points were also awarded for the distance from which you sprayed the red liquid into your mouth. The farther you held the *boot* from your mouth, the more points.

When it came time for them to head back to Bariloche for the night, they left the keys to the cabin with us.

"Tomorrow, please lock up and leave the key under this rock," the patriarch of the family said before they drove off.

Toti and I awoke early and fed the horses.

"Man, I think I drank too much wine last night," I said to my Argentinian friend as he laughed and danced and screamed. What I learned very quickly is that Toti only had one gear: sixth. No matter what time we went to bed or how tired we were, he sprang out of bed and began his day with a bright smile. He put water on to boil, began cooking breakfast, and organized everything. Toti was a machine!

"Okay, brother. I'm going to drive ahead and find somewhere nice for us to have lunch. I'll come check on you soon," Toti said before fixing his dark blue beret over his shaggy hair.

That day, we trekked a huge mountain that had us snaking our way downward for hours. The highway became very dangerous with many blind turns and little space for the horses and me. Luckily, there was a beautiful old road that made its way to the other side of the mountain. It was full of overgrown trees and large rocks that had fallen from above.

At the bottom of the mountain, we found refuge in the quaint log home of a forest ranger. In this area of Argentina, there were national parks everywhere. The road from Bariloche all the way to El Bolsón, a 120-kilometer stretch, was made almost entirely of national parkland.

Every park has one or many rangers protecting these natural gems. They live in the most beautiful wooden cabins in the middle of the forested mountains. For a moment, I wanted to be an Argentinian park ranger!

We turned out the horses in a small corral nearby and made a fire. With fall quickly approaching, the nights had begun to cool very quickly. Accompanied by the park ranger who lived there and another ranger who lived nearby, we ate some burgers and chatted the night away. They told us about their work ensuring that forest fires didn't start, and we told them about our ride. It was a great night.

Before we bid them farewell, Chino, one of the rangers, an Asian-looking man with a long ponytail, invited us to eat dinner with his family when we arrived in El Bolsón.

"You have to meet my stepdaughters," he told us. "They love horses." We agreed to the invitation and retired to the van for the night. The thought of having dinner with Chino and his family sounded nice, but we still had seventy hard kilometers ahead of us. Before the park ranger who hosted us awoke, Toti and I had the horses tacked and were moving south once again.

That day, I rode through the stunning village of Foyel in the early morning. I stopped at an outdoor market that sold sweets and keepsakes to tourists and bought a cup of weak coffee. Very quickly, we were swarmed by curious travelers who fired questions my way. They all wanted to pet the horses and know their names.

Like a proud parent, I announced, "Sapito Gonzales and Pablo Picasso!"

Before I rode out, a short woman with curly hair and a pretty smile approached me and asked if I was Brazilian. I said yes and her face lit up. She told me she was originally from Brazil. After marrying an Argentinian man, she had lived in the small village for the past five years.

"Oh, how nice it is to speak Portuguese," she said after I finished telling her about my trip.

For lunch, Toti and I found a corral to leave the horses and drove to a nearby river for a much-needed bath. The water flowing down from the glaciers was freezing, but after three days on the road with no shower, our desire to bathe was stronger than our fear of cold water. The water was clear, revealing rounded stones of different shapes and colors.

On the banks of the river stood *lupinos* flowers in varying shades of pink and purple and yellow. The plant had a tall green stalk, and the tip opened up into a shape like a cornstalk with hundreds of bean-shaped flowers. Due to its height and the weight of the flowers, it swayed in the Patagonian wind back and forth, never stopping, like the golden arm of a lucky cat found behind the cash register of every Asian restaurant.

To my left behind a small bridge stood a rugged cordillera with various shades of green racing up its face. Farther up, it turned to dark gray stone and, finally, white with snow. The freshness of the air and the water, the sound of the birds chirping all around, and the natural beauty swallowed me.

All of a sudden, a Ringed kingfisher, flying low above the river, dove into the clear water like a torpedo, only to shoot out seconds later with a flailing fish in its long beak.

Feeling clean and refreshed, we drove back to the ponies and tacked them up. Before I rode out, a mammoth of a man in an old blue truck stopped and asked what we were up to. After a short chat, he invited us to camp at his mother's farm that afternoon, fifteen kilometers south.

I rode through a forest of pine trees before a giant rock-faced mountain. The road was absolutely breathtaking.

In the late afternoon, we arrived at the farm. A small lady in her late seventies with bright eyes welcomed us with a kiss on each cheek. Her son towered next to her. I wondered how she had birthed such a large being. She told us we could turn the horses out in the pasture behind her home with the sheep and offered an empty garage for us to sleep in. The cute little lady placed two mattresses on the ground for us and bid us goodnight while we munched on noodles with boiled eggs.

The next morning, I began a hard trek down a rocky back road. It was nice not having any cars flying by, but the rocks made it hard for the ponies to walk. Since entering Patagonia, their front feet had suffered daily due to the endless pointy rocks and stones plaguing the road. With the gorgeous views of the mountains and valleys all around us, it was hard to keep focused on the dangers of the road in front of us.

In the late afternoon, we arrived in the jockey club of El Bolsón. It felt invigorating to have finished this first journey with my brother Toti. The Universe had sent me another angel. After those first four days together, I was sure we would make it to Ushuaia together.

The man in charge of the grounds had no idea we were coming but quickly opened a corral for Sapito and Picasso. He gave me a bale of alfalfa and invited Toti and me to eat lunch with him. Over mashed potatoes, rice, and sausages, we chatted about our combined love for the horse and the rewards of that love. During lunch, he told us we had arrived just in time for the hops festival.

"You guys should go tonight. Tons of beer and girls," our host said with a wide grin on his swollen face.

Toti and I looked at each other, smiling from ear-to-ear as if we had just won the lottery. We raced to town to buy materials to shoe the horses over the weekend. Already Friday afternoon, we feared the shops would stay closed due to the festival.

Speaking to my high school roping coach, good friend, and farrier back in Canada, Jason Thomson, I asked him for help with the horses' feet.

"There is a plastic pad you can buy in North America that comes with a special gel for the horses' soles, but I doubt you will find it in Patagonia," Jason explained to me over WhatsApp. He went on to tell me I could buy hard leather, the same used to make the soles of shoes, cut them to the same size as horseshoes, and then purchase silicon used to seal windows from any hardware store. "Nail the leather pad in between the shoe and the hoof and then slide the silicon gun at the back where the horses' frogs are. Fill the area between the sole and the leather pad with it."

According to Jason, this concoction would save my life and the horses' front feet during our ride through Patagonia. Toti and I spent two hours driving around El Bolsón, and once we had purchased everything we needed, we returned to the horses. All we talked about was the kick-ass party we would attend that night.

"I never arrive in a town during any festival. I'm always two weeks too late, or one week early," I told Toti.

As soon as we pulled up to the jockey club, we saw Chino standing in front of the horses' corral.

"Oh, no, this guy is going to invite us to eat dinner at his house with his family," Toti protested before turning off the van. "How are we going to say no? I want to go to the beer festival."

With fake smiles, we marched toward the park ranger. Before we reached him, two goddesses turned the corner, making our backs straighten and hearts skip a beat.

"Filipe, Toti, you guys made it! Welcome to El Bolsón," Chino said before giving each of us a hug. "This is Clara and Azul, my stepdaughters I told you two about," he said before we shyly said hello to the two girls.

I wanted to give Chino another hug! As soon as I laid eyes on Clara, I fell in love. She had the eyes of a cat, and her irises were bright honey with a darker spot on the bottom of her left iris. She had thick dark eyebrows, pouty lips, and dark skin that made her look like a Spanish princess from another era. Her hair was jet-black, and her body was perfect. Her gaze was that of a lioness, strong and intense. She wore a black tank top and ripped jean shorts with paint splattered all over them. She was Salma Hayek in her heyday!

"We don't know if you two have plans tonight, but we would like to invite you to eat pizza at our place," Sandra, the girls' mother, said. She had eyes that seemed to be made from the waters off the coast of the Bahamas, light turquoise. Her hair, curly and silver, running down to the middle of her back.

"Pizza? I love pizza. We would be delighted," I said, smiling like an idiot. Toti shot me a comical look with a sly smirk. It was official, we had ditched the beer festival for these two girls.

When the family left, Toti and I almost died laughing at our pathetic display of not sticking to our plan. "'Pizza, I love pizza,'" Toti mimicked me as I rolled on the dirt floor howling. After wiping the tears from our faces, we talked about the chances of these twenty-something, beautiful girls actually being single.

"Slim to none," I concluded, "so you're saying there's a chance."

After a shower in a filthy gas station bathroom nearby, Toti and I followed the directions to our future girlfriends' house. That was what we titled their abode. Built in the foothills of the Piltri Mountain, the house was gorgeous. It had large windows instead of walls on the lower and top floors that made it look and feel like the mountain was inside the house. A stunning vista.

I spent all night talking to Clara about my journey, life, food, Argentina, and horses. Every second that passed made me fall deeper and deeper in love with this girl. She reminded me so much of the princess from *A Knight's Tale*, the one the late, great Heath Ledger falls for.

At some point, someone pulled out a camera and set it on a tripod to capture a group photo. I didn't remember this happening in the moment, but later looking at the photo, Clara and I had our faces locked, cheek to cheek, as if we were a longtime couple.

After drinking too much beer and eating some delicious homemade pizza with vegetables from Sandra's garden, Toti and I bid our hosts farewell and drove to the horses.

"Brother, I am in love with this girl," I said as soon as we closed the doors to the van.

"I'm in love with Azul. Let's sell the horses and stay in El Bolsón," he said, making us both laugh hard.

"*Yiiiipoooo!*" we yelled out loud while Toti slammed on the horn repeatedly.

After talking about how much we were in love for about fifteen minutes, we realized neither of us had asked for their numbers, emails, Facebook, or Instagram. We were idiots. We had no way of messaging the girls and trying to set up something the following day.

Luckily, Argentina is large in landmass, but small in population. Toti had a mutual friend with Clara from Buenos Aires and managed to find her Facebook account. I sent her a friend request and wrote her a message right away.

When we woke up the next morning, the first thing I did was check Facebook. Not only had my new love not messaged me, she had yet to accept my friend request. I was heartbroken. It was obvious she didn't want anything to do with me. I was an old saddle tramp. She was a twenty-two-year-old beauty who probably had a lineup of guys after her.

Depressed, I went to feed the horses before Toti and I drove off to get breakfast. After eating *medialunas* at a local cafe, we drove to the center of town to see the hippie market. During the seventies, the small town was flooded with hippies from all over Argentina and the world. They wanted to build a community in this gorgeous place where peace, happiness and freedom could strive. To this day, there are many traces of this commune. It was on full display at the hippie market downtown. Vendors could only sell handmade things like knives, clothing, dreamcatchers, and food. The smell of marijuana smoke permeated the air, along with various flavors of incense.

After a stroll through the market, I got into the van to make our way back to the horses. I opened my Facebook, and to my surprise, there was a message from Clara.

Her message read: *Sorry, I don't get internet at my house. I'm downtown. Where are you guys?*

My heart stopped. I shut off the engine and opened my door to announce to Toti, who was still outside finishing his cigarette, "There really is a God!"

In that moment of extreme ecstasy, I leapt out of the van and shut the door, only to realize that the keys were inside, still in the ignition. The door was locked. I yelled a curse.

"*What?* What happened?" Toti asked, confused. "She messaged you or she didn't message you?"

"I locked the van with the keys inside," I replied, feeling even more stupid hearing the words spoken aloud.

"No, no, no!" Toti burst into laughter.

While trying several different ways to open the door, Clara announced we had to meet in the next five minutes because she had to go back home. I had to drive to see her.

I smashed the window.

"What men do for women," Toti observed, laughing hard.

Clara and I met and made plans to go out for beer that night. My heart was mended. My window was still broken.

That afternoon, we shod the horses just as Jason had instructed and allowed the silicon to dry before releasing the boys. I hoped it would work because if not, I didn't know how the boys would continue walking over all that rocky terrain.

Toti and I taped clear plastic on the van's door as a temporary window and went to meet the girls for drinks in the late afternoon. We were happier than two teenage boys going to the prom. It was another great night that left me in a deeper state of desire for this gorgeous woman. However, when I tried to steal a kiss, I was shut down hard.

The following morning, it was time to hit the road, Jack.

I rode out of El Bolsón on a beautiful sunny morning, but it felt like a dark cloud was following me. I couldn't stop thinking about Clara and how I would never find another love traveling on horseback.

At ten a.m., a solar eclipse made the morning cooler and everything turned yellow. To my surprise, Clara and her family met me on the side of the road to bid me farewell and to allow me to see the solar eclipse using a round *obsidiana* stone.

I was happy to see her one final time, but it only made my feeling of sadness multiply deep in my core. I just wanted to get off Picasso and stay with this gorgeous brunette for the rest of my days. I didn't want to keep going but, like many times before, I put my feelings aside and kept riding south.

CHOLILA

Wondering if I would ever see Clara again, we rode toward the small town of Cholila. As with the road from Bariloche to El Bolsón, we continued to traverse large stunning mountains.

"I can't wait to see Butch Cassidy's cabin," I said to Toti while we ate dinner on the side of the road late one night. We were both super excited to see where Butch, the Sundance Kid, and Etta Place hid when they made a run from the United States in the early nineteen hundreds. The law was after the notorious gang, and they thought Patagonia would serve as the perfect hiding spot.

When I entered the valley where the cabin they lived in for several years still stood, I was transported to the Western United States: the rolling hills, the tall dark yellow grass, and the rugged mountains in the backdrop. I could have been riding in Wyoming or Montana. To see this view from the saddle made me believe this was what made those gangsters choose this location to live when they arrived in Patagonia. It must have felt like home.

Toti had arrived a few hours earlier and found a great ranch where we could rest. It happened to be the land where Butch's cabin was. I shook the hand of Don Peppe, the owner of the ranch.

"Nice to meet you, sir. Thank you for allowing us to rest here."

In his mid-eighties, the elderly man was a gentleman's gentleman. He wore a blue button-up shirt with a gray sweater on top and a brown wool hat covering his milk-white hair. After untacking the horses and feeding them, Don Peppe showed us his very own museum. Housed inside the town's first supermarket, the antique building held many artifacts from the days of Butch Cassidy and many more from Don Peppe's childhood.

"My favorite piece? That's a hard question. It's probably this wooden rocking horse. My parents gave it to me when I was a little boy. It was my first pony."

After showing us the museum, Don Peppe told us his wife had passed away a few days earlier. It was heartbreaking. His eyes filled with tears as he told us how lost he felt. "You live with someone your entire life, and then one day they are gone. I still don't know what to do when I'm home alone."

The truth was, I couldn't imagine the pain he felt at that moment. Having the love of your life taken from you must be one of the worst pains the human heart had to endure, especially after living by their side for over sixty years.

We tried to keep Don Peppe busy and his mind off of the death of his great love, but it had a profound effect upon me. That night, I fought to fall asleep as I contemplated how hard it must be to lose one's spouse after a lifetime together. I was an emotional mess, especially since I had discovered a great love only to leave her behind.

The next morning, Toti and I woke up early and rode the horses to Butch's cabin. Dressed in traditional western gear, holding a pistol and sawed-off shotgun lent us by Don Peppe, we played cowboys for an hour. On the property, there was the cabin where the group lived and a small barn next to it. They were both made from thick slabs of wood cut from the nearby forest. The windows were all very low to the ground to make it easy for them to escape in case of an ambush.

Toti and I shot photos with the pistol and shotgun on display atop the horses inside the cabin and in the barn. For a couple of minutes, we felt like gangsters ourselves.

"They say that Etta was such a good shot, she could put out a man's cigarette and not hit him with the bullet," Don Peppe told us when we returned from our fun. He also explained how the group had horses strategically set up, every thirty kilometers for hundreds of kilometers as part of their elaborate escape plan to Chile. If someone found them, they would be able to gallop thirty kilometers and get fresh horses and gallop thirty more and so on.

"They weren't dumb, that's for sure," the elderly gentleman let out one of the few smirks we saw on his face.

Eventually, after robbing trains and banks in Argentina, Chile, Peru, and Bolivia, the gang was discovered, and Butch and the Sundance Kid were killed in a cave in Bolivia by the Bolivian Military. Or not. Some people believe Butch Cassidy was never killed and died of old age.

∽

In Cholila, we were forced to leave the horses resting on Don Peppe's ranch to go on a different adventure. Not only did I have to ride and care for my horses on the road, I was also required to play journalist every day. I shot everything and wrote blogs for *Outwildtv*. I wrote monthly articles for Canada's largest daily newspaper, the *Toronto Star*, and for *Country Fever*, a magazine in Brazil. I needed to upload photos to my social media as much as possible. It wasn't easy juggling my rugged cowboy lifestyle with my profession, but I loved sharing this experience with people.

Because the memory cards I used for the camera were eight GB each, it was impossible to transfer the footage to the United States through an internet connection. The files were too large, and with the terrible internet found in Latin America, it would take days. So, once a month, when the cards filled up, I would FedEx them to Nashville, TN. When the footage was safely copied to the production company's hard drive, they sent the empty cards back to me.

To prevent footage from being lost, I shot everything with two cards. Once I knew the A cards arrived safely and that the footage had been copied, I could shoot on the B cards. On my first journey from Canada to Brazil, things couldn't have gone better. We never lost cards. FedEx packages always arrived in the countries I was crossing. It was fabulous. This time around, things couldn't have gone worse.

In the state of Paraná, Brazil, I ran out of cards and was forced to start shooting with the B cards. When I sent the package to Nashville, it was opened by Customs in the US and never closed properly. By the time it arrived, four cards were missing. That was eighty minutes of footage lost. I wanted to cry.

Recordings ate up a lot of time and energy: getting off the horse, setting up the tripod, riding by the camera only to have to step off the saddle again to pack up the camera. After long days in the saddle when all I wanted to do is rest and sleep, I shot interviews with people. I awoke early to catch those epic sunrises. It was all gone.

Almost a year after this episode, I still lost sleep over those ruined labors. But this was not the only hiccup we had on the journey. Argentina was a country plagued with bureaucracy, and the further south I rode, the harder it became to get the video cards into the country. Three different times, the government did not allow the package to enter. That left me without cards and shooting as little as possible. An awful situation for a video journalist like me!

After all of the failed attempts to get the cards into the country, I managed to buy some in Bariloche, but they weren't enough.

The production company sent a package and a new camera along with a fellow journalist to Santiago, Chile. (The camera I was using had been malfunctioning.) She then shipped the package to Osorno, Chile, a six-hour drive from Cholila where we were staying. The idea of driving back to Bariloche and into Chile sucked, but it took me through to the one place I wanted to be — El Bolsón.

"I'm so happy I get to see you again." Clara blushed after we hugged in front of her home.

I wanted to melt like butter in her arms. That night, we went camping with Clara and Azul next to a river on the road to Cholila. It was a Friday night, and the camera would arrive in Osorno Monday afternoon, so we had some time on our hands.

We barbecued sausages on an open fire, drank Fernet with Coke, and laughed way too hard at anything and everything. At one point,

Toti went to get more firewood with Azul and left Clara and me alone sitting on a blue cooler, arms touching, the fire dancing in front of us.

"I really like you, you know," I said to her after rehearsing the line in my head for what seemed like an eternity.

"I like you, too," she said nervously before taking a sip of the Fernet. When she finished, without giving her time to think, I moved in and stole a kiss. My lips touched hers ever so smoothly.

It felt heavenly, but it didn't last long. After a few seconds, her head shot back. "Now, now, we won't be having any of that. You are going to leave me and go to Ushuaia, remember? Then what?"

"I like you, Clara, I'm sorry I travel on horseback. I can't change that, but I haven't felt this way about someone in a long time."

Toti and Azul finally returned after what felt like twelve hours. I later discovered they took extra time so we could be alone. We continued our party until we laid our sleeping bags under a willow tree and crashed.

The next morning we said goodbye to the sisters and drove off to Bariloche where we would spend the night with a friend of Toti's until Monday when we would cross the border into Chile.

Driving out of El Bolsón, Toti and I chanted, "Never again ... never again ... never again ..."

Toti had discovered Azul had a boyfriend she loved dearly, and I was tired of being frustrated by Clara. She made me feel like I was in grade three again, trying to steal my first kiss. My Argentinian brother and I swore never, ever to enter El Bolsón again!

Only eight hours later, I was in the van, driving back to El Bolsón. Clara invited me to watch a band play in a local brewery, and I couldn't say no. Clara had that kind of effect on me. Toti laughed for about twenty minutes and then announced he would stay in Bariloche with his friend. I made the two-hour drive alone.

When I parked the van, I went into my bag and fished out the bracelet Ramon's daughter had given me. As I fingered the silver band, her words repeated in my mind like a mantra: *I want you to give this bracelet to your soulmate.*

Could this be her? Clara Victoria Davel? A twenty-two-year-old Argentinian born in Bahía Blanca and raised in Patagonia? Why did we meet Chino? Why did he come to find us and invite us to eat those pizzas? Why had I ridden to the cordillera, instead of saving time and effort and simply followed Highway 3 to Ushuaia? I couldn't answer those questions. I stuffed the bracelet into my jacket pocket and made my way to the bar.

"You came!" Clara gave me a big smile as she stood up. She wore a brown leather jacket with fringes running down both her arms and back and wore her hair in two heavy braids that fell over each shoulder. There wasn't a lick of makeup on her face. No blush. No eyeliner. No lipstick. Her nails weren't painted. She hadn't bothered to put on any perfume. Yet, she was the most beautiful woman at that bar. At that moment, I realized why I fell in love with this girl so quickly. She was so pure, so genuine. Naturally gorgeous like a Patagonian sunrise. It was as if I could see through her skin and into her soul. An old soul, her name was Truth.

"Of course, I came." I said, "There was no other option!" She blushed after I gave her a long kiss on her left cheek, secretly wishing it was her lips.

The band sucked, but I told her they sounded great. After they finished, we scarfed down a pizza with Azul and then went to a different bar, a club of sorts called *El Sol*. I discovered Clara was not a big drinker. A Beatles cover band was playing their suit-wearing hearts out while Azul and I hammered back drinks.

After trying to kiss Clara for the fifteenth time that night and with the alcohol already sloshing inside me, I'd had enough. I said goodbye to Azul and told Clara I was leaving.

She grabbed my jacket as I tried to walk away. "Filipe, please don't go. I want you to stay."

"I can't play this game anymore, Clara. I've professed my love to you over and over again. I don't know what else I can do to prove that I like you," I said, freeing myself from her grip and leaving the place.

I made it three steps outside before I felt her hand grab my right arm and turn me around. When my eyes met hers, she was only a few inches away. First, I felt her warm breath touch my face. Then her lips touched mine. I closed my eyes, and we shared the greatest kiss of my life. Finally, she had freed her soul and allowed herself to act on the feelings she felt in her heart.

We walked to a nearby bench where we continued to make out and talk about our strong feelings for one another only to start kissing again. I would kiss her and then hold her face with both of my hands and stare deep into her caramel eyes, trying to read her soul. Digging deep into my jacket pocket, I pulled out the bracelet and gave it to her.

"I was given this bracelet a few weeks back and told to give it to my 'flor del pago,'" I said, placing the band around her left wrist. She smiled as she inspected her gift.

After some time alone, we returned to the bar where Azul had made new friends. We continued drinking and laughing until the early hours of the morning. Just before four a.m., we walked out of the bar to call it a night. I was as drunk as a skunk with alcohol and love. I held hands with Clara, fingers intertwined.

Standing on the curb, I saw four people huddled around a little white dog a few feet away. With the curiosity and bravado of an intoxicated individual, I walked up to the group to see what was going on.

"A car just ran over this little street dog," one woman told me.

They were all staring down at this little white-yellow-gray ball of fluff. I could kind of see his yellow eyes, but the hairs on his face nearly covered them. With the alcohol taking over all basic instincts, I reached down, picked up the little dog and announced I would nurse it back to health. Cradling the shaking pup in my arms like a baby, I returned to Azul and Clara announced my new acquisition. "I just adopted a dog," I said with conviction.

"Oh, my God, he's so cute! Why is he so scared?" Azul said, petting his little face.

"He was just hit by a car. He's a street dog."

"Oh, we have to get him to a vet." Clara took him into her arms immediately.

It was 4:30 a.m. and all of the vets were well asleep along with the rest of the town. We agreed to call it a night and figure out what to do with our new friend later that morning. I found a cheap hotel that accepted dogs, and the girls drove home. They wanted me to sleep at their house, but I was too embarrassed.

A few hours later, I woke up with a splitting headache and a dog next to my face. I smelled him before I even opened my eyes, a mixture of garbage and earth. When I fought to open my eyes, he was lying right next to me, his little snout tucked into his tail, just as I had placed him a few hours earlier.

"Hey, buddy. Good morning." My eyes barely opening, I petted his fluffy little body.

I opened the blinds and let the sunlight in the room. Seeing him for the first time in the light, I analyzed my new best friend. He was likely a mixture of Shih Tzu, Maltese, and Puma. He had long, off-white hairs that dropped to the ground and covered his face. In the middle of his back, the fur got darker, a yellowing beige color. Near his butt, he had a black oil stain and what looked to be a bright streak of yellow paint. I tried to touch his back legs, but when my hand got near his right paw, he cried in pain.

"It's okay, little guy. We're going to get a vet to fix you up. You'll be a new dog in no time."

His body shook.

I took a quick shower and drove to Clara's house. When I arrived, they were in worse shape than me. Azul looked like a rodeo clown. She had slept with her makeup on which was now all on the wrong parts of her face. Clara had been puking.

"Your mom must think I'm the devil," I said to Clara, letting out a nervous laugh. She was still wearing the bracelet I had given her a few hours earlier. She tried to laugh, but it only made her feel sicker.

Clara took the little dog from my arms and began talking to him in a baby voice. The plan was for him to stay at her place until I came back from Chile. I couldn't take him over the border without the proper shots.

"Don't worry. I'll take care of this little cutie until you return," Clara said, holding the dog tightly in her arms. She knew a vet who would come by later that day to treat the dog's broken leg and give him all of the shots and medication he needed. I bid my new friend farewell, gave Clara a kiss, and drove off to Chile.

~

After spending twenty-four hours in Chile, Toti and I drove back to El Bolsón with a new camera and thirty new memory cards. I told him about our new dog, and he couldn't wait to meet him. We were already thinking of names for the little guy. Perrito Moreno, Puma, and Butch Cassidy were the favorites.

"I hate little dogs," Toti kept saying as we approached Clara's house.

We arrived just after lunch to find our new pup with a little splint around his back right leg. He was still really quiet and looked sad, but he was now walking around a step or two and, most importantly, eating a little. His tail even began to wag.

"Thank you so much for looking after him," I told Clara after giving her a hug. I knew something was wrong immediately. She wasn't wearing the bracelet, and her hug was as cold as glacier ice. I paid her for the vet and, when Toti went outside with Azul to see which name the little dog liked most, Clara dug into her pocket and pulled out the silver bracelet.

"Here, I want you to take this back." She held the band in front of my face. A lump the size of a bowling ball rose in my throat. It was as if I had given her my heart, and now she was handing it back to me.

"Clara, I'm not taking the bracelet back. It was a present." I sounded angrier than I'd meant to.

"Filipe, I know you go from town to town kissing girls, giving out bracelets to the first one who kisses you back. I'm not going to be made a fool. You are leaving now, and I'm never going to see you again," she said before locking her jaw and giving me an intense gaze, still insisting I take the bracelet back.

I couldn't believe what she was implying, as if what we had shared and felt meant nothing to me, that I was lying to her. That I had a box of made-in-China bracelets in the van, which I was handing out from Barretos to Patagonia.

"The bracelet is a present, and I will not take it back. Thank you for looking after my dog. Goodbye, Clara." I stormed out the door without looking back.

I announced to Toti it was time to go, and picked up Perrito Moreno or Puma or Butch Cassidy or whatever his name was going to be, said goodbye to Azul and trotted toward the van. Toti started it up. With the little dog in my lap and staring straight ahead, I murmured, "Never again."

We had fixed the van's broken window in Bariloche before returning. Now, it was my heart that needed mending again.

MEET BUTCH CASSIDY

On our drive back to Cholila, Toti and I chose the name for our smelly little dog. Since we were staying on the same property where Butch Cassidy had lived, it was the obvious choice.

"Butch Cassidy will live to see the end of the world!" I said, holding him up as if he were Simba and I, Rafiki.

After a week's rest at Don Peppe's, Sapito and Picasso were fat and fresh. It took us more than an hour to catch them in the pasture we had turned them out in. We were only able to do so using grain and a large rope we tied in one of the corners.

We said an emotional goodbye to Don Peppe on a beautiful Patagonian morning. The air crisp and the sky various shades of pink, purple, and red, we began our trek into Los Alerces National Park.

In only a few days, I would celebrate my eleventh month on the long road south. As I rode past the small picturesque town of Cholila and into the national park, I thought about all of the people I had met on this adventure, the places seen, the experiences lived. Riding down a wide gravel road flanked by thick forest on both sides, a smile grew on my face as a gorgeous rainbow appeared right in front of us. Arching my neck back to take in its colorful arch, only the sound of the saddle creaking and the crunching of the horses' hooves hitting the gravel beneath accompanied us. I simply gave thanks.

On our first week of having a dog, we crossed a patch of land where dogs were not allowed to enter. As soon as I entered the National Park, a large yellow sign with the silhouette of a dog inside a black circle with a line running through it made me shrink in the saddle.

"Did you know dogs couldn't enter the park?" I asked Toti when he stopped next to me with the van.

"I had no idea. Never heard of this in my life," he replied, lighting a cigarette.

With no other option, Butch would have to stay clandestine during our ride through Los Alerces. Luckily, he needed the rest because of his broken leg. We placed the silent dog under the passenger seat of the van. As far as we knew, Butch didn't have vocal cords. He had yet to let out any sort of bark.

The gravel road we followed south had large stones everywhere, and I was glad to have followed Jason's advice with the leather pads. They seemed to be making the horses' lives a lot easier! Both were walking with confidence over the rocks and stones without missing a beat.

That evening, while we camped next to Lake Rivadavia, a white park ranger vehicle stopped behind us. Toti and I were in the back of the van, hiding from the rain. It had started in the afternoon, so we'd taken shelter to warm up a can of chicken soup.

Worried, I asked Toti, "Do you think they saw Butch?"

"Hello, gentlemen, how are you?" the park ranger asked as he removed his flat-rimmed green hat to expose his balding head. He was a tall, skinny man in his late forties.

"We are fine sir, warming up from this cold rain. How are you?" Toti shook the man's hand.

"The temperature certainly did drop quickly. It's the norm around here in the park due to the cordillera. Can I please see your horses' papers?" he ordered, eyeing the inside of the van with interest.

I flashed a worried look toward Toti. I had their *libretas* (health papers) but hadn't been keeping up with the exams. By law, horses being transported in Argentina must get their blood tested for anemia every three months. Because I was walking the horses, I had been told I didn't need to follow this rule.

"Since you are riding, no one will ask you to see the *libretas*," several gauchos had assured me. Now, I was screwed.

I fished the *libretas* from the front of the van, asking Butch to please stay put under the seat. Luckily, he didn't move or bark. Praying somehow everything would be okay, I returned to the back of the van. I didn't know how much trouble we were about to get in, but I knew it wasn't going to be good. I was already imagining having to return to Don Peppe's ranch and staying put for another week or two until we took their blood, sent it to a lab in Buenos Aires, and waited for the results to return. That was the best-case scenario. The worst possibility was a hefty fine and the horses being taken from me, perhaps even put down.

Swallowing hard, I passed the blue booklets to the park ranger, who was now standing in the van chatting to Toti. He leafed through Picasso's papers first, looking at the photo of the horse on the second page (taken at El Cardal days prior to my departure). Then he looked at the vaccines page, leafed through the rest of the booklet, and moved on to Sapito's.

Toti and I shared a short look with a smirk on our faces. It very quickly dawned on us that this guy had no idea what he was looking for. After a few more seconds looking over Sapito's booklet, he handed both back to me. "Thank you, gentlemen."

"No problem, sir," I said, letting out a sigh of relief and rushing the books back to the front of the van before he changed his mind.

The next morning, when I went to brush my teeth on the shores of the stunning Lake Rivadavia, I found the three colossal mountain peaks that surrounded the sparkling water were covered with bright white snow. It was as if someone had sprinkled confectioner's sugar on the dark gray rocks overnight. Low, heavy clouds drifted over the tip of the mountains to reveal occasional glimpses of blowing snow. It was a magnificent moment that left me worried about how early the snow had arrived in southern Argentina. Unable to do anything about it, I brushed my teeth using the freezing water and enjoyed the view fit for a *Planet Earth* documentary.

That day, I almost froze as I rode under heavy freezing rain. The truth was I was not ready for this cold this early. My cowboy boots quickly filled with the cold water, and my fingers went numb through my drenched, dark yellow leather work gloves. My toes and fingers burned as if they were on fire. Freezing water dripped down my back toward my ass. My face felt like someone was slicing it with a sharp knife. I was in pain, already broken. I knew that this was only the beginning. If I was to make it to Tierra Del Fuego, I would have to get used to this suffering because it would soon become the norm.

At lunchtime, I switched socks and boots and warmed my hands next to our little cooking oven. Eating a warm bowl of pumpkin soup, my spirit lifted. We followed the gravel road all the way through the stunningly wild park. Mountains and lakes appeared at every turn, 1000-year-old Alerce trees all around, until we finally reached the pavement again.

With the cordillera's white peaks glowing behind me, I made my way out of Los Alerces wishing Clara could have seen its majesty with me. It was by far one of the most beautiful places I had ridden through since leaving Calgary, and it reminded me a lot of Glacier National Park in Montana. Yet even immersed in this natural beauty, I could not stop thinking about the girl from El Bolsón. Clara had stolen my heart.

We arrived in the picturesque town of Trevelin in the late afternoon and had a hard time finding a place to rest the horses. In the north of Argentina and all of the other Latin American countries that I crossed, when I arrived on the outskirts of a new town or city, someone always stopped me to offer a place to stay, food, a barbecue, and alfalfa for my horses.

In some places, grown men would fight to see who got to host me. In a small Mexican town, for example, I was put in a super awkward position when two groups of horsemen, who hated one another, made me decide who would host the horses and me. I didn't know what to do. At that moment, I felt like the child of divorced parents, having to pick who I would live with. In the end, I expressed to both groups that

I was tired, hungry, and didn't have the time nor the energy for this childish game. I agreed to stay for two days, one day at Mom's house and one day at Dad's house. In the end, everyone was happy.

In Southern Patagonia, this kind of problem was nonexistent. Toti and I spent two hours trying to find a place to rest the horses in Trevelin. When we finally got hold of the fellow who ran the rodeo grounds, he came, opened the gate for us, and left. No barbecue, wine, mate, or chat was offered. From our combined experiences traveling on horseback, Toti and I came up with a theory that people seem to emulate the climate they live in. We started to understand that people weren't rude or mean. They were simply more introverted. Colder.

"When I crossed the northern part of Argentina on my Long Ride, the people were as warm as the days," Toti told me while we downed a box of *Vino Toro* and cooked chicken on our small grill. I had to agree. In Mexico and Central America, the people I met wanted to offer me the shirts off of their backs. In the northern United States and Patagonia, although people were helpful, they lacked warmth.

Toti and I explored the small town and learned of its rich history. At the local museum, we learned about how Welsh settlers arrived in that sweeping valley in the eighteen hundreds. They wanted to start a colony of Welsh citizens outside of England where they had been treated as second-class for many generations.

The museum was built in an old mill and told a lovely story of how the settlers, unlike many of the colonizers who arrived in the new world, had a positive relationship with the native people in this area. They helped one another and lived in complete peace. This was nearly unheard of in other parts of the Americas where the colonizers used the natives to survive the first few months only to carry out some of the worst genocides in modern history.

In other parts of Patagonia, for instance, General Roca, who in 1880 became president of the country, paid one pound sterling for those who brought him the ears of native people they had killed.

After the museum, we drove to the grave where a special horse, Malacara, is buried. In 1883, John Daniel Evans, a Welsh explorer, rode out of Trevelin with a group of men from the community to discover new fertile lands in the cordillera for harvesting crops.

A year later, on March 4, 1884, Evans and his crew ran into a native tribe who thought the Welsh men were spies for the Argentinian military. The tribe killed all of the explorers but Evans and three of his friends. They tried to escape, but eventually, only Evans was left alive. With the natives about to catch and kill him as well, he arrived at a precipice over a high canyon. The length of the gap was six meters, impossible to make on horseback. With the natives closing in, Evans was left with no choice. He kicked his steed on and jumped the canyon clean. Malacara not only made the impossible jump, he galloped all the way back to Trevelin, saving Evan's life. It was surreal to stand over the tomb of this great horse and imagine this insane feat.

While resting for two days in Trevelin, still brokenhearted from my final exchange with Clara, I checked my messages to see if she had said anything. While crossing Los Alerces, I spent a lot of time thinking about her, but with no cell phone connection or internet, thinking is all I could do.

As soon as I got a signal, I opened my text messages and found nothing. I checked my Facebook inbox. Nada. She really did hate me. I fought the urge to message her with all of my might and decided it was over.

My flor del pago didn't want anything to do with me, I thought to myself as I fell asleep.

Moping and feeling way too bad for myself, I worked on blogs and filmed interviews on our second day of rest. The ponies happily munched in a field of tall clovers. After lunch, much to my surprise, my phone lit up with a new message from Clara. My heart stopped, only to kick into an energy-drink induced frantic rhythm seconds after.

Do I read it now? No, no, I should wait. What does she want from me?

Holding the phone with both hands, staring at the black unlit screen, my reflection stared back at me. My palms became clammy with sweat. After about a minute, I decided to read her message:

Hey Filipe, how are you guys? I sent you a few texts this week and you never responded. I guess you're mad at me, rightfully so. I really want to talk to you, I feel really bad about what happened :(

. . .

I read the message over and over again, trying to take in her meaning, but it was as if it was written in another language. My mind was blank, so I called her. We spoke for two hours. Clara apologized for being so stubborn and hardheaded, but she was afraid I would break her heart.

"I knew I was falling for you, and it made me feel so stupid. I didn't want to be left brokenhearted again," she told me, her voice cracking. Clara had just escaped a terrible relationship and did not want a repetition of that drama.

"I really, truly like you, Clara. I know this isn't the best-case scenario, me being a Brazilian cowboy who crosses continents on horseback, you living in Argentina. But we have something special here, and I don't want to lose it."

We decided to take things slow. We would continue to chat over the internet and by phone as much as possible to get to know one another with the promise she would join me on the road for a week or two farther south.

I was ecstatic. I was falling in love with Patagonia. I was falling in love *in* Patagonia.

CAMINO DE LAS MULAS

The road from Trevelin to Río Pico was a long, lonely desert. We got off Highway 40 and rode on an old gravel route called *Camino de las mulas* (The way of the mules).

Along the way, I met two gauchos riding with about twenty dogs each, following close by. At first, I didn't understand why they needed so many canines. My first instinct was that they were out hunting. After asking a local rancher, he explained that because the ranches were full of large bushes and low trees, the dogs were needed to get the cattle out. It was impossible to see and find the critters otherwise.

The road took us across the Andes cordillera in one of the scariest mountain passes we had crossed on the journey. It was a fifteen kilometer climb that snaked up a massive mountain. Toti, who drove it first in the old van, told me he nearly didn't make it. With my super Criollos, I never had a problem. It took us about four hours to climb the rugged mountain. Slowly, but surely, we made it up.

On the large plateau, Toti and I ran into a character fit for a novel. Julio was as thick and tall as a centennial tree trunk. Beneath bright green eyes, he had a long handlebar mustache that looked like it was cut using a dull cleaver. The faded tattoos on his arms, containing simple, crooked lines, looked like they'd been drawn in prison. During the summers, he lived in a small shack on the mountain caring for about 800 head of cattle. Julio had seven loud dogs tied to nearby trees.

"Here, have a sip of wine, my friend," the big man said, passing me a box of *Toro* red wine even before I stepped down from the saddle. Julio not only made us drink way too much wine, he offered us a delicious barbecue. The gaucho had a love for singing improvised ranch songs and wouldn't stop all night. He sang about his horses, cattle, fishing, women, our arrival — he sang about everything. Or rather, he yelled about everything.

"I should have been a famous singer, but missing teeth make it hard to pronounce certain words," our host said, running his tongue through the few black and yellow teeth left in his mouth.

At one point, he instructed Toti to grab a new bottle of wine he had stashed in the middle of the river that ran behind his one-room shack. Sure enough, in five minutes, Toti returned with the wet bottle.

"I thought he was joking, but it was under a rock in the middle of the river just like he told me," Toti said as we both laughed at the ridiculousness of the situation.

Suddenly, Julio announced it was time for an arm wrestling competition. He obviously came out the champion, easily beating Toti and me.

"The champ is here!" he yelled out, arms raised in the air, head tilted back in glory.

Heads throbbing, we left the next morning before Julio awoke. I'm not sure if my head hurt from the wine or from Julio's singing or both.

The temperature began to drop drastically on this stretch of the journey. Not only were we at a very high elevation, but winter crept ever closer. The night after Julio's concert, Toti and I camped on the side of the gravel road near a small stream. The next morning when we awoke, everything was white with frost including the horses' manes. A thin layer of ice covered the stream's flowing water. We fought to warm up. It was a painful breakfast.

During this stretch, we removed the little cast from Butch's broken leg. It was starting to smell like a dead body, and the little dog spent hours biting at it. We worried it would become infected. He'd worn it for a month already, so we felt it was time to cut it off.

Butch looked immediately relieved to lose the cast and began to walk a lot better. Every third or fourth stride he would toss up his rear end in a funny little hop that made us laugh. Having spent more than a month with us already, he was becoming a different dog. He was more trusting of Toti and me and had lost his depressed look. One thing he never got over was his fear of feet. Any time our feet went anywhere near Butch, he would cower or run off scared. "Poor little guy must have been kicked all the time," I told Toti.

After a long week in the saddle, we arrived at a stunning ranch deep in a vast green valley. Tres Valles was a cattle ranch and fishing lodge for tourists. Fat Red Angus cows grazed in the tall grass while Sapo, Picasso, and I rode down the long driveway toward the main home.

Guille Etchebarne, a slim, pretty blonde, welcomed me with a strong hug. "My husband will be here soon, but you guys make your-selves at home. We have prepared the lodge next door for you two to rest. You can stay as long as you need."

With the leather pads under their feet, I worried about a fungus growing in their frogs due to the dark and dank environment it created. After removing their shoes, we turned the horses out in a beautiful pasture. Once the ponies were fed and happy, we carried our things to the lodge.

We were in heaven. The cozy home had a fireplace, four bedrooms, and a spacious living room with a gorgeous view of the ranch. Most importantly, it had a shower with warm water. After taking a three-hour shower, Toti and I went outside to drink mate with Guille and eat some *torta fritas*. At this stage of the journey, I was addicted to both. Maybe I was slowly becoming a true Argentinian.

While we sat on the front lawn, her husband Simon arrived with their five children. I had met a lot of families since leaving Barretos, but I must say, Simon and Guille and their kids stole my heart. If there was ever a perfect family, they would take the prize.

The kids were absolutely adorable, extremely polite little gauchos. Wearing berets, *bombachas,* and *alpargatas*, they grew up riding horses and working cattle and sheep.

While we rested at the ranch, we had the opportunity to help the kids cut the tails off of their sheep. Every year they did this to the young animals to keep the wool clean when they defecate. Because they have so much wool in their rears, the tail can trap the stool and create a terrible infection.

"The kids run the sheep operation, and I simply give them a hand," Simon, a light-skinned gaucho with silver Elvis-like sideburns, told me proudly.

After wrestling with about thirty head of sheep, castrating some, vaccinating all, and cutting their tails, the kids placed the cut tails on top of a small fire. After a few minutes, they pulled the burned wool off and proceeded to eat the meat. They sucked on the thin white bone after eating all of the meat as if it was licorice.

"I love this so much," the youngest girl said with a big smile, showing three missing teeth, her reading glasses sliding down to the tip of her button nose. I melted inside.

On our final day at the ranch, Simon made a delicious barbecue for us in the middle of the woods. We ate, drank beer, played with the kids, and shared stories. With a light wind blowing and our bellies full, it was the greatest afternoon I'd had in a long time. Being around that beautiful family made me yearn deeply to begin building my own. That recurring thought had become the theme of my ride.

The next morning, rested and happy, we nailed the shoes back on the horse's feet (including the leather pads) and began our trek south to Río Senguer along a small dirt road. It was a desolate and complicated ride that took us into Chile for a few kilometers before turning back into Argentina. We camped almost every night in the middle of nowhere, except for one night where we arrived at a police station. The cops offered us mate, food, and a corral for our ponies. They seemed to be extremely bored in the middle of those mountains guarding the border from I didn't know what. I was not sure they knew either.

On our third day out, we came to a fork in the road and had no idea which way to go. I chose the wrong path and rode four kilometers in the wrong direction. We spent half an hour trying to figure out on which side of the cordillera we should be. Having to ride the extra hour back toward the fork was terrible, but at least we discovered the mistake before I had ridden any farther.

～

In Alto Río Senguer, I arrived exactly one year after leaving Barretos to a wonderful surprise. It was in this small town that Mancha and Gato, the horses I grew up reading about, were born. The Criollos that traveled from Argentina to New York in 1925, and shared the same origins as Sapito Gonzales and Pablo Picasso, were foaled in a ranch near the town.

The mayor of the one-road town, a quirky fifty-something historian, took us to see the statue that was built to honor the two horses and gave us a history lesson.

"In the early 1900s, Emilio Solanet traveled to this region of Patagonia in search of horses with the bloodlines of the animals brought from Spain to Argentina by Pedro de Mendoza in 1535. After losing his battle with the Indians, Mendoza returned to Spain with his soldiers, but they left forty-four horses behind," the mayor told us.

He went on to explain how in the first half of the following century, there were believed to be 10,000 equines in the Pampas. Sixty years later, that number grew to millions. According to the mayor, the horses adapted to the land and traveled as far as Patagonia. The natives fell in love with the wild beasts, eventually learning to tame and ride them.

"Solanet, on three different trips to Patagonia from 1911 to 1919, handpicked and purchased eighty-four mares and studs from the local natives and took them back to *El Cardal*. The arduous journey on foot and by train took six weeks." Mancha and Gato were said to have been in that original herd!

After our history class, he explained how every year the town hosted the Mancha and Gato Festival at the beginning of January and that the people there were extremely proud of the horses.

"These two Criollos put Alto Río Senguer on the map," he said, pointing at the statues with pride.

After all of the surprises this journey had awarded me, I couldn't believe I was in the birthplace of Mancha and Gato while celebrating one year on the road. Another gift from the Universe.

However, when the time came to leave, my good fortune also came to an end. I woke up at 7:30 a.m., ate breakfast (crackers with jam washed down by a strong cup of instant coffee), and began tacking Picasso. After resting for a day in Río Senguer, it was time to continue our ride. Once Picasso was ready to go, I jumped into the saddle and made my way toward the statue of Mancha and Gato to snap a photo.

As I neared the statue, I knew something was wrong with Picasso. He was walking strangely, lame on his back end. I immediately got off the tall pony and inspected his back legs. There were no cuts or scrapes, nothing lodged in his hoof, but when I walked him around, it was obvious he was sore.

With no other option, I walked the horses back to the rodeo grounds and began feeling his back legs to identify the injury. After feeling for heat in his hooves and legs, Toti and I concluded the pain came from his hindquarters. It was a muscular pain, and there was no way of knowing how long it would take for him to recuperate.

We called a local vet and he concurred. He advised us to give Picasso four days of anti-inflammatory injections and a week off. Spending a week in the town of 1,500 people didn't sound very enticing, especially with all of the kilometers we had left to ride — 1,688 kilometers to be exact. Winter was fast approaching. Still, there was nothing to do but be patient and wait.

Sleeping in the van parked on the rodeo grounds, we spent the long week trying to find things to do. What made it even harder was the fact that although we were in the birthplace of Mancha and Gato, no one seemed to care about us being there. One family invited us for dinner one night and that was it. No one offered us a warm bed, a shower, or an afternoon of mate. Often, a car would drive onto the rodeo grounds, stop, take photos of the horses, and leave without saying a word to us. It was a hard few days. To make matters worse, in the middle of the week, it started pouring rain and it never stopped. We were left frozen and spending the majority of the days sitting in the van watching the raindrops hit the windshield, trying to stay dry and sane.

The week in Río Senguer did give me a chance to talk to Clara regularly and even organize her trip to meet us. She would come down with one of Toti's friends who was driving to Patagonia from Buenos Aires. They would meet us in the small town of Río Mayo in a week. I couldn't wait to see her again.

After seven days, Picasso was 100 percent recuperated and ready to head south under heavy rain. The road to Río Mayo, the last city we would cross in the province of Chubut, was a muddy mess. I rode through puddles that were rivers, my feet just inches from the water beneath my stirrups. At some points, I wondered if Toti would make it through with the support van.

"Man, we almost got stuck in that last one," he said to me during lunch as we ate warm pumpkin soup. The rain, mixed with the cold temperatures, made the week hell. Every night we tied the horses to the fence line and slept in the van. We never saw another car or human during this leg of the journey. We did ride through a small village called Pastos Blancos, but very early in the morning, so we were met by closed doors and lowered blinds. No smoke rose from any of the chimneys.

When I rode into Río Mayo, I was tired, sore, frozen, dirty — the usual, a mess. Luckily, we were welcomed by a radio host who arranged for the horses to rest at the local police station. He also secured two beds in the town's gym for Toti and me. The gym had several beds in case of a town emergency. Due to the recent rains, several families had been evacuated from their homes. Many were with relatives, but one elderly gentleman was also calling the gymnasium home.

"We have never seen rains like this," the lady who opened the gym for us said. "The city is one step away from announcing a state of emergency. Heavy rains and mudslides had ruined 80 percent of the city of Comodoro Rivadavia (the capital of Chubut). It was a catastrophe."

Because Toti and I had spent the last several days in the middle of the desert, we had no idea the rains had caused so much damage. We worried about what would happen to our plans if it continued raining. We had already heard that many roads in the region had collapsed. Others were flooded.

With the love of my life about to arrive, I had no time to think about collapsed roads right then. I needed to contain my nerves. Pacing outside the gymnasium, unable to sit still with the news that Toti's friend Lúcio was about to arrive any minute with Clara, I tried to keep calm. I hadn't seen Clara in weeks. The last time we saw each other, it had not ended well.

Trying to ease the butterflies in my stomach, I thought about how to say hello to her. Should I kiss her on the lips? Kiss her on the cheek? Just hug her? I had no answers. I was too excited and too scared to think. Luckily, Lúcio's black Amarok truck pulled into the parking lot before my heart exploded out of my chest.

"Thank you so much for coming," I said to Clara as we hugged tightly.

"Thank you for inviting me," she replied as we continued to hold one another, neither wanting to let go. We didn't kiss right then, but at the first opportunity I got to be alone with her, I pounced on her lips. It was better than warm blueberry pancakes with homemade maple syrup and vanilla ice cream. Heavenly.

That night, we used the large grill at the back end of the gym to make an *asado*. Holding up his glass of Fernet with Coke, Toti announced, "We need to celebrate the arrival of Clarita Davel and Lúcio and his dog Moro!"

We all cheered as Moro, a big boxer, and Butch smelled each other nearby. The truth was, the past few weeks were hard on our minds, bodies, and souls. We'd faced freezing temperatures, torrential rain, terrible road conditions, the Andes over and over again, and Picasso's injury. Having Lúcio and Clara with us seemed to give us new life and take our minds off the journey for at least a few hours. After eating, Clara and I retired to our room and left Lúcio and Toti drinking.

"I've been dreaming about this moment," I told Clara as we lay on the single bed, legs interlaced, noses touching, eyes locked. I kissed her lips softly before biting her bottom lip gently.

Afterward, we lay in each other's arms, hearts beating against one another, out of breath, sweating, kissing, and staring into each other's eyes.

I almost couldn't believe what had just happened, how magical it felt, how in tune our bodies were. I wanted to stay in that bed with Clara in my arms for the rest of my days. I wanted to marry her. Have children with her. Make her happy. Grow old next to her. I had fallen deeper in love than I ever imagined I would.

Hard, wet snow slashed me in the face like tiny razor blades. My toes were cramped and numb inside my cowboy boots. My fingers ached in my drenched, icy gloves. All I could feel was pain. I closed my eyes and focused on the rhythm of Sapo and Picasso's hooves hitting the slick pavement.

One year and two weeks after leaving Barretos, Brazil, I found myself in the middle of the Patagonian desert, 6,000 kilometers from my starting point and in the middle of a terrible snowstorm. I allowed the memories of the past 379 days to transport me far away from my suffering. I tried to concentrate on the adventures lived, the friends made, the lessons learned, and the inspiration for making this journey: the Barretos Children's Cancer Hospital.

I let the image of the children I met at the hospital take over my thoughts. Their powerful smiles. Their suffering. Their fight. Many had lost all of their hair, some their limbs, but none lost their hope that they would beat this monster, that they would survive.

I don't cry at the needles anymore because my mom told me they will turn me into a superhero.

I remembered my conversation with little Arthur prior to departing from Barretos. His remarkable strength and warm smile carried me for the rest of the day as I pushed the suffering aside and continued on.

By late afternoon, I arrived in the small Argentinian town of Perito Moreno, Santa Cruz. I was frozen like Lake Louise in February. The strong Patagonian winds, the recent rain, snow, and freezing temperatures had taken their toll. My frustration worsened when Toti announced that the van was making a strange noise.

"I talked to a mechanic, and he said we may be stuck here for a few days. They don't have the parts we need."

I felt defeated. We had already lost one week in Alto Río Senguer. This set us back terribly on our race to beat the harsh Patagonian winter. Luckily, I had Clara by my side. She had spent the week traveling with us, some days riding Sapito while I rode Picasso and others in the support van with Toti. Lúcio and Moro had returned to Buenos Aires.

"Everything is going to be okay. You'll see," she comforted me while we tried to warm up in a gas station drinking warm coffee.

We were forced to wait four days in Perito Moreno. Every day we went to the mechanic to find that the part we needed had yet to arrive. It was coming from Comodoro Rivadavia, which was still in total chaos from the devastating rains. It was frustrating.

One day, while I wrote blogs in a gas station that had free Wi-Fi, a Brazilian couple walked up and asked if I, too, was Brazilian. They had heard me on the phone with my parents. When I told them I was, they burst out laughing.

"A few days ago we saw a horseman on the side of the road while we drove into town and we were like, 'Wow, look at that native from Patagonia riding in this snow,'" the husband said. "We never imagined it would be someone from our country. You're crazy, brother!"

They were traveling the Americas in a white Volkswagen hippie van. We ended up chatting all afternoon, sharing stories from the road. As it turned out, they were from Ribeirão Preto, only one hour from Barretos. Small world!

By the time our van was repaired, my patience had been tested and my wallet drained. To top it off, Butch Cassidy had disappeared. Every time we got to a new town, the ex-street dog would wander off for a few minutes or hours but had always returned. This time, he never did. We searched and searched for the little white ball of fur, but he was gone. I was heartbroken.

With one less member to the team and a lot less money, we started out again. We headed south into the most arduous part of the journey: 900 kilometers of nothing but desert and wind, toward Río Gallegos, the capital of Santa Cruz. Luckily, I had Toti and Clara by my side to begin this difficult stretch. As we trekked over the pink and red hills (created by minerals) toward the village of Bajo Caracoles, Clara thanked me repeatedly.

"I love horses so much, but it's been a long time since I last rode," my muse said from atop Sapito's back while I rode next to her on Picasso. "Their smell, beauty, friendship. They make me so happy."

The raw beauty we encountered in this part of Patagonia was intense. The sky was lit on fire with every sunrise and sunset. Shades of neon blue, purple, and pink danced alongside dark yellow and deep red clouds. Every day, we rode by hundreds of *guanacos* (a camelid native to South America) and wild ostriches grazing peacefully.

In Bajo Caracoles, we were welcomed into a town that seemed like it belonged in a model train world. Literally built in the middle of the desert, fifteen people lived here. Their homes sat in a perfect tiny grid in front of a large hill beside Highway 40. There was a hotel with a gas pump in front as well as a police officer. A campground had a hand-painted sign that read: *Campin Gratis*.

They had misspelled *camping*, but the second word meant free, so I wasn't complaining!

We stayed in the campground with two Argentinians from the North who had recently quit their bike journey south due to the unforgiving winds. When we arrived, they were taking the bikes apart and placing them in large cardboard boxes. We also met two Brazilians who were riding their badass Harley Davidson motorcycles to Ushuaia and shared stories over a cheap bottle of whiskey and a cup of noodles. We all agreed that without adventure, life was not worth living. It was like a mini-adventurer summit in the middle of the desert.

Toti, who was battling a terrible cold, went to try his luck with the local nurse. The obese man served as a doctor of sorts for the small community. When the gaucho told the man his symptoms, he offered the only medication he had, a tube of nasal spray.

"Put your head back, place the opening in your nostril and squeeze the tube," the nurse gave Toti the instructions slowly, pronouncing each word carefully, with a break in between each as if he were deaf and needed to read the man's lips. Toti grabbed the tube and followed the directions just as dictated. But when he went to squeeze the tube, it came undone, and the entire thing (it was about half full) went up his nose.

"Oh, my God!" the Argentinian finally spoke after coughing for about five minutes straight.

For the next hour, Toti was climbing the walls. He couldn't breathe properly. He said his brain felt like it was itchy. His ears rang.

"I think I might die!" he told Clara and me. We laughed while he paced nonstop. It was as if he had snorted cocaine.

In Cueva de las Manos, just seventy kilometers north of Bajo Caracoles, we traveled back in time more than 9,000 years by taking in the cave paintings from the first Patagonian nomads. The cave system, which lay in the valley of the Pinturas River, was alive with artwork from about 7,300 BC. It got its name from the many paintings of hands stenciled on the rock walls. Archeologists say early hunters and artists used mineral pigments from the area mixed with water to create not only the hand stencils, but also illustrations of animals and hunting techniques.

Instead of painting the palms of their hands and placing them on the rock face, they would put the paint into their mouth, place their hand on the cave wall, and proceed to blow the liquid, creating a perfect stencil of their hands.

Visiting Cueva de las Manos once again made me question our existence as much as seeing the dinosaur tracks in northern Patagonia had. This land was truly magical, full of history, mystery, raw beauty, and suffering. It was like no other stretch of land I had ever crossed.

After traveling nearly 300 kilometers with Clara, it was time to say goodbye. I drove her back to Perito Moreno, where I needed to pick up more memory cards for my camera and take the van to the mechanic — again. The front left wheel bearing was now making a terrible racket, as if a screw was loose or a metal piece had fallen off. It was a horrible metal-grinding-on-metal sound that made us cringe, like nails on a chalkboard.

I left Toti with the horses at a cattle ranch, the first we had come across since leaving Perrito Moreno, and promised to return as soon as possible. I felt bad leaving him behind in the middle of that desert, but it was the only way. Toti had to take one for the team. As soon as we arrived back in Perito Moreno, I took the van to the mechanic.

He laughed when he saw me. "Back already? What happened? Miss us?"

He took the wheel off and got to work. In the afternoon, he announced it would take two days for the part to arrive so I took the van back and found a place for Clara and me to sleep. The next day, while I worked on a new article for the *Toronto Star*, Clara got to work on finding Butch.

"Before we left, I posted about Butch in a Facebook group for lost dogs in Perrito Moreno. A woman said she saw him yesterday in a neighborhood ten minutes from here."

Clara charged off on her rescue mission, but I never expected she would find him. I mean, what were the chances? He had gone missing a few days before we left the small town. Since then, a full week had passed. To top it off, Patagonia was plagued with little street dogs that looked just like Butch. Two hours passed and no sign of Clara.

Then, while I wrote away, I heard her yell in triumph, holding Butch up in the air while she ran toward my table. I couldn't believe it. I stared at them with my jaw on the floor. In a kind of a miracle, she'd found Butch Cassidy wandering the streets.

Taking the little dog in my arms, I asked, "Where did you go, Butch? We missed you!" He stared up at me with his yellow eyes. Clara had parked the van in the neighborhood where the woman said she had seen him and began searching. She asked a few kids playing on the street if they had seen him, using a photo of Butch on her phone. To her surprise, they said they had. Sure enough, a few minutes later, after turning down another street, she spotted the little dog walking on the side of the road.

He smelled terrible and looked worse. Dirt covered his body and leaves dangled from his fur along with small twigs. Under his tail, dried shit hung from his fur in several different spots.

"He must have had diarrhea from something he ate, poor little guy," Clara said, petting him. "All kinds of vermin around here could kill you."

We took him back to the small cabin we'd rented and gave him a bath. Once he was clean again, we gave him a bowl of food and water, but he didn't want anything. He had the same depressed look as when I'd found him the first time.

The next day, the part finally arrived for the van. Before it was replaced, I dropped Clara off at the bus station.

"I'm going to miss you so much, but I'll see you in Ushuaia. Please be safe out there," Clara said, hugging me tightly before boarding her bus.

I smiled broadly. After one year on the road, the Universe had given me the greatest gift a lonely Long Rider could ever ask for: someone to miss.

SOUTHERN PATAGONIA

"For a second I thought you had left me with the horses and made a run for the Brazilian border with Clara," Toti said when I finally made it back. After telling him about the saga at the mechanic, I told him to open the front door of the van.

"What?! No! I can't believe it!" he said as he grabbed Butch and gave the little dog a hug. I guess he liked little dogs, after all.

That night, we organized the van while I told Toti about how Clara had found Butch. He explained how he helped the owner of the ranch fix some fence posts, organized the small cabin he was sleeping in, and tended the fire so it wouldn't die. We drank a six-pack of beer before crashing.

The following morning, we thanked the family for hosting Toti and the horses for so many days. Continuing south, I suffered in the saddle once again. Powerful 120-kmph winds blew for days at a time. Below-zero weather froze us through the desert nights. I rode for ten days straight without showering. I fought my way south swaddled in long johns, jeans, knee-high rubber boots, T-shirt, a button-up shirt, a hoodie, a windbreaker, a thick outback jacket, scarf, tuque, face mask, and gloves topped by a black plastic rain poncho with a hood. Only my eyes, covered by black sunglasses, were exposed to the elements.

I looked like a homemade superhero who fought against the wind. And I was definitely losing! Some days, the wind was so strong I was forced to lean forward and hug my horse's neck. The wind made Sapo and Picasso stumble with every third stride. Even Toti suffered through the cold, stark terrain. The van didn't have heat. When we woke up in the mornings, a thick layer of frost covered the ceiling. We nicknamed it "the fridge."

Every night, Toti would sleep in the back of the van, and I would make my bed in the front seats with Butch under me. Some nights, it was so cold we went to sleep unable to feel our feet.

"Can you feel your feet, brother?" I would yell back to Toti.

"No, can't feel them," he shot back.

"Perfect."

Through this region of Patagonia, we rode by hundreds of kilometers of empty pastures. No cattle. No sheep. No horses. In many parts, the fences lay on the ground.

The only thing that inhabited this raw desert was the *guanaco*. When they felt in danger, they would make a high-pitched bleating sound. While watching me ride by, they held their heads high like their cousin, the llama.

Thousands of *guanacos* had run free through this land. Some were still alive, caught on the top wire of the fence they tried to jump, waiting to die. Others had died long ago, their carcasses decaying under the midday sun.

Every night we were forced to tie the horses to the fence posts that were still standing and sleep next to the road. There were no ranches or people to take us in. It was an incredibly lonely and challenging stretch. We relied heavily on "the fridge" during this portion of the journey. Without the water and feed it carried, the horses would have suffered immensely to cross this southern part of Santa Cruz.

With no cell phone signal or internet, we depended on a small, rectangular black, battery-operated radio Toti had purchased in Perito Moreno for entertainment (the van's radio did not work, and we only had one CD: *Best of Bruno e Barreto*).

During lunch and dinner, Toti would first light a smoke, take a deep drag, then pull out the radio's tall, silver antenna before fiddling with the round dial in search of our favorite radio station. As he surfed the different stations — Argentinian country music going to announcers with deep voices talking politics then back to music again — he would slowly blow the smoke out of his nose and mouth until he finally found *the* station. It was a signal that came from Río Gallegos. Three times every day, it offered messages to the few ranches that still existed in the area. It was the only way to communicate with the workers.

"What messages do we have today?" Toti would ask excitedly, rubbing his hands together. Most days, the same messages would repeat all three times. Often, they were the same for two or three days. But it didn't matter, every time they came on, we went silent and listened carefully.

"For *Estancia la Quebrada*, close the horses in the corral tonight because tomorrow Don Rodrigo will arrive at 10 a.m. to check the cattle" was typical of the many messages we heard on this station. They were usually about work. Dropping off materials. Picking up a worker to bring to town.

Every once in a while, we got a gem. "For *Estancia La Laguna*, Mom and Dad, I got the exams back from the doctors and I am okay."

That was by far our favorite message we'd heard, it made Toti and me die of laughter. We created our own versions during the next few days: "For *Estancia El Toteiro*, I got the exams back from the doctor, and my STD is cured."

"For *Estancia El Cavaleiro das Americas*, the DNA test came back, and Carlitos is not your son."

Who needed Netflix?

One hundred kilometers south of the small town of Gobernador Gregores, we were rescued from this never-ending desert by a ranch called *Estancia la Verde*. The main house was surrounded by tall *alamos* (poplars), used in this region as a natural barrier against the unforgiving winds. Growing twenty to thirty meters high, these towering green trees signified that there was life up ahead.

Where there's alamos, there's people! I thought to myself atop the saddle every time I spotted the treetops waving in the wind. It was as if they were waving me in.

Another clear sign there were people up ahead was a thin line of chimney smoke climbing the sky. We rode by so many torn-down ranches and homes, the only way to truly know if someone lived there was to look up at the chimney. If there was smoke, there was life within those walls.

Much to our delight, La Verde had both *alamos* and a chimney spewing smoke! We had passed many empty ranches so the thought of being with a real family lifted our spirits.

The afternoon we arrived, Jorge Villalba, the ranch manager, invited us to a lamb barbecue. With kind eyes, dark skin, and black hair, he had the same bowl haircut as Bolivia's ousted president, Evo Morales. Sitting down for dinner with this gracious gaucho and his lovely family (his wife and two cute little girls), he explained why we were crossing hundreds of kilometers of ranch land without seeing a single family in the homes or animals in the fields.

"These lands are plagued by government-protected guanacos. The animals overgraze the pastures, eating the same amount of grass as four sheep," Jorge told us. "The winters are hard. The volcano erupted a few years back, covering everything with a thick layer of ash and killing thousands of sheep. Finding people to work is nearly impossible. Most families picked up and left because it's simply too difficult to ranch in Santa Cruz."

One of the most important parts of Jorge's job was tracking and killing pumas. These large gray felines preyed on the ranch's livestock, a significant threat to the flock of over 2,000 sheep. They can kill up to twenty sheep in a night. Judging by the remarkable number of puma pelts in his barn, Jorge was an even match for the predator.

"They teach their kittens to hunt using the sheep," the soft-spoken ranch manager explained over warm mate. "They won't eat them, just wound them badly, and strike the next. They do this all night, wounding and killing twenty to thirty head of sheep."

The next morning, Jorge took us hunting. After he carefully cleaned his rifle, we jumped into his white pickup truck and drove through the ranch's long pastures. He slammed on the brakes on a steep hill, turned off the truck, and pointed his rifle out the window.

With a loud explosion, a guanaco about fifty meters to our left dropped to the ground. In a heartbeat, we drove up to the wounded animal. Carefully grabbing its left ear, Jorge jabbed the sharp blade of his knife into the animal's soft neck.

"You have to be careful it doesn't bite you. They have sharp teeth." The guanaco twitched for a few seconds while it bled out. Jorge butchered the animal on the spot, and we drove back to the ranch with the meat. Every ranch can legally kill one guanaco a month for food. As we packed up to move on, Jorge handed us the two hindquarters and top loins.

"You guys take this for the road. With these cold temperatures, you need to eat a lot of protein."

We gladly hung the meat in the back of the white van, giving its nickname "the fridge" even more value. The rest of the guanaco went to feeding the dogs that helped Jorge hunt the pumas. The hungry pack ripped the animal's dead body apart in minutes. It was both fascinating and sad to watch the dogs devour the guanaco.

From *Estancia La Verde*, we continued through that desolate, cold, and windy province eating guanaco meat every day. We made fried guanaco with mashed potatoes, barbecue guanaco, boiled guanaco with pasta, and guanaco sandwiches. It was a welcome addition to our cuisine which normally consisted of soup and noodles.

Butch Cassidy, who was now back to his happy self once again, also benefited from the meat. All day Toti would cut little parts for the hungry little dog who became addicted to the red meat. The meat even made Butch speak — a miracle! We heard his sharp, high-pitched, annoying little dog bark for the first time!

When Toti held a little piece of guanaco in his hand, Butch would stand on his back legs and begin to dance, spinning and barking and wagging his tail nonstop.

"Eat your guanaco, boy!" Toti would say while the little ball of fluff munched. "You're a wild puma hunter from Patagonia! You need your red meat!"

In La Leona, one year and one month since leaving Barretos, we rested the horses at a restaurant and hotel which had hosted Butch Cassidy and his gang for a night back in the day. For a few days, I got to play tourist and go on an excursion to raise funds for the Barretos Children's Cancer Hospital.

First, we visited the Perito Moreno Glacier. Standing seventy meters high and thirty kilometers in length, the colossal ice field left me in awe. I sat in front of the glacier for more than an hour in silence. Ice plates, at times larger than a car, broke off every couple of minutes and crashed into the icy green water, echoing like deep thunder. The bluish white ice atop the glaciers raced toward the mountains on the horizon, making their way up steep faces until reaching the light blue sky, not a cloud in sight.

Interestingly, while most of the glaciers left on earth are receding more and more every year, Perito Moreno continues to stretch its icy grip over Patagonia. Scientists believe this is due to the glacier's steep angle.

The next morning, we drove to the trekking capital of Argentina, El Chaltén. Surrounded by mountains, the town attracts thousands of tourists from all over the world to climb the nearby peaks.

On a cold and cloudy Sunday morning, I put on my cowboy boots and decided to take on Fitz Roy, the peak that inspired the Patagonia logo (the outdoor clothing brand also known as Patagucci for its expensive prices). It's one of the most famous mountains in the world.

After four hours trekking up the steep mountain in rain, ice, and thick snow, we finally reached Lagoon de los Tres. Cowboy boots do not make very good hiking footwear. I was frozen numb and extremely fatigued by the time we reached the lagoon, but the turquoise water we discovered at the top left me feeling lucky to be a witness, lucky to be alive. Unfortunately, I couldn't stay up in the clouds for very long because I had a flight to catch.

A month prior, my agent Marcos Silva contacted me and asked if I could take a couple days off and fly to Brazil for a talk.

"It's an amazing opportunity for you, Filipe. The event will be held at the Sheraton Hotel in downtown São Paulo with over 2,000 people in attendance."

I didn't buy it at first. The thought of leaving Picasso and Sapo for a couple days and flying back to Brazil did not entice me. It felt weird to stop in the middle of the journey, in which I traveled at four kilometers an hour, thirty kilometers a day to jump into an airplane, fly at 900 kilometers an hour, 38,000 feet in the air, back to where I started. It felt almost as if I was cheating. Two things made me change my mind. First, Marcos told me we could use the talk to raise funds for the Barretos Children's Cancer Hospital.

"We may be able to raise upwards of $10,000 Reais," he stated during a second chat. I liked that idea!

The final push came from another phone call. While chatting with my mother, who was unaware of this opportunity, she told me my grandmother's ninetieth birthday was coming up, and they were planning a surprise birthday party for her. She asked if I could record a video message so they could play it for her on the day. When I asked my mother when the party would take place, I couldn't believe the coincidence. It fell on the same weekend as the talk! I immediately called Marcos and told him to book my flight, I would be there. For some reason, the Universe wanted me back in Brazil that weekend.

While the horses rested in La Leona and Toti in a hostel in El Calafate, I flew to Buenos Aires and then São Paulo. What took me more than a year to ride south on horseback, I traveled in a day, flying north on two different airplanes. Mind-boggling.

I arrived in São Paulo late on a Thursday night and went straight to Marcos' apartment. The Brazilian/Japanese businessman was like a father to me. The following morning, we awoke early and drove to the posh hotel where the event would take place. After so many months living in such a wild and desolate land, it was strange being in the middle of a city of twenty-two million people: the chaotic sounds, array of smells, crowded streets. Looking out of the car's window, I felt a little claustrophobic.

The talk couldn't have gone better. Sharing the stage with some of Brazil's top speakers, my speech was voted the best one of the day. To top it off, we raised $11,000 Reais for the hospital.

From São Paulo, a driver took me to my hometown of Espirito Santo do Pinhal. I can't begin to explain how nice it was to see my sisters, my parents, my friends, and of course, my kids: Frenchie, Bruiser, and Dude, the three horses I traveled with from Canada to Brazil on my first Long Ride.

Already in their stalls for the night, I went to say hello to them. In a trance, they were half asleep. I hugged the three horses and told them how much I missed them. Their familiar aroma lifted me.

With friends and family, I ate a delicious barbecue that night while I told everyone about Patagonia, Sapito Gonzales, Pablo Picasso, Butch Cassidy, Toti, and Clara. Everyone wanted to meet Clara. I loved being wrapped in the warmth of my family. My infuriating family. I had missed them all and couldn't wait to introduce them to Clara.

The next morning, my dad told me he thought Dude was acting weird.

"He was lying down all morning and seemed to struggle to stand up," he said while we got ready for my grandma's surprise party.

I went down to see him, and Dude was standing near his stall. I pet his little golden face, asking him what was wrong. Dude, a Mustang given to me by Karen Hardy (my American mom) and the Taos Pueblo Native People from New Mexico, was always the most loving of the three horses.

He would stand with you for hours if you pet him or played with his mane. He loved it. Standing at 14.1 hands, Dude had a thick white blaze on his golden face, a three-quarter cannon on his front right leg and back right and a full pastern on his back left. Unlike the Quarter Horses, the hairs on the Mustang's fetlocks were long like that of a Spanish horse, a true testament to this pony's blood relation to the first equines brought to the Americas by the Spaniards.

His eyes, only half-open, made him look like he had just smoked a joint. His long blond mane could have belonged to a Californian surfer, messy, curly, and wild.

I'd watched this mustang roll down a mountain in Mexico three full times, get up, shake off the dust and start grazing as if nothing had happened. Under Dude's tough exterior, there was a gentle, caring, and loving little pony. He had the most heart out of all of the horses I have ever ridden. In the heat, snow, on the highest cordilleras and the deepest rivers, he always gave me 110 percent. He had no quit in him and was nothing short of a great warrior.

While I was checking on him, I raised his upper lip and pressed my index finger on his gums, making the flesh turn white, to see if it took a long time for the natural pink-reddish color to return. If it took too long, it could mean he had anemia. By my test, he looked fine. The color returned quickly.

I pushed him away so he would walk a few steps. He was reluctant to walk, and after he took three steps, I noticed he walked strangely, as if he was drunk. My heart sank for I knew what this could mean.

"We need to call the vet right away, something is definitely wrong with Dude," I told my dad when I returned to the house. He called the local vet and, since it was Sunday, he was out of town. The vet promised to come first thing the following morning. Since the mustang was eating, drinking, and breathing normally, we agreed the next morning was fine.

We went to my grandma's birthday party. It was heavenly seeing her comforting face and feeling her strong embrace. Iolanda Lobo's photograph should sit next to the word grandmother in the dictionary. The most loving woman I have ever met, she had light brown hair, cut short, a slight hunch, and was always wearing jewelry on her neck and fingers. When you visited her, any day of the week, you would find an array of homemade cakes sitting on her table along with bread, cookies, salty treats, and more.

"My son! You are here!" the petite ninety-year-old beauty said, holding my face with both hands. She was so surprised by my presence and all of the relatives and friends there, over one hundred people, at one point she almost fainted and had to lie down.

"We almost killed grandma," my sister Paolla said as we all laughed.

After the party, we drove back to my house so I could gather my things before driving back to São Paulo to catch my flight to Patagonia. Before I got on the road, I went back down to the barn to say goodbye to the horses. As I combed Dude's bleach-blond forelock using my fingers, a deep sadness took hold of me. I hugged him tightly and dug my face into the right side of his neck. I took a deep breath and let his wild aroma — a mixture of wood chips, fresh rain, and honey — fill my soul. I didn't want to let go. Something told me, this was the last time I would see my little surfer Dude in this life.

That night I slept in São Paulo and began my trek back to Patagonia early the next morning. First, I flew to Buenos Aires and spent seven hours waiting at the airport before boarding the second flight to El Calafate. I finally landed in Patagonia in the late afternoon. When I stepped off the plane and opened my WhatsApp, I read the message from my father I knew was coming.

"Filipe, unfortunately, the vet has been here all day. In fact, three vets have been here all day. There is nothing they can do. Dude contracted a virus that attacked his nervous system."

The words on the screen sucked the air from my lungs. I had to sit down to understand what the message actually meant. I called my dad immediately, and he told me the vets thought Dude had contracted rabies.

"They can't say for sure, but they think it's rabies. There are a lot of vampire bats down here, and this year there has been a recent spike in rabies cases in this region."

Dude was now lying down, unable to get up, having terrible spasms. My dad held the cell phone up to Dude's ear as the vet gave him an injection to stop his heart and end his suffering.

"Hey, Dude, I love you so much, buddy." I whispered. "Thank you for everything. You're the best horse I could have ever asked for. You rest now, okay? I love you so much, I'll see you soon."

Heavy tears strangled my voice while images of my little surfer Dude with his bleach-blond mane flowing wild in the wind filled my mind. I now understood why the Universe summoned me back to Brazil that weekend. Dude could have passed away any day during the more than 365 I had spent away from home. He waited for me to come home. He needed to say goodbye to an old friend before he departed this life for the next.

Since the Brazilian vets feared Dude had died of rabies, my entire family had to get rabies shots. Since I touched the inside of his mouth and came in contact with his saliva, I needed to get shots immediately or I, too, could face a terrible death.

From the airport, Toti and I drove to the El Calafate hospital only to discover Patagonia was free of the virus, and therefore, they didn't have the shots.

"You will have to fly to Buenos Aires, sir," a lifeless nurse said. Her words hit me like rocks.

The next morning, sitting inside the fourth airplane in just four days, I tried to understand just what had happened. I had one shot pricked into the fat in my arm inside a fancy medical clinic and purchased the rest I needed to take.

In a sort of present from the Universe amidst so much suffering, Clara was also in Buenos Aires. We met outside of the clinic, and I broke down in her arms. We spent the night together in a cheap hotel. I laid my head on her lap for hours, telling her stories about Dude while she played with my hair.

"I'm so sorry for your loss, *amor*. I wish I had met him."

The next day, with a foam cooler filled with rabies shots sitting on ice under my arm, I boarded my fifth flight in five days. Toti ended up having to give me the other injections in the middle of the Patagonian wilderness. With only 150 kilometers of Argentina's mainland left to cross and 300 kilometers in Tierra del Fuego, I dedicated this journey to the mightiest horse I have ever met.

I will never forget you, Dude!

Finally, we left La Leona with the wind screaming uncontrollably once again. With sad eyes and a broken heart, I fought my way south until we found refuge a couple of kilometers short of a small town called La Esperanza (Hope). God knows I needed some at that moment!

"You guys are lucky I didn't shoot your dog," Frederico, the worker of the Estancia said when Toti and I made our way to the house. Butch Cassidy had run down the small hill to the ranch before we started our trek down. Out there, a random wandering dog was a danger to the sheep. If a worker saw a dog that didn't belong on a ranch, he shot first, then he asked questions. The ranch owner offered a hefty amount of cash for the hide of every dog and puma killed.

"I noticed he was too small to be a wild dog eating sheep, so I called him, and he ran to me. When he got closer, I realized someone had trimmed the hair in front of his eyes," Frederico said. That was when he put his shotgun down and came out looking for his owners.

Feeling lucky Butch Cassidy had literally dodged a bullet, we got to know our host. Frederico was in his twenties. He looked like a smaller version of Mr. Bean with a big nose and a mole the size of a dime on his pale face. His clothes were ripped to shreds, and he wore black rubber boots that went up to his knees. He allowed us to rest our horses at the ranch for two days.

Frederico, whose first child, a healthy baby boy, was born only days before our arrival, had us over for dinner every night. As always, the main course was lamb. He was a tremendous host who told us about his hard life in the north of the country.

"Before I came down to the south, I couldn't find any work where I'm from. I used to cut wood and sell it to feed my family," he said, looking down at his baby boy sleeping peacefully in his arms. Frederico was now making monthly payments for his soon-to-be-new car thanks to the salary he received. His life had changed drastically and he was so happy to have this opportunity. "I want my boy to have a different life than I've had."

Working as a ranch hand in the far south of the country was not an easy job. Toti and I heard many horror stories of *Puesteros*, the men who worked these deserted ranches with little contact with the outside world. One man killed all of his dogs, his two horses, and then committed suicide. His boss brought his worker food once every three months. When the owner arrived, he was horrified at what he found. Being isolated in such harsh conditions takes a toll on the strongest of men. Luckily, Frederico had his wife and baby with him and a fair boss.

The night before we rode out, Dannie Fernandez, the owner of the *Estancia* arrived for the next day's sheep shearing. He invited us to eat dinner with him and promised to take care of us when we arrived in Río Gallegos, where he lived 150 kilometers to the south-east.

"I will do whatever I can to help you, boys," the bald man with light blue eyes said while we enjoyed a delicious lamb dinner. It was hard to believe we were so close to Río Gallegos, the last city we would cross in mainland Argentina. Santa Cruz had taken its toll on me, and I was extremely relieved to be so close to the end of this unforgiving province.

But as we all know, it was not over till the fat lady sings or better, till the Patagonian wind screams!

RIO GALLEGOS

As with every part of my journey through the Americas, it was obvious that the final one hundred kilometers through mainland Argentina would be a grueling adventure. The days got colder and colder while the wind continued to blow. Mentally, I was ready to be done with it all. After being on the road for more than a year, I was burned out. However, quitting was never an option. I found great comfort in the handwritten letters Clara sent me during this period. After she left from Perito Moreno, we started mailing letters to one another.

In one of her letters, she sent me a dried flower. "This flower is called *amancay*," she wrote. "It's my favorite. The *Mapuche* tell a tale in which a native woman called *Amancay* trades her heart for the yellow flowers with a *condor*, the guardian of the mountains, to save a great love."

She went on to explain how the native woman's blood stained the flowers. That's why the flowers had little red dots on their soft yellow petals.

"The *Mapuche* believe that when you give someone an *amancay* flower as a gift, you are giving them your heart," she wrote. "I choose you, Filipe. Take care of my heart."

I loved everything about those letters. Going to the post office in those wind-swept Patagonian towns to pick up a small envelope covered with stamps. Opening it to see what treats were inside. Reading Clara's small and neat handwriting. Seeing her drawings, scattered all over the page, in the empty spaces her words had not covered. I would read and re-read those letters a million times over before falling asleep with the pages hugged tight to my chest. In a way, it felt like those pieces of papers carried her essence, a piece of her.

In one of my letters, which I wrote on graph paper one night in the van forty-five kilometers from El Calafate, I started by apologizing.

"It's going to be hard to write this letter in Spanish. I'm sorry for my bad grammar and my sloppy handwriting." After telling her it was -3°C that night and that I was freezing my ass off, I professed my love for her. "This region of Santa Cruz is beautiful, Clara, I just wish you were here to see it with me. I miss you and think about you often." Inside the white envelope, I included a chunk of Sapito's black and dirty-blond mane. She loved the little frog-like Criollo.

"I will save Sapito's mane forever, it even smells like him," she wrote back in another letter before drawing a cartoon version of the little Criollo. Her words brightened my days and warmed my nights.

Unfortunately, she didn't have the power to change the weather. With heavy, wet snow falling and the thermometer reading -5°C, I finally rode into the ranch where we would rest, two days before arriving in Río Gallegos. I was frozen stiff and numb. After turning the horses out, we were welcomed into a toasty home for a delicious barbecue.

"Any man who arrives on horseback deserves an *asado*," an elderly gentleman said, passing me a shot of *aguardiente*. I immediately shot it back. Its fiery liquid warmed me from the inside out.

Our host was a retired *puestero* who still lived on the ranch and worked a few days a week. With his deep eyes, cloud-white hair, and *bombachas* tucked into his knee-high gray wool socks, I liked him right away. We spent the afternoon hearing stories of his days working with the cattle and sheep on the open range. I sat close to the wood-burning heater, trying to get the feeling back in my fingers and toes.

"This is not an easy life," the old man told me, looking far off into the distance before taking a swig of the *aguardiente*. "One day I almost died when heavy fog kept me disoriented in the field. When I finally found the house, it was midnight and I was nearly frozen... I looked like you when you arrived today!"

The following morning, after chipping at the horses' frozen water, I rode out early and waited all day for Toti to meet me. I waited and waited and waited until I realized something was wrong. *The van must have broken down again,* I thought to myself.

In the early afternoon, I met my fears. A blue truck pulled over in front of me and Toti jumped out. "The van won't start, brother. I'm going to get a ride to the ranch ahead where we will rest tonight, and we can figure out what to do." He jumped back into the vehicle and disappeared.

Damn. Damn. Damn. I couldn't take it anymore. This journey just kept getting harder and harder. The wind, weather, solitude, lack of basic hygiene, the death of Dude ... the van that broke down every three days. I was so tired of having to deal with so many problems.

When I arrived at the ranch where we would rest, Toti had already made friends with the employees. It took him all of twenty seconds to befriend complete strangers. We untacked the boys, fed them a bale of alfalfa, and hitched a ride to Río Gallegos. We got dropped off in front of an internet cafe, and I called the insurance company in Brazil. It was a painful ordeal. When we finally got through to them, after waiting on hold being tortured with the worst elevator music in the world for half an hour, they said they would send a tow truck. It was midnight.

"Hopefully, it comes," I said to Toti while we waited in the freezing cold. Thick white vapor cut the darkness of the night with every word spoken. After an hour and a half, much to our relief, the driver finally showed up. Thank the Lord!

Toti and I said hello and quickly jumped inside the cab in search of heat. The driver asked where the van was parked. We proceeded to tell him it was about sixty kilometers outside of town.

"Oh, I can't drive out of town, they told me it was in Río Gallegos," he said, staring at us blankly.

I wanted to cry. I pleaded with him. "Please, sir. I'm tired, sore, and cold. Tomorrow I have to wake up early and ride thirty kilometers to town." I tried to make a case, but he wasn't having any of it.

"I can't leave town with this truck. You have to call the insurance company back and explain to them that the van is not in Río Gallegos."

Now two in the morning, we climbed out of the truck. Toti and I wandered the streets of Río Gallegos looking for a place to sleep, hoping not to get robbed. It wasn't a welcoming city in the light of day, never mind in the darkness of the night. We found a cheap hotel to rest our tired bodies for a few hours. We rose at six a.m. to try to figure out what the hell we would do.

"I'm going to message Dannie from La Esperanza," Toti announced over breakfast. "Maybe he can help."

Dannie ran a sand and stone quarry. Luckily, he always awoke at the crack of dawn for work. In a few minutes, we were sitting in his truck, driving toward the horses.

"Why didn't you clowns call me last night? You two idiots could have slept at my house," he said, lightening our dark mood a little.

Dannie looked like an Italian and talked like one too! Flailing his arms to make a point and yelling more than speaking, he seemed like an uncle more than a stranger we had just met. Dannie dropped me off with the horses and drove to see the van with Toti. A self-taught mechanic, he promised to either fix it or, in the worst case, tie a rope to the back of his truck and haul it to his quarry in Río Gallegos.

Still in the dark, I tacked the horses and began my ride to the last city in mainland Argentina. With the first light of day brightening the world around us, I heard the van's diesel engine creeping up behind me. I couldn't believe it. When I looked back, Toti was driving the old fridge with a huge smile on his face and a cigarette hanging from his lip. As he passed me he slammed on the horn while I yelled at the top of my lungs with relief. Dannie passed me close behind, also laying on the horn. A few kilometers ahead, Toti was waiting on the side of the road with mate ready.

"Brother, Dannie is a genius!" Toti announced. "In a few minutes, he knew exactly what the problem was and fixed the starter using wire and pliers. Once he found out we were traveling without heat, he said he would fix us up once we arrived, too!"

"I love Dannie!" Toti yelled, his legs spread as if sitting on top of a Harley motorcycle and his head cocked back.

~

Having survived the grueling desert of Santa Cruz, we were met with equal parts love and bureaucracy in the provincial capital, Río Gallegos.

"We are honored to be hosting someone who has come from so far on horseback," said Miguel O'Byrne, president of the Río Gallegos Rural Society. "Whatever you need, just let us know."

Toti and I were ecstatic to finally arrive in the capital of Santa Cruz. In the months we spent together on the road, usually camping in the middle of nowhere in Patagonia, we would open the map and imagine how it would feel to arrive there. It seemed so distant, nearly impossible. Now, there we were.

Río Gallegos would be as far as we would be allowed to ride in continental Argentina. To enter Tierra del Fuego, we would have to put the horses into a sealed truck and cross 200 kilometers of Chilean soil and only unload them once we arrived on the Argentinian portion of the island. But first, we celebrated our arrival like two thirsty sailors back on land after months at sea.

"Cheers brother, you made it," Toti said, Fernet raised in the air, a wide smile on his face.

"*We* made it!"

We spent an entire week running around like headless chickens trying to get all of the paperwork ready to ship the horses to Tierra del Fuego, off the southernmost tip of the South American mainland. We had to get the horses' bloodwork done and bring their vaccinations up to date, hire a logistics agent to deal with the Chilean and Argentinian customs officials, and find a trucker to haul the horses south for free.

After a year and two months on the road, I was broke. It was a week of hell, but with the help of several members of the Río Gallegos

Rural Society, things moved much quicker than imagined. The process ended up costing a lot less than expected, too.

The only problem was Butch Cassidy. For a dog to cross Chile, even without ever stepping foot on Chilean soil, it needed to have been vaccinated at least one month prior to the trip. Because Butch was a street dog we picked up in El Bolson, he didn't have any shots. We didn't even know how old he was. We were sad to leave our puppy behind, but our friend Sophia from the Rural Society offered to take care of him until we returned.

"Don't you boys worry at all. I'll take care of this little cutie," the tiny, but strong, horsewoman assured us. I couldn't thank her enough. Sophia and her boyfriend Frederico helped us tremendously while we were trying to get the paperwork in order, as well.

Now entering the heart of the Southern Hemisphere's winter, we took the van to Dannie's shop to get the heater fixed.

"You guys are crazy driving this thing in southern Santa Cruz with no heat," Dannie said with a smirk on his pale face. It took him a little over an hour to install the parts needed to pump the hot air from the engine into the van.

"You are my hero," I said, giving him a big hug.

"Don't thank me yet. Wait until you get to Ushuaia alive," he laughed, wiping his grease-stained hands with an even greasier cloth.

That night, our final day in Río Gallegos, we ate dinner at his house with his gorgeous blonde wife and two kids. They told us about how the teachers in the province hadn't received their payment in months and were on strike.

"It's very sad. Politics ruin this country." Dannie spoke the words I had heard around dinner tables all the way from Mexico to the bottom of South America.

On a chilly, gray Monday morning, nine days after riding into Río Gallegos, we finally loaded the horses into a large cattle truck and made the drive to Tierra del Fuego. The trip took us across two borders and down a slippery, muddy road that almost stopped us in our tracks several times. Finally, we came to a somewhat disappointing ferry full of trucks that transported us across the Strait of Magellan.

After twenty-five hours, including a sleepless night at the final border, we unloaded Sapo and Picasso one kilometer from the Chile-Argentina border at *Estancia San Martin*.

The truck driver who hauled the horses free of charge to the island was named Jorge López, a ginger who looked more like a Scotsman than an Argentinian. "Welcome to Tierra del Fuego!" he said enthusiastically.

Tierra del Fuego. The Land of Fire.

I looked out at the Atlantic Ocean as a high, cold, salty breeze kissed my dry cheeks. I was 300 kilometers from ending a journey of more than 7,000 kilometers. I was on the southernmost island in the Americas with my horses. From Calgary, Canada to Barretos to here. We were so close to the end, literally and mentally.

TIERRA DEL FUEGO

We drank mate with the manager of *Estancia San Martin*, while we watched Picasso and Sapito happily grazing on the first green grass they had seen in months.

The stocky manager told us that when the first explorers arrived on the coastline by boat, they saw large bonfires across the island. To survive low temperatures and long winters, the indigenous people never let the fire die, which was why the island is called Tierra del Fuego (Land of Fire), a tradition that remained true to this day. Every home we entered on the island, had one or more fires burning in wood heaters, fireplaces, or wood ovens. Those flames burned twenty-four hours a day, seven days a week.

That night, we were treated to a traditional lamb barbecue and five bottles of champagne. You know those gigantic bottles of Jack Daniels you see on the top shelf at the airport duty-free shop and wonder who the hell buys those things? We got one of those, too! I felt like I had won a Formula 1 race!

The next morning, I felt like I had crashed into a wall at 300 kmph. Hungover, I saddled Sapito under heavy, wet snow to begin our final 300 kilometer push to Ushuaia, the southernmost city in the world, and our finish line. I wanted to feel excited about entering the final stage of this journey, but with the thermometer reading -3°C, all I felt was pain.

On the road to Río Grande, the largest city on the island, we spent a night at one of the oldest and most important ranches in Tierra del Fuego. With 65,000 sheep, 300 cows, and 120 horses, the legendary *Estancia Sara* employed more than twenty families and even had its own rural school.

"We run the largest sheep operation on the island today," Jorge Barria, the manager of the estancia told us over a glass of Cabernet Sauvignon.

Barria, who looked like a high school English teacher and always wore pullovers atop neat button-up shirts, explained just how hard ranching was on the island. Long winters, freezing temperatures, snow, and *guanacos* were the sorts of problems we'd heard about during our travels in the province of Santa Cruz. But here, they had a terrifying factor: wild dog packs.

Between the murder of Cluck Norris and a panicky skirmish of two or three nipping at our heels, I'd had my fill of wild dogs. In Tierra del Fuego, it was estimated that these beasts kill 10,000 head of sheep a year. An average rancher slaughtered sixty to seventy wild dogs each year in that region, yet the population continued to grow.

Speaking to a rancher who ran a ranch sixty kilometers southwest of Río Grande, we were able to understand just how big the problem was. "I used to have a flock of 22,000 sheep in 2010. Today I have only 4,000 animals left," the elderly gentleman with sad eyes told us.

If they were hungry, a large pack of wild dogs could take down a horse. More than 600 people reported being attacked by wild dogs every year on the island. The stats were terrifying and left Toti and me worried for our horses and our lives. With 210 kilometers of freezing temperatures, ice-covered roads, heavy snow, and howling winds ahead of us, we also had to worry about packs of vicious wild dogs!

We truly were at the end of the Earth.

~

On a sunny and chilly afternoon, I finally arrived in Río Grande, the first city of three we would cross on the island.

"You made it to Río Grande," Julio Rocha, a local gaucho with a strong love for the horse, announced as he shook my hand. A colossal Argentinian flag flapping way up in the pale sky behind him. Julio had a large head and an even bigger heart. He had set up a room at the local rodeo grounds for us to rest and a corral for the horses. "Whatever you need while you are here, just ask," the gaucho told me.

The road took us first through the center of town and finally across a long bridge to what looked like a shanty town. Unpaved roads with large holes wound their way to small houses built from cement or wood. Some were more like shacks. When we finally arrived in the late afternoon, I spent a few minutes petting and thanking my brave Criollos. My children. My heroes. I was so proud of them.

"Thank you so much for bringing me this far, boys," I said before putting their checkered blankets on for the night. "We are almost done! Almost!" We spent two days resting the boys and getting ready for the final 200-kilometer push to Ushuaia.

A local rancher loaned Toti a stocky, lazy mare called Ona, named after the indigenous people on the island, so we could ride together. "Oh, man, this is going to be epic!" Toti said when he went to pick up the chestnut from a nearby feedlot.

Before we rode out toward the small town of Touhlin, we shod Sapito, Picasso, and Ona with special horseshoes that had sharp spikes on both sides of the heel of the shoe.

Julio helped us shoe the animals. "Without these, it will be impossible for you two to cross the island. There's ice everywhere."

He was right! Just to walk the horses from their corral to where we would shoe them was a struggle. They tried to walk but slipped and fought to hold themselves up. Now in the middle of winter, the island was covered almost entirely in a thick layer of ice. It was like trying to walk a horse in a skating rink.

On a cold Thursday morning, Toti and I saddled our mounts and began trekking south. Instead of following Highway 3, which ran down the coast of the island, we traveled down a dirt road that cut the island in half. It was full of *estancias* and offered a quieter ride with almost no automobile traffic.

Due to the extremely cold temperatures, anywhere from -5°C to -16°C, the plan was to ride only about fifteen to twenty kilometers a day, about three to four hours in the saddle. Unfortunately, because of a locked gate on our second day out, that plan went straight out the window. At about five p.m., we rode up to the ranch where we would stay that night as the sun set. When we dismounted and walked up to the gate, my heart almost stopped. A large lock sat on a thick chain, preventing us from opening the wooden gate.

"What the heck are we going to do now?" I asked Toti. He had no answers. We jumped the gate and walked around the ranch calling out. Only a crippled dog came to greet us. Our friends in Río Grande had assured us all of the ranches we arrived at would be open, with people waiting. We asked several times because, with the short days and freezing temperatures, any mistake could cost us our lives. We didn't have the van to sleep in. We had nothing but the essentials in the packsaddle.

After a few minutes contemplating what to do, we decided the only option was to trek to the next ranch – eighteen kilometers south. We were desperate and frozen. Our fingers and toes burned with pain. With the sun now under the horizon, we knew the real pain had only begun.

"Man, I hope the next ranch is open because we are going to arrive after ten o'clock!"

With the locked gate behind us, we trekked in the dark through a narrow road covered with snow and ice. In mid-June, the sun set around 5:10 p.m. Every three kilometers or so, we were forced to stop, get off our horses, and clean out their hooves. The wet snow would create a frozen ball under their feet that made it both difficult and painful for them to walk. At times, the egg-shaped clump was so frozen, removing it required several heavy blows using our knives. The temperature was around -8°C, and our bodies, hands, and feet were frozen.

We walked a lot that night to try to stay warm, but feeling cold was inevitable. Both looking over our shoulders constantly, fearful of being attacked by a pack of wild dogs, we trod on. After about two hours trekking in the darkness, a truck drove toward us. To our relief, it was the manager of *Estancia Rubi*, the ranch that was our new destination.

"What the hell are you guys doing out here? I thought you were arriving tomorrow," Dennis MacLean said with wide eyes. When we shook hands, his hand was so toasty from the truck's heat, I didn't want to let go. We explained what happened, and he drove Toti to the ranch while I continued with the three horses alone. Because we would arrive late, he wanted to let the worker know we were coming and show Toti where we could turn the horses out.

Riding alone, in complete darkness through that frozen frontier, was both petrifying and exhilarating. The thought of a pack of wild dogs attacking us was difficult to shake, but I lost myself in the starry sky. I have seen few skies like the ones I witnessed in Tierra del Fuego. It was as if there were more stars than dark spots in the sky. Falling stars, comets, and satellites streaking across the sky formed a mesmerizing dance.

After about an hour, Toti returned with Dennis and we continued together. I must say, having Toti riding with me instead of driving the van was astounding. We chatted, laughed, and shared stories constantly. His companionship not only made every day go by faster, dangerous situations like this one seemed less serious.

For Toti, it was also a welcome break. The natural horseman felt way more at home in the saddle than in that clunky van.

At eleven p.m., we finally arrived at *Estancia Rubi*. We walked the horses to a half-frozen stream to offer them water. The snow was deeper compared to Rio Grande. At some points, I sank up to my knees as I walked next to Picasso and Sapito. Ona and Sapo dropped to their knees to drink the cold liquid. Picasso didn't want to drink from the stream, so I was forced to find a bucket and scoop water up for him. My fingers felt like someone was pushing a sharp knife into them.

While we walked them to the barn where they would spend the night, I was in so much pain I wanted to cry. Had Toti not been there, I probably would have wept.

Finally, at 12:30 a.m., we were in a container house with no heat, eating a lukewarm bowl of angel hair soup we had prepared while the horses munched on alfalfa in the barn. As the one light in the building flickered above us, not many words were exchanged between Toti and me. It had been a treacherous day. We simply focused on eating and hoped tomorrow would bring a better day.

As always, it didn't. We awoke to the coldest day yet, -16°C. It was a terrible morning, and our suffering would continue.

~

On our second last day toward Touhlin, a massive snowstorm hit the island, and we were left looking like snowmen. The heavy sheets of wet snow hit both our bodies and our horses with force. Instead of disappearing, it created a thick white coat over our bodies. The already cold day felt even colder. We were as white as the land surrounding us. Just after three p.m., we arrived at the ranch where we would rest that night. When we rode up to the gate, we almost had a heart attack. It was locked.

"Touhlin is twenty kilometers from here," Toti said, shaking his head. "We are going to freeze if we have to ride to town today."

Before continuing on, we decided it would be smart to walk to the home to check if anyone was there. I waited with the horses while Toti made the trek down the long driveway. In seconds his footprints were covered by the heavy snow. It was as if he had never walked down the path. Much to my relief, about ten minutes later, he returned in a white truck with Carlos, the Paraguayan who ran the ranch.

We untacked the horses under a shed while a family of pigs watched us curiously. A fire burned in a half barrel nearby. We gave Sapito, Picasso, and Ona a bale of hay and went to warm up near the flames. It felt heavenly to be near the heat and out of the snow. The storm continued outside, and I curled up in my sleeping bag. Grateful to be wrapped in warmth, I pondered this journey. I was blessed to have so many people help and ground me. The horses, too.

Sapito Gonzales became my safety blanket. He was a sturdy, calm horse that kept his slow but powerful stride going the entire day. While Picasso jumped and fidgeted in fear at the weirdest things, from shadows to burned cars, Sapito never even flinched, simply bobbing his big ugly head while trekking south unfazed. Unable to tire the short Criollo, even on super long days, he would go anywhere I asked. Across anything. Sapito was braver than most horses I had met. He was the horse you wanted to ride into the battlefield. I knew he would never let me down, but he was also a crusty old man! Often with his ears pinned back, biting the young gun Picasso if the bay got too close or did something he deemed as wrong.

In many ways, Sapito Gonzales was like my mustang, Dude. They were both reliable, short, but stocky, and full of heart. The best part was that they both enjoyed getting loved! Just like with Dude on my first Long Ride, I spent countless hours petting Sapito's soft golden brown face and neck. Scratching his cheeks. Hugging his neck, while he leaned his jaw on my shoulder, letting his powerful odor, a mixture of earth and alfalfa, permeate my body. Or simply sitting by his side while he slept lying down, twitching every once in a while from his dreams or nightmares.

It wasn't just Sapito and Dude who made for interesting comparisons. On this journey, all three sets of horses I rode were in a way polar opposites of one another.

In Brazil, for instance, Life was the obedient and reliable Quarter Horse with calm eyes while Doll was the spicy redhead of the team. With the whites of her eyes always showing, the red roan was dashing yet a ball of nerves — ready to go off at any second, sassy but with unpredictable mood swings.

In Uruguay, the chestnut Cautiva took Life's trusting role while Andariega was as sassy as Doll but somehow even more coltish, long-legged, and paranoid. Now Sapito and suspicious Picasso were my yin and yang.

The next morning, we saddled up early and began our final day toward the heart of the island: Touhlin. Toti and I were so happy, so excited. When we arrived, we had huge smiles on our frozen faces. After trekking 7,400 kilometers from Barretos, Brazil, I was only one hundred kilometers from the finish line. I could hardly believe it. It felt so good to be nearly done with this Long Ride, especially after all of the suffering I had endured the past few months crossing Patagonia and now Tierra del Fuego.

Feeling like I was dreaming, we rode to the pasture where the horses would rest in the small town. Our host led the way in his truck. The entire town was covered under a thick blanket of snow. It was a marvelous scene that made me feel like I was in a classic Christmas movie.

"Welcome to Touhlin, Filipe!" our host exclaimed with a smile and a handshake. He was a big man with shaggy silver hair and a pep to his step. We untacked the horses as he filled a large feeder with alfalfa cubes.

The three munched happily on the cubes while we watched. I was so proud of my boys. They were only 100 kilometers from becoming legends like their distant relatives Mancha and Gato and being retired. I gave both a pat on the neck and walked away.

Had I known the nightmare tomorrow would bring, I would have spent all night with my boys.

FROZEN HELL

On the morning of Saturday, June 24, a day after arriving in Touhlin, my dream turned into a nightmare. When I went to feed the horses, I noticed that the boys didn't want to eat. We thought it was weird but figured Sapito and Picasso were full. However, when we went to check on them again during lunch, we quickly realized something was terribly wrong. Both horses had diarrhea and were breathing heavily. We needed a vet — fast.

Our host said there was only one, and he was currently on vacation in northern Argentina. We called vets in both Río Grande and Ushuaia. None would agree to come see the horses. "Sorry, I don't treat emergencies, and I only deal with small animals... I work with cows and sheep," were their useless answers.

By late afternoon, after giving both horses a 10 cc injection of Banamine (a muscle relaxant we carried with us) and a 500 ml IV of saline, Picasso began breathing better and defecating normally. Sapito kept getting worse.

That night, I didn't sleep. It was -17°C, and the ground was covered with a thick coat of ice and snow. A cold wind made my hands turn deep red and my fingers burned with pain. It was the worst night of my life.

Sapito fought for his life like I have never seen a living being fight before. We continued to put IV bags into his veins all night, but he kept getting worse. He peed continually and had terrible diarrhea. Every hour that passed, he seemed to lose weight and motion in his body. Eventually, he started drooling severely, and his muscles started seizing more until eventually, he could no longer stand. He lay down on the frozen ground.

At seven a.m., he rose for the final time. Using all of his might, he shot his stocky golden body up. He stood shaking. Then, while I held his head with everything I had left in my exhausted and frozen body, he began to walk forward. It was like his heart was moving his legs, as if he wanted to get far away from me.

Sapito was getting ready to die.

Running my right hand down the soft hair on his forehead, I thanked him for his hard work these past few months and asked him to rest. The sun was up, but he was still fighting.

Toti and I had spent all night trying to save him. Our host, who had fed the horses alfalfa cubes, had gone to sleep at ten p.m. He left us to fend for ourselves. It was hard to understand why. He was a horseman himself.

Finally, at 4:01 p.m., Sapito lifted his head off the snow and tried to bite the air. Then his eyes went matte-black. Seconds later, he took one short, final breath. He was gone. I sat next to him on the frozen ground crying like a father who had lost his son. I was angry. I blamed myself.

Praying for Sapito's soul, I cut a piece of his mane to keep with me forever.

Our host's dog, who had been circling the dying horse for hours, started biting at his legs the second Sapito took that last breath. It was unbelievable how he knew death had come right away. It showed me that this dog was used to eating horse meat regularly. At a barbecue at our host's house, I later found out the main course was horse. They loved eating equine meat on the island.

"Oh, this is the best meat there is," our host said as he grabbed another piece of the oily meat. There were horse hairs all over the silver pan where the meat sat. In that part of the world, many would think we should have left Sapito to Nature's will, gone to sleep, and if he didn't make it, cooked him the next morning.

The night of Sapito's passing, having not slept for over twenty-four hours, a vet finally agreed to come to Touhlin to check on Picasso. He medicated the tall bay and said he would be okay. The vet had several possible theories. There might have been something wrong with the alfalfa cubes.

"Either a rat urinated inside the bag, or some of the cubes had gone moldy, or they came bad from the factory. Sapo must have eaten most of the bad cubes and Picasso ate less. This was intoxication from those cubes."

I would never know the truth. All conjecture. It could have been any number of things. Poison even crossed my mind. The only thing I knew for sure was anger and the pain of his loss.

For the first time since leaving Brazil, I honestly thought about quitting. I asked the Universe, *Why did you take him from me now? Only one hundred kilometers from the end?* I received no answers.

Although I was exhausted, I couldn't sleep. The previous day's endless nightmare overwhelmed my thoughts. All I knew at that moment was that this was my fault. No one else was left to blame but me. I tried to stop thinking so I could sleep, but then Dude's image would creep in. Both horses dead less than a month apart. What had I done to deserve this? It felt like a part of me had died, too.

I did not want to continue riding. I did not want to finish.

THE END... OF THE WORLD

After several days of reflecting and speaking to my family and Sapo's owners, I decided to finish the ride in memory of my boy.

"Filipe, we understand what happened," Roque Solanet consoled me. "We are horsemen and we know that, just like people, horses, too, die. It was not your fault. I know how well you treated Sapo and Picasso. Now please, finish this journey for Sapo."

He was right. Sapito had fought too hard to get us this far for me to quit. So had his brother. Picasso and I would ride the final stretch of this journey for him and for Dude.

~

The final one hundred kilometers of the Americas held the biggest test of the journey: Paso Garibaldi.

From Touhlin, Toti and I rode from fifteen to twenty kilometers each day, with someone taking the van ahead of us every night. On our first day, we slept in a rock pit with the horses tied to a big yellow tractor. It was not the most comfortable sleep, but it was what we had.

The following day, we rode to a police station that sat in front of a beautiful frozen lake flanked by two snowcapped mountains. Toti and I rode up to the lake and allowed the horses to drink from a flowing stream. I took in my surroundings from atop Picasso. It was a stunning view.

That night, we were offered a delicious barbecue by the policemen and women who hosted us. "Tomorrow, we will help you two cross Paso Garibaldi," the chief said while cooking meat on the grill.

I was relieved to hear we would have help. It would be a perilous crossing. The next morning we woke up early, saddled the horses, and walked over to a school a few meters from the police station. With the sixteen kids who studied there sitting on the cement floor of the main hallway, I used a map of the world to explain my ride. I tried to act enthusiastic, but I was a mess. I was sad. I was nervous. For the past few nights, the nightmare I had before starting this journey, where my dark horse would leap over the railing of a tall bridge once again plagued my dreams. I was afraid that after losing Dude and Sapito, I would be the third casualty.

It's always in the end that something bad happens, I kept thinking to myself. *Bad things happen in threes.*

I tried to shake these thoughts, but I could not. After the children met the horses, we said goodbye, mounted our steeds, and began the steep climb.

The final time we would cross the Andes cordillera (mountains) took us to 450 meters above sea level. Riding up a narrow road, with a frozen rock cliff to our left and a precipice to our right, switchbacks made it impossible for cars to see us. Trucks hauling giant containers flew by us on their way to the port in Ushuaia. I rode in front while Toti followed close behind. The white and green police SUV trailed him with the lights flashing.

About halfway up the mountain, a freezing torrential rain, utterly unheard of in winter, drenched us. It was hell.

I kept my black felt hat tipped down as the wind blew punishing raindrops into my face. Toti put his rain poncho on, but I was too afraid Picasso would freak out with the flapping plastic in the strong wind to wear mine. With Sapito's halter tied to a mesh of his mane hanging on the saddle horn, I asked for his protection during the entire ride. I knew he was there with us. I could feel his warrior spirit.

On the way down the mountain, on one of the final switchbacks, we were forced onto the shoulder by a vehicle coming our way and one trying to pass us. A thick layer of ice covered the entire shoulder to the guardrail. It was a skating rink. As soon as Picasso stepped on the ice with both front feet, he slipped and fell to his knees. The hooks on the back of his shoes had nearly wasted away completely after so many days on the road from Río Grande.

"Whoa, boy! You're ok!" I leaned back while placing my right hand on the saddle horn. With a car passing us only inches from his ass, I prayed for him to stay quiet. Thankfully, he did and slowly he stood back up and put one foot back on the pavement. He stood still for a few seconds before I neck-reined him over so he was completely on the road again.

"Wow, that was close," I said, looking back at Toti.

He couldn't hear me. The torrential rain drowned my words.

By the time we finished the grueling ride, I was drenched and close to hypothermia. My thick goose down jacket, lent to me by Sophia's boyfriend Frederico in Río Gallegos, weighed a million pounds. Ice-cold water flowed down my spine as if there were a river running down my back. My jeans were glued to my frozen legs like a wet suit.

"Thank you very much for all of your help," I said to the police chief before he took off with Toti, who would bring the support van to our resting spot.

We were on a government road management site. The plows and tractors that cleaned the road during the winters stood all around me. We found a fenced-off area to turn out the horses and slept in the van after eating dinner in the mechanic shop. We drowned our sorrows with a cheap bottle of red wine.

Our final night on the road was spent at a dogsledding business only sixteen kilometers from Ushuaia. The owner, a dark, handsome man with long hair, was fascinated by our journey and offered to take Toti and me on a ride.

"Hold on!" he yelled down to us as he asked the dogs to run on. We sat in the sled with huge smiles on our faces as the dogs took us into a beautiful valley. It was an awesome experience that took some of the edge off the past few days.

After the ride, the owner yelled out a few words in what sounded like an indigenous language. Magic happened. All of the dogs, over fifty stunning huskies, arched their noses up to the afternoon sky and began howling like a pack of wolves. The loud and deep chorus of howls gave me chills.

The following afternoon, just after 3 p.m., we finally rode into Ushuaia. When I crossed the gates to the city, it was as if the weight of a piano was removed from my back. I was alive. We had made it. The suffering was over. Finally!

The day we arrived in Ushuaia, so did everyone else. Toti's parents flew in from Buenos Aires with Don Carlos Solanet and his brother. I was so pleased to see them even though I didn't believe they thought I was going to make it. They were so kind to me when I told them about Sapito's death.

My parents, along with eighteen other Brazilians came, too. My welcoming committee included Mario, who drove the support van for me through Uruguay; the President of the Barretos Rodeo, Lincoln and his family (who lent me Doll), Neto and his family (who owned the ranch where I trained the mares in Barretos), Mariana (a good friend and adventurer) with her father, Flavio, my boot sponsor and his girl-friend Jordana, and others from my home country made the journey.

The Canadian photographer, Barbara Nettleton, who had attended my arrival in Barretos flew for over twenty-four hours from Canada with her son to be there. Dannie and his family from Río Gallegos drove in. Clara flew from El Bolón.

I couldn't believe all of these people had traveled to the end of the world just to be with me. When we all met for dinner that night, the sorrow I'd felt in my core lifted. Being with my family, seeing all of these familiar faces, feeling their positive energy, and their love made me feel a happiness I had not felt in days.

Speeches were made that night, too many drinks were downed, and several tears of joy shed.

The next morning, we went to a nearby beach to film for *Outwildtv*. The company sent a cinematographer from the US. It was another windy, miserable day, but we managed to get through it.

There was even a wedding proposal to warm up the afternoon. "Jordana, I want to take this special moment to ask you if you will make me the happiest man in the world. Will you marry me?" Flavio asked his stunning blonde girlfriend, many years younger than him, before taking out two rings from a knapsack nearby.

"What? Did he just ask her to marry him?" Barb protested, not believing what had just happened. We popped champagne that night and celebrated life.

On a gloomy Saturday, July 8, exactly five years after leaving the Calgary Stampede and one year and three months into this journey, I saddled Pablo Picasso for the final time. With a terrible wind making it hard to saddle the horses, Toti and I looked at one another and smirked.

"Why would the last day be sunny and beautiful?" Toti asked.

We laughed.

Accompanied by four gauchos on horseback, my little sister Izabella on a loaned Overo, and Toti on Ona, we rode the final seven kilometers to the port of Ushuaia. With family and friends from Brazil, Canada, the United States, and Argentina waving me in, I arrived at the port just after noon.

A woman from the tourism department handed me a Brazilian flag that I tied on my back. With the Beagle Canal behind me and a small marching band playing, I stepped off Picasso's back. Holding Sapito's halter and mane in my right hand, I dropped to my knees, raised my hands to the sky, and thanked my horses.

"Thank you, thank you, thank you... I love you all, and I will never forget what you have done for me."

As I spoke these words, images of all of the horses I'd ridden on this journey filled my mind and heart. Heavy tears ran down my face while I looked up at my beautiful pony who made it with me. Picasso, a train wreck who feared his own shadow a few months back, now stood proud and muscular, as steadfast as a warrior. I touched his muzzle with both hands, closed my eyes tightly, and prayed.

I stood, embraced my new brother Toti and gave Clara a warm kiss. I hugged my family. After everything we faced these past sixteen months, after losing my son, Sapo, after so many days suffering, their love was all I wanted. These experiences made me forgive and forget everything that had happened before I climbed into the saddle in Barretos. It made me realize just how short life can be. There was no time to hold grudges or wonder what if. I loved my parents and ultimately realized all they ever wanted was the best for their son.

I made my way to the End of the World sign where a small ceremony was held. Politicians spoke before I was handed the microphone to say a few words. I mostly cried then thanked everyone for coming all that way. When the ceremony ended, a photo shoot began.

Everyone wanted a picture beside Picasso and me next to the large brown sign. When all of the photos were taken, we remounted our horses to ride back to the corral where they would rest.

As soon as we began our trek, a monsoon hit us and it hit hard. It left us drenched, but passed rather quickly. When the first rays of sunshine pierced the dark clouds, a gorgeous rainbow rose from the Beagle Canal. Behind orange, blue, and dark red containers stacked atop a sizeable blue ship, the rainbow went from violet to a pool blue, light yellow, and neon pink. I stopped Picasso and took in its beauty. Something told me that two old friends were smiling down on us at that moment. I gave my pony a few pats on the neck and reflected on all that had happened.

I still didn't have answers to why I lost Dude and Sapito in such a short time at such an important moment in my life. However, when I first saw my mom in Ushuaia, she brought a message from my loving ninety-year-old grandmother that gave me hope in the Universe and its plan.

"She said that when she was little and lived on the farm, her father used to tell the kids that everyone should have a dog, a horse, and a rooster. The elders believed that when something bad was meant to happen to the owner, if the person was pure of heart, the animals would sacrifice their lives instead."

According to my grandmother, Dude and Sapito had lost their lives to save mine. I pondered this thought. I had never told my grandmother or my mother about the deep premonition I felt during the entire journey that I would die. I didn't know if these animals actually died so I could live, but I did know that having the opportunity to know them changed my life.

Seeing how quickly everything can come to an end, made me want to enjoy this opportunity to *live* even more.

Had I let the fear of dying hold me back from taking this journey, I never would have met Toti, Ramon, Dannie, and the hundreds of friends I made for life. I never would have seen Patagonia's beauty and felt its wrath. But most importantly, I never would have met Clara, my *flor del pago*.

I left Brazil an emotional mess. I believed I would never fall in love again. For a long time, I blamed my parents for splitting up Emma and me. I blamed myself. I harbored much hate in my heart, much pain in my soul. I felt lost. Depressed. But thanks to the horse and the open road, I learned to forgive and to love once again.

The night I finished my journey from Canada to Brazil, Emma said to me, "Promise you will never go on another adventure again."

Looking deep into her green eyes, I lied to her, "I promise, babe."

She hated my nomadic spirit, but I was like a wild horse. I could never be broken or fenced in. I must wander the land. To me, happiness was freedom and freedom was happiness.

During my journey, in those moments of suffering and solitude, I realized my parents didn't break up Emma and me. It wasn't my fault, nor was it hers. The Universe brought us together, and it split us apart. It was already written long ago. We learned an abundance from one another, but our Long Ride had to come to an end so we could follow our own dreams and find our peace.

Out in that Patagonian desert, I found my peace. The experience allowed me to feel real happiness again. Sometimes we must travel to the depths of hell before we can be lifted into heaven.

That night, Clara turned to me and said, "Promise you will never go on another adventure like this without taking me with you."

Looking deep into her caramel eyes, I told her the truth, "I promise, *amor*."

Love always wins.

EPILOGUE

From Ushuaia, Filipe returned to Brazil, where he donated the $60,000 USD raised for the Barretos Children's Cancer Hospital, and once again entered the Barretos Rodeo to 40,000 screaming fans.

He released his first book *Cavaleiro das Americas*, in Portuguese with Harper Collins and *Long Ride Home* in English, telling of his first journey from Canada to Brazil. Both works became bestsellers with the Brazilian version spending thirteen weeks on the list and was voted the number one book for young adults that year.

Shortly after its release, the book was picked up by one of Brazil's most renowned production companies, Total Filmes in partnership with the Canadian powerhouse, Mythic Productions. It will soon become a major motion picture.

The footage Filipe shot for *Outwildtv* is currently being edited into a three-season reality series due out in 2020.

When the journalist is not in the saddle crossing continents, he is on stages around the Americas, giving his powerful motivational talk. Filipe has spoken in Argentina, Brazil, Uruguay, the United States, and Canada, inspiring thousands of people to follow their dreams.

Butch Cassidy and Nevada (the border collie Filipe was given on his first journey) live at his parents' ranch in Espirito Santo do Pinhal in the interior of São Paulo. Butch loves Nevada to death. The border collie has learned to live with the little dog. They chase birds, swim in the pond, and run around the forest behind the stunning ranch all day.

Frenchie and Bruiser are also there, living the dream in full retirement thanks to Filipe's father, Iso, who takes care of the horses every single day.

After arriving in Ushuaia, Pablo Picasso spent the winter in Río Gallegos before being trailered back to *El Cardal* by Sophia and her boyfriend Frederico. Andariega and Cautiva are back at the Lanfranco ranch in Uruguay. Life and Doll are in São Paulo.

Mark, Toti, and Mario are all doing well! Mark is back in Toronto working at Mark's Work Wearhouse. Mario is finishing medical school and is now a licensed pilot, and continues to run his ranch. Toti traveled with Filipe to the Barretos Rodeo after their journey and then — get this — rode a bicycle back to Argentina! He arrived in his parent's *estancia*, one month after leaving from the state of São Paulo. Toti is a machine!

Believe it or not, as this book was published, Filipe was back in the saddle! The thirty-three-year-old was completing his final Long Ride from Fairbanks, Alaska back to the Calgary Stampede Rodeo, where it all began, with two wild horses from the Osoyoos Indian Band.

When he arrives on July 3, 2020 in Calgary, the cowboy will become the first Brazilian to cross the Americas on horseback. And only the third in the world to do so. On that same day, he will be honored to be named the Parade Marshal for the Calgary Stampede Parade.

What about Clara, you may be wondering? Clara is out with Filipe on the trail, driving a motorhome, carrying water, hay, and feed for the horses. The motorhome was lent by Rocky and Marie Aitken from Clairsholm, Alberta, a couple who have been following Filipe since 2012.

Filipe and Clara are deeply in love and hope to settle down and start a family after this adventure.

Stay tuned for Filipe's third book on this final journey full of adventure as he navigates through massive grizzly bears, mighty bison, rugged mountains, and bloodthirsty mosquitoes in the extreme north.

All while trying to stay on top and control his two *wild* horses, Smokey and Mac!

Thank you for spending your valuable time reading this work. Now get out there and make life count. Go on your own Long Ride!

We all have a horse to ride, a path to follow, a sunset to ride off into, or an end of the world to conquer. But how do you know what it is? It's the first thing that came to your mind just now.

Gulp. Scary thought, right? But that's precisely what makes it worth it. Write it down. Start planning. Set goals. Make lists. Meet dates. *Go!*

Life is waiting.

ACKNOWLEDGMENTS

Thanks to:

My family for the continuous love and support. I love you and I know you love me.

Peter Hawkins, the project manager of this book and my mentor.

John Honderich, who championed this project from the earliest days.

Mary Maw, my Canadian mother, who helped turn me into the man I am today.

My sponsors and partners, without you this journey would not have been possible:

Barretos Children's Cancer Hospital (Hospital de Amor), Os Independentes, MELLOHAWK Logistics, NC2 Media Pralana, Goyazes, Selas PRO-HORSE, The Toronto Star, Added, The Long Riders' Guild, Marcos Silva, Dana Peers, CuChullaine O'Reilly, Basha O'Reilly, Comitiva Água do Peao and Milton Liso, ABQM, João Rozeta, RG Rural,

Velho Selvagem, Os Moiadeiros, Radade, Sofia Rudd, Municipalidade de Ushiaia, Agência Brasileiros em Ushuaia, família Aitken, família Ferrari, Mariana Britto, Barb Nettleton, Marcelo Murta, and Rodrigo DeMollay.

My support drivers and brothers: Mark Maw, Mario T. Luna, Ramon Bastias and Sebastián "Toti" Cichero.

Lincoln Arruda, Fabio Pinto da Costa, Nicolas Lanfranco, and the Solanet family who lent me my wonderful mounts.

And all of the selfless families who took me into their homes and helped me raise funds for the Barretos Children's Cancer Hospital and arrive in the Land of Fire.

Thank you.
   - Filipe
   days

TO FIND OUT MORE

This is the second book in the *Journey America* trilogy. Have you read the first book?

Long Ride Home

is available as an ebook and in paperback.

Stay tuned for the third and final volume of the *Journey America* trilogy.

Read his monthly column in the Lifestyle section of *The Toronto Star*'s website and watch videos from his journeys at www.outwildtv.com.

To stay up-to-date with Filipe and his adventures, follow him on Instagram @filipemasetti.

Manufactured by Amazon.ca
Bolton, ON